PRAYING LEGALLY

Program in Judaic Studies
Brown University
Box 1826
Providence, RI 02912

BROWN JUDAIC STUDIES

Edited by

Mary Gluck
David C. Jacobson
Saul M. Olyan
Rachel Rojanski
Michael L. Satlow
Adam Teller

Number 364
PRAYING LEGALLY

by
Shalom E. Holtz

PRAYING LEGALLY

Shalom E. Holtz

Brown Judaic Studies
Providence, Rhode Island

© 2019 Brown University. All rights reserved.

No part of this work may be reproduced or transmitted in any form or by any means, electronic or mechanical, including photocopying and recording, or by means of any information storage or retrieval system, except as may be expressly permitted by the 1976 Copyright Act or in writing from the publisher. Requests for permission should be addressed in writing to the Rights and Permissions Office, Program in Judaic Studies, Brown University, Box 1826, Providence, RI 02912, USA.

Library of Congress Cataloging-in-Publication Data

Names: Holtz, Shalom E., author.
Title: Praying legally / by Shalom E. Holtz.
Description: Providence, RI : Brown Judaic Studies, [2019] | Series: Brown Judaic studies | Includes bibliographical references and index. | Summary: "In the Hebrew Bible and related ancient sources prayer is an opportunity to make one's case before divine judges. Prayers were formulated using courtroom or trial language, including demands for judgment, confessions, and accusations. The presence of these legal concepts reveals ancient Near Eastern thoughts about what takes place when one prays. By reading ancient prayers together with legal texts, this book shows how speakers took advantage of this opportunity to have their day in the divine court, and even sue against divine injustice"-- Provided by publisher.
Identifiers: LCCN 2019037938 (print) | LCCN 2019037939 (ebook) | ISBN 9781946527394 (paperback) | ISBN 9781946527400 (hardcover) | ISBN 9781946527417 (ebook)
Subjects: LCSH: Bible. Old Testament--Prayers--History and criticism. | Judgment of God. | Trials in the Bible. | Justice, Administration of, in the Bible. | Jewish law--Language. | Metaphor in the Bible.
Classification: LCC BS1199.P68 H65 2019 (print) | LCC BS1199.P68 (ebook) | DDC 221.8/34--dc23
LC record available at https://lccn.loc.gov/2019037938
LC ebook record available at https://lccn.loc.gov/2019037939

Printed on acid-free paper.

לאבא ולאמא, שיחי'

שותפיו של שומע תפילה החונן לאדם דעת

Contents

Preface ix

Acknowledgments xi

Bibliographical Abbreviations xiii

Introduction to Pursuing a "Social Analogy" 1

1 • The Idea of Praying Legally 17

2 • Praying as a Plaintiff 39

3 • Prayer, Procedure, and Protest 63

4 • The Audience in Prayer's Courtroom 93

Conclusion: Why Pray Legally? 127

Bibliography 135

Indexes 147

Preface

All translations are my own, made in consultation with published translations. Citations of the Hebrew Bible are based on the Masoretic Text of the Aleppo Codex and related manuscripts, available from the electronic corpus of Mechon Mamre (www.mechon-mamre.org). Citations of Hebrew High Holiday liturgy come from Daniel Goldschmidt, ed., מחזור לימים הנוראים: לפי מנהגי בני אשכנז כולל מנהג ענפיהם לכל אשכנז (המערבי), מנהג פולין ומנהג צרפת לשעבר, 2 vols. (Jerusalem: Koren, 1970). Medieval Jewish commentaries are cited from Menachem Cohen, ed., *Mikra'ot Gedolot 'Haketer': A Revised and Augmented Scientific Edition of 'Mikra'ot Gedolot' Based on the Aleppo Codex and Early Medieval MSS* (Ramat-Gan: Bar-Ilan University, 1992–).

Citation conventions and abbreviations follow those published in *The SBL Handbook of Style*, 2nd ed. (Atlanta: SBL Press, 2014) and *CAD*.

Acknowledgments

אֲבָרֵךְ אֶת-ה' אֲשֶׁר יְעָצָנִי (תה' טז:ז)

I begin by formally discharging my duty to acknowledge two sources of financial support for my research on this book. In 2014–2015, I received the Memorial Foundation for Jewish Culture's International Fellowship in Jewish Studies. A grant from the Chelst, Schreiber, and Zwas Yeshiva College Book Fund aided my work in 2016–2018. It is an honor to be included among the recipients of both of these grants.

For some fifteen years now, one main focus of my research has been ancient Mesopotamian trial procedure, primarily as it is attested in the Neo-Babylonian cuneiform corpus. During this time, I served as a consultant to the Neo-Babylonian Trial Procedure project, funded by a Collaborative Research Grant from the U.S. National Endowment for the Humanities and led by Bruce Wells, Cornelia Wunsch, and Rachel Magdalene. While the project itself has ended, and my research interests have migrated toward divine, rather than earthly, courtrooms, my scholarly relationships with Bruce, Cornelia, and Rachel remain. All three have, in one way or another, contributed something to the present work.

Bruce and Rachel welcomed me to the Biblical Law section of the Society of Biblical Literature's Annual Meeting. Over the years, I have presented most of the research for this book at this section's sessions, first as a newcomer, then as a steering committee member, and now as a co-chair (with Hannah Harrington). Among the other scholarly venues in which I have shared the work published here, I should single out the Columbia Bible Seminar, whose stimulating meetings are always a monthly highlight for me. At all of these forums, audience responses to my presentations have definitely improved this publication in ways impossible to enumerate.

Similarly, conversations with teachers and colleagues have contributed to this work. Many thanks to Tzvi Abusch, Shawn Zelig Aster, Marc Brettler, Simeon Chavel, Tova Ganzel, Edward Greenstein, Peter Machinist, Moshe Shoshan, Benjamin Sommer, Jeffrey Stackert, David Vanderhooft, and Avi Winitzer, all of whom took an interest in this project and offered criticism and encouragement, as needed. Saul Olyan and the anonymous referees of Brown Judaic Studies made valuable suggestions that have improved the book in its present form. My sincere apologies and thanks to those whose names I neglected to mention.

For someone of my research interests, few intellectual environments rival Yeshiva University, my academic home since 2006, where I am a member of the faculty of the Bernard Revel Graduate School of Jewish Studies and of the Robert M. Beren Department of Jewish Studies at Yeshiva College. Among my colleagues there, I wish to single out Moshe Bernstein, Barry Eichler, Aaron Koller, and Ari Mermelstein, on whom I can always rely to serve as sounding boards for my ideas. This work owes a special debt to Ari and his involvement with the Yeshiva University Center for Jewish Law and Contemporary Civilization, where I was a fellow during the 2009–2010 academic year and where my first thoughts on prayer and the courtroom took shape. Lauren Fitzgerald, Professor of English and Director of the Wilf Campus Writing Center at Yeshiva University, read drafts and provided other welcome support for my writing. Alongside the names of the living, I record the memory of Yaakov Elman, with whom I shared many powerful conversations on my research. His passing is a loss to the entire world of Jewish Studies, most keenly felt at YU.

As this book took shape, the ideas it contains became a unit in my graduate-level course on prayer in the Hebrew Bible. Classroom discussions have certainly impacted what now appears in print, and I am grateful to the students who have shared their thoughts with me. Special thanks to the following students who worked as my research assistants when they were undergraduates: Jacob Yisrael Ben Pesach, Yakov Ellenbogen, Eliav Grossman, and Shlomo Wadler. Their undergraduate careers are well in their pasts, but this work remains a testament to their abilities. I am especially grateful to Yael Landman for reading and commenting on most of the manuscript, chapter by chapter, and contributing her expertise as a scholar of the ancient Near East and as a writer.

From this book's very inception, my wife, Leebie Mallin, has provided consistent interest and encouragement. Our three children, Zev (Billy), Avigayil, and Tal have grown up knowing that "Abba is writing a book called *Praying Legally*." They are always sources of delight and reminders that the second (or third) millennium c.e. is at least as interesting as the second (or first) millennium b.c.e. To all of them go my deep appreciation for tolerating my ultimately offbeat interests and for welcoming me into their worlds.

Finally, my parents, Avraham and Toby Berger Holtz, have been at my side throughout my life. The phrase "at my side" can be understood both idiomatically, as it usually is, and quite literally, for we have, in fact, occupied adjacent seats in library reading rooms. My parents are models of devotion to Jewish scholarship who nurtured and supported me every step of the way. I dedicate this book to them. May they continue to enrich the lives of our family and of all who know them.

בשמחה רבה, עש"ק פ' שקלים כד באדר א' התשע"ט

Teaneck, New Jersey
March 2019

Bibliographical Abbreviations

A.	Tablet Signature of Texts from Mari
AB	Anchor Bible
ABAW	Abhandlungen der Bayerischen Akademie der Wissenschaften
ABL	*Assyrian and Babylonian Letters Belonging to the K. Collection of the British Museum*. Edited by Robert Francis Harper. 14 vols. Chicago: University of Chicago Press, 1892–1914.
AfO	*Archiv für Orientforschung*
AMD	Ancient Magic and Divination
ANEM	Ancient Near East Monographs/Monografías sobre el Antiguo Cercano Oriente
AnOr	Analecta Orientalia
AOAT	Alter Orient und Altes Testament
ArOr	*Archív Orientální*
ASAW	Abhandlungen der Sächsischen Akademie der Wissenschaften
AYB	Anchor Yale Bible
BASOR	*Bulletin of the American Schools of Oriental Research*
BaF	Baghdader Forschungen
BaghM	*Baghdader Mitteilungen*
BCOTWP	Baker Commentary on the Old Testament Wisdom and Psalms
BE	*The Babylonian Expedition of the University of Pennsylvania, Series A: Cuneiform Texts*. Edited by H. V. Hilprecht. 31 vols. Philadelphia: University of Pennsylvania Press, 1893–1914.
BEATAJ	Beiträge zur Erforschung des Alten Testaments und des antiken Judentums
BETL	Bibliotheca Ephemeridum theologicarum Lovaniensium
BibInt	Biblical Interpretation
BIN	*Babylonian Inscriptions in the Collection of James B. Nies*. 10 vols. New Haven: Yale University Press, 1918–1987.

BJS	Brown Judaic Studies
BM	Tablets in the collection of the British Museum
BMes	Bibliotheca Mesopotamica
BMS	Leonard W. King, *Babylonian Magic and Sorcery*. London: Luzac, 1896.
Boyer, Contribution	Georges Boyer, *Contribution à l'histoire juridique de la 1re dynastie babylonienne*. Paris: P. Geuthner, 1928.
BTS	Biblical Tools and Studies
BWL	Wilfred G. Lambert, *Babylonian Wisdom Literature*. Oxford: Clarendon, 1960.
BZ	*Biblische Zeitschrift*
BZABR	Beihefte zur Zeitschrift für altorientalische und biblische Rechtsgeschichte
BZAW	Beihefte zur Zeitschrift für die alttestamentliche Wissenschaft
CAD	*The Assyrian Dictionary of the Oriental Institute of the University of Chicago*. Chicago: Oriental Institute of the University of Chicago, 1956–2006.
CBQ	*Catholic Biblical Quarterly*
CM	Cuneiform Monographs
COS	*The Context of Scripture*. Edited by William W. Hallo. 3 vols. Leiden: Brill, 1997–2002.
CT	*Cuneiform Texts from Babylonian Tablets, &c., in the British Museum*. London: The Trustees of the British Museum, 1896–.
CTH	Emmanuel Laroche, *Catalogue des textes hittites*. Etudes et commentaires 75. Paris: Klincksieck, 1971.
Cyr.	J. N. Strassmaier, *Inschriften von Cyrus, König von Babylon (538–529 v. Chr.) von den Thontafeln des Britischen Museums*. Babylonische Texte 7. Leipzig: Eduard Pfeiffer, 1890.
DÖAW.PH	Denkschriften Österreichische Akademie der Wissenschaften. Philosophisch-historische Klasse
EANEC	Explorations in Ancient Near Eastern Civilizations
EJL	Early Judaism and Its Literature
FAOS	Freiburger altorientalische Studien
FAT	Forschungen zum Alten Testament
GKC	*Gesenius' Hebrew Grammar*. Edited by Emil Kautzsch. Translated by Arthur E. Cowley. 2nd ed. Oxford: Clarendon, 1910.
HAT	Handbuch zum Alten Testament
HBS	History of Biblical Studies
HSM	Harvard Semitic Monographs
HTR	*Harvard Theological Review*
HUCA	*Hebrew Union College Annual*

JANER	*Journal of Ancient Near Eastern Religions*
JANESCU	*Journal of the Ancient Near Eastern Society of Columbia University*
JAOS	*Journal of the American Oriental Society*
JBL	*Journal of Biblical Literature*
JEOL	*Jaarbericht von het Vooraziatisch-Egyptisch Genootschap Ex oriente lux*
JJS	*Journal of Jewish Studies*
JNES	*Journal of Near Eastern Studies*
JNSL	*Journal of Northwest Semitic Languages*
JSOT	*Journal for the Study of the Old Testament*
JSOTSup	Journal for the Study of the Old Testament Supplement Series
JSS	*Journal of Semitic Studies*
JTS	*Journal of Theological Studies*
KAR	*Keilschrifttexte aus Assur religiösen Inhalts*. Edited by Erich Ebeling. Leipzig: Hinrichs, 1919–1923.
Köcher BAM	Franz Köcher, *Die babylonisch-assyrische Medizin in Texten und Untersuchungen*. Berlin: de Gruyter, 1963– .
Kültepe	Tablets from Kültepe
LHBOTS	Library of Hebrew Bible/Old Testament Studies
MRS	Mission de Ras Shamra
Nbn.	J. N. Strassmaier, *Inschriften von Nabonidus, König von Babylon (555–538 v. Chr.) von den Thontafeln des Britischen Museums*. Babylonische Texte 1–4. Leipzig: Eduard Pfeiffer, 1889.
NJPS	*Tanakh: The Holy Scriptures; The New JPS Translation according to the Traditional Hebrew Text*
OECT	Oxford Editions of Cuneiform Texts
OPBIAA	Occasional Publications of the British Institute of Archaeology in Ankara
ORA	Orientalische Religionen in der Antike
OTE	*Old Testament Essays*
OTL	Old Testament Library
RA	*Revue d'assyriologie et d'archéologie orientale*
RB	*Revue biblique*
RIDA	*Revue international des droits dans l'antiquité*
RS	Texts excavated at Ras Shamra (Ugarit)
SAAB	*State Archives of Assyria Bulletin*
SBLDS	Society of Biblical Literature Dissertation Series
SBLSymS	Society of Biblical Literature Symposium Series
StBoT	Studien zu den Boğazköy-Texten
StPohl	Studia Pohl
TCL	Textes cunéiformes. Musée du Louvre

UET	Ur Excavations, Texts
VT	*Vetus Testamentum*
VTSup	Supplements to Vetus Testamentum
WAW	Writings from the Ancient World
WBC	Word Biblical Commentary
Wiseman, Alalakh	D. J. Wiseman, *The Alalakh Tablets*. OPBIAA 2. London: British Institute of Archaeology in Ankara, 1953.
WMANT	Wissenschaftliche Monographien zum Alten und Neuen Testament
WO	*Die Welt des Orients*
WUNT	Wissenschaftliche Untersuchungen zum Neuen Testament
YOS	Yale Oriental Series, Babylonian Texts
ZAW	*Zeitschrift für die alttestamentliche Wissenschaft*

Introduction to
Pursuing a "Social Analogy"

When people prayed in biblical Israel and the ancient Near East, what did they think they were doing? This book offers one answer to this fundamental question by exposing a forensic theology of prayer, in which speakers imagine themselves as petitioners making their case before divine judges. Throughout biblical and ancient Near Eastern literature, and even in postbiblical Jewish texts, prayers are framed as courtroom speeches. In this form, prayers evoke an entire legal system analogous to the one that operates in the human sphere.

In postbiblical Jewish tradition, the connection between prayer and the courtroom is perhaps best known from the liturgy for Rosh Hashana, the New Year Festival, and Yom Kippur, the Day of Atonement. God's judgment of humanity is an important theme of these holidays. Referring to God's own written decision, the words of one prayer, *Untannê Toqep*, express the theme of judgment as follows: "On Rosh Hashana they are written down, and on the fast of Yom Kippur they are sealed."[1] This same "writing" plays a part in the litany-like prayer known as *ʾAbînû Malkênû* ("Our Father, Our King").[2] In this prayer, the speakers, as a community, make several requests for God to "write us down in books" for a favorable future, as well as for God to "cancel our debt-notes" and "tear up the evil sentence decreed against us." As in earthly courtrooms, ancient and

---

1. Daniel Goldschmidt, ed., מחזור לימים הנוראים: לפי מנהגי בני אשכנז לכל ענפיהם כולל מנהג אשכנז (המערבי) מנהג פולין ומנהג צרפת לשעבר, 2 vols. (Jerusalem: Koren, 1970), 1:169–72. For an overview of the prayer, see Lawrence A. Hoffman, "*Un'taneh Tokef* as Poetry and Legend," in *Who by Fire, Who by Water*: Un'taneh Tokef, ed. Lawrence A. Hoffman (Woodstock, VT: Jewish Lights, 2010), 13–25. For the text of the prayer, with translation and annotations, see Joel M. Hoffman, "*Un'taneh Tokef*: Behind the Translation," in Hoffman, *Who by Fire*, 33–48.

2. Goldschmidt, מחזור לימים הנוראים, 1:131–32. For a historically oriented introduction to this prayer, see Lawrence A. Hoffman, "The History, Meaning, and Varieties of *Avinu Malkeinu*," in *Naming God*: Avinu Malkeinu—Our Father, Our King, ed. Lawrence A. Hoffman (Woodstock, VT: Jewish Lights, 2015), 3–15. For a conflated text, based on various liturgical traditions, with annotated translation, see Joel M. Hoffman, "*Avinu Malkeinu*: A New and Annotated Translation," in Hoffman, *Naming God*, 41–58.

modern, God's own courtroom makes extensive use of writing; judgment comes in written form.³ Sins are recorded in "debt-notes" and God's own decree can be "torn."⁴ By incorporating these legal images in the petitions, the speakers imply that they are addressing God as a judge, even as they explicitly address God as father and king. The legally tinged prayers reflect the speakers' position as a community on trial and awaiting a verdict.

Conceptual analogues to these courtroom-style requests in ʾAbînû Malkênû occur throughout the long tradition of Hebrew petitionary prayer, and, beyond that, in the religious literature of the ancient Near East. Here let us consider just one such analogue, part of the long Babylonian anti-witchcraft ritual *Maqlû*. In broadest strokes, this ritual's words and accompanying acts symbolically put the inimical witch (not actually present) on trial and execute her by burning.⁵ The motif of the witch's trial manifests itself in the use of legal terminology. Several times in the earlier part of the ritual the patient demands judgment from the gods: "judge my case, decide my decision" (*dīnī dīn purussâya purus*).⁶ In fact, comparison with ancient Near Eastern trial records shows that the patient's demand finds parallels in the language of human courtrooms. In other words, the patient speaks to the gods much as a petitioner would before a human adjudicator.

This book's title, *Praying Legally*, refers to the kind of terminological and conceptual overlaps between the courtroom and prayer that we see in ʾAbînû Malkênû and *Maqlû*. Incorporating legal language, especially from the human courtroom, into prayer occurs throughout the long history of the Hebrew prayer tradition, beginning with the Hebrew Bible.⁷ Biblical prayers, especially the psalms known as individual and communal complaints or laments, use forms of speech that connect them to the process of adjudication. Indeed, some of these psalms contain a demand

---

3. For heavenly analogues to the "Book of Life" from the cultures of Mesopotamia, see Shalom M. Paul, "Heavenly Tablets and the Book of Life," *JANESCU* 5 (1973): 345–53.

4. For more on this metaphor and its origins in ancient Near Eastern ideas of royal bureaucracy, see Joseph Lam, *Patterns of Sin in the Hebrew Bible: Metaphor, Culture, and the Making of a Religious Concept* (Oxford: Oxford University Press, 2016), 88–101.

5. Tzvi Abusch, *The Witchcraft Series Maqlû*, WAW 37 (Atlanta: SBL Press, 2015); and Abusch, *The Magical Ceremony Maqlû: A Critical Edition*, AMD 10 (Leiden: Brill, 2016).

6. *Maqlû* I.114; II.24, 108, 131. In *Maqlû* I.14, part of the ritual's first incantation, the same phrase occurs, but with a changed second half: *dīnī dīn alaktī limdā*. The force of the phrase is the same.

7. There are Greek "judicial prayers" or "prayers for legal help," surveyed and analyzed by H. S. Versnel, "Beyond Cursing: The Appeal to Justice in Judicial Prayers," in *Magika Hiera: Ancient Greek Magic and Religion*, ed. Christopher A. Faraone and Dirk Obbink (Oxford: Oxford University Press, 1997), 60–106. At nearly every level, Versnel's Greek examples offer intriguing parallels to the ancient Near Eastern texts. The relationship, if any, between these prayers and the ones from the ancient Near Eastern tradition remains beyond the scope of this book.

for judgment just like the one that occurs in *Maqlû*. The presence of this demand and other legalisms, such as oaths and even counter-accusations against God, in Hebrew prayer reflects a basic conception of prayer as a legal petition. As the next chapter will show, this basic conception underlies even the common Hebrew word for prayer, *təpillâ*, which denotes not only communication between humans and the divine realm, but also an argument in court.

The Prayer–Courtroom Connection in Modern Biblical Scholarship

This book takes its cue from brief remarks in Moshe Greenberg's important study of prose prayer in the Hebrew Bible.[8] In one section of this work, Greenberg pursues what he calls "the social analogy," or the "inter-human speech patterns" that constitute the model for speech between humans and God.[9] There Greenberg writes that "the affinity between suit and petitionary prayer is worth pausing over."[10] In this "pause," Greenberg concentrates mainly on the terminology of prayer, with observations about the legal valences of the Hebrew words *təpillâ* ("prayer") and *hitpallēl* ("to pray"), as well as *ṣ-ʿ-q* ("to cry out"), often used to denote prayer.[11] He also clarifies the theology implicit in these terminological associations: God's response to prayer is perceived as a favorable legal verdict.[12]

In keeping with his focus on prose prayer, Greenberg does not discuss the "affinity between suit and petitionary prayer" in poetic prayers, such as those in the biblical laments. One purpose of this book is to extend the pursuit of this "affinity" into these other texts. With Greenberg, this study will focus largely on "petitionary prayers," rather than on other, nonpetitionary types of prayers. This is because connections to the courtroom are most explicit and pervasive in the petitionary genres, mainly the laments

---

8. Moshe Greenberg, *Biblical Prose Prayer as a Window to the Popular Religion of Ancient Israel*, Taubman Lectures in Jewish Studies (Berkeley: University of California Press, 1983).
9. Ibid., 19–37.
10. Ibid., 21.
11. Ibid., 21–22.
12. Ibid., 21. Greenberg bases this theological observation on Rachel's explanation of Dan's name in Gen 30:6. Greenberg translates that verse, "God has passed judgment on me and indeed has heard my prayer." The verb for judgment (*d-y-n*) is clearly present in the verse and certainly justifies Greenberg's conclusion. For accuracy's sake, at least, it should be noted that Greenberg's "my prayer" (compare "my plea" in NJPS) corresponds to the Hebrew *bəqôlî*, which could also be rendered "my voice." Thus, from the strictly philological or lexicographical perspective, the verse is more valuable as evidence for the legal valence of God's hearing (see ch. 4) than for explicating the terms denoting prayer.

or complaints.[13] Indeed, in many cases, they are even more explicit than Greenberg's examples from prose. I have already mentioned demands for judgment and other forms of speech that connect prayers to courtrooms. Apart from these, the Psalms, in particular, contain rather concrete references to various aspects of litigation. Speakers in psalms complain of false witnesses, refer to God as an expert investigator, and even mention heavenly analogues to written records that apparently accompany judgment. As important, they do so by means of locutions familiar from descriptions of human litigation.[14]

The manifest connections between petitionary prayers and lawsuits have even raised the possibility that some of the more explicitly legal prayers were spoken during actual trials. The most fully developed expression of this understanding is the study by Hans Schmidt, published in 1928, and entitled *Das Gebet der Angeklagten im Alten Testament*.[15] As his short book's German title indicates, Schmidt interprets many of the individual lament psalms as "the prayers of defendants," spoken by people standing trial before temple tribunals. For Schmidt, these psalms show "affinities" (in Greenberg's terms) to the courtroom because the courtroom is where the psalms themselves originate. The courtroom is not merely the "analogy" (again in Greenberg's terms) on which prayer models itself; the courtroom is nothing less than the very setting in which prayers were uttered.

For example, consider Schmidt's interpretation of Ps 69. The speaker in this psalm complains, "I must restore that which I have not stolen" (69:5), so Schmidt situates the entire chapter in the context of a trial for theft. Thus, the speaker's cries for salvation from drowning (69:2–3, 15–16)

---

13. Prayers of praise refer to God's judgment too (see, e.g., Pss 33:5; 48:12; 67:5; 96:13; 97:2, 8; 98:9; 99:4; 103:6; 146:7; 147:19), but this is the main extent of their legal associations.

14. On witnesses, compare Pss 27:12; 35:11 with Deut 19:15–18. On investigation, compare Pss 10:13–15; 44:21–22; 139:1, 23–24 with Deut 13:15; 17:4; 19:18. See Pietro Bovati, *Re-Establishing Justice: Legal Terms, Concepts and Procedures in the Hebrew Bible*, trans. Michael J. Smith, JSOTSup 105 (Sheffield: Sheffield Academic Press, 1994), 244–45; and F. Rachel Magdalene, *On the Scales of Righteousness: Neo-Babylonian Trial Law and the Book of Job*, BJS 348 (Providence, RI: Brown Judaic Studies, 2007), 108. On written records, see Pss 69:29 and 109:13–14 (see Paul, "Heavenly Tablets"). Note that biblical trial legislation does not mention these records as part of the adjudicatory apparatus, although references like Job 19:23–24; 31:35, together with those from the Psalms, suggest as much. See Magdalene, *Scales of Righteousness*, 180.

15. Hans Schmidt, *Das Gebet der Angeklagten im Alten Testament*, BZAW 49 (Giessen: Töpelmann, 1928). A shorter version of this study, with fewer examples and no notes, appeared shortly before: "Das Gebet der Angeklagten im Alten Testament," in *Old Testament Essays: Papers Read before the Society for Old Testament Study at Its Eighteenth Meeting, Held at Keble College, Oxford, September 27th to 30th, 1927* (London: Charles Griffin, 1927), 143–55. Many of Schmidt's observations are reiterated in Hans Schmidt, *Die Psalmen*, HAT 15 (Tübingen: J. C. B. Mohr, 1934).

indicate that the speaker faces the death penalty. The speaker complains of illness too (69:27, 30) and also mentions alienation from family and community (69:9–13, 19–22). Together, these latter two elements indicate an evidentiary dispute during the trial between the speaker and the speaker's enemies or accusers. All parties share the assumption that the illness must stem from some guilt on the speaker's part. For the accusers, the illness itself proves the speaker's guilt in the present matter. The speaker, on the other hand, maintains innocence, claiming that the illness has no bearing on the question at hand. God knows why the speaker is sick (69:6), but it is not because of the theft.[16]

While Schmidt's reading of Ps 69 can never be thoroughly disproven, it also exposes the main weakness in reading this and other psalms as "prayers of defendants." Legal language is not the only kind of language we find in these prayers, and Schmidt's position fails to account for all the language that does not immediately evoke the courtroom. More accurately, Schmidt actually does account for this other language but forces it into the courtroom. In the nearly one hundred years since the publication of *Das Gebet des Angeklagten*, scholarship has recognized that the variegation of motifs within biblical laments, such as, in Ps 69, the references to sickness and enemies alongside the denial of theft, precludes any confident assignment to a specific context or occasion for prayer.[17] Somewhat paradoxically, then, mentions of witnesses and the like lead us directly from prayer into the courtroom, but we cannot really be sure how, or even if, the prayers that contain these mentions would have functioned in that setting.

Despite this fundamental problem, Schmidt's work is valuable for its sustained attention to the occurrence of overtly legal language in biblical prayers. Instead of approaching this language as the key to recovering these prayers' original setting or when they might have been recited, this language is best understood as the reflection of a fundamentally legal conception of prayer itself. The courtroom is a conceptual or metaphoric framework, rather than the actual venue, for prayer.

---

16. Schmidt, *Das Gebet des Angeklagten*, 32–34; and Schmidt, *Die Psalmen*, 132–33.
17. For a convenient summary of this methodological aspect, in general, see James L. Kugel, "Topics in the History of the Spirituality of the Psalms," in *Jewish Spirituality from the Bible through the Middle Ages*, ed. Arthur Green, World Spirituality 13 (New York: Crossroad, 1986), 113–44, here 115–17. For early critiques of Schmidt's specific position, see Hermann Gunkel and Joachim Begrich, *Introduction to Psalms: The Genres of the Religious Lyric of Israel*, trans. James D. Nogalski, Mercer Library of Biblical Studies (Macon, GA: Mercer University Press, 1998; German original, 1933), 188–89; and Sigmund Mowinckel, *The Psalms in Israel's Worship*, trans. D. R. Ap-Thomas, 2 vols. (1962; repr., Grand Rapids: Eerdmans, 2004), 1:228 n. 5. A convenient account of Schmidt's ideas and their reception can be found in Giovanna Raenger Czander, "'You Are My Witnesses': A Theological Approach to the Laws of Testimony" (PhD diss., Fordham University, 2008), 113–26.

This approach to the prayer–courtroom connection is implied in Greenberg's use of the terms "affinity" and "social analogy" to describe how Hebrew prayers make use of legal language. It views prayer within the broader sphere of what an earlier scholar, Berend Gemser, termed "the rîb- or controversy-pattern in Hebrew mentality."[18] Gemser demonstrates how the legal dispute, or rîb in Biblical Hebrew, is a pervasive "frame of mind" through which biblical Israelites understood their religious world.[19] Communication between humans and the divine, in both directions, makes use of lawsuit terminology: in prophecies, God speaks to Israel as a plaintiff, and, in prayer, humans turn to God as plaintiffs too.

In light of this, Gemser offers the following explicit critique of Schmidt:

> [The rîb terminology's] occurrence even where the distress of the psalmist clearly arises out of sickness (Pss 31:10–13; 35:13–15; 69:2–3, 15–16, 21, 27, 30), prove[s] that the rîb-pattern is often, if not mostly, used metaphorically, although not as a purely literary style-motif, but rather as a form of thinking and feeling, a category, a frame of mind. There are at least twenty-five Psalms in which parts and expressions of this pattern occur. To interpret this class of Psalms as representing a real lawsuit and trial before a temple tribunal with decision by ordeal looks like a hermeneutic "transubstantiation" or substantializing of metaphor into reality. Undoubtedly the phraseology is thoroughly judicial, but with this metaphor other comparisons vary. The "scarcity of motifs" to which H. Schmidt has drawn attention finds its explanation in the use of the controversy-imagery for all kinds of distress, and this results in a distinct frame of mind.[20]

According to Gemser, Schmidt correctly identified the prayer–courtroom connection in the psalms but interpreted it incorrectly. Through his "hermeneutic transubstantiation," Schmidt, in effect, reduced the psalms to legal jargon. Gemser, in contrast, advocates for restoring the relevant psalms to their proper place as prayers. Courtroom terminology in prayer attests to something much more profound than just the workings of Israelite courtrooms or the patterns of Israelite legal speech. Prayers sound like courtroom speeches because, fundamentally, they participate in biblical literature's broader network of the controversy "frame of mind."[21]

---

18. B. Gemser, "The rîb- or Controversy-Pattern in Hebrew Mentality," in *Wisdom in Israel and in the Ancient Near East*, ed. M. Noth and D. Winton Thomas, VTSup 3 (Leiden: Brill, 1960), 120–37.

19. On the survival of this worldview in rabbinic prayer, see Joseph Heinemann, *Prayer in the Period of the Tanna'im and the Amora'im: Its Nature and Patterns* [Hebrew] (Jerusalem: Magnes, 1964), 121–30 (English summary, IX–X). Heinemann himself refers to Gemser's study.

20. Gemser, "The rîb- or Controversy-Pattern," 128.

21. Compare the interpretation of Mowinckel himself, who referred to examples of

Rather than focusing primarily on prayer, however, Gemser's article takes a broader look at this "frame of mind." He demonstrates that legal terminology appears across the Hebrew Bible's literary genres. For Gemser, prayers are just one strand among several that, in the aggregate, attest to the wider literary-theological phenomenon.

One corollary of the pervasive presence of courtroom imagery across biblical literature is that the imagery itself can inform us about the workings of interhuman disputes in ancient Israel. Simply put, if prophecy and prayer, for example, reflect the courtroom, then we can learn about Israelite courtrooms from their reflections in prophecy and prayer. Thus, in the subspecialty of biblical studies commonly known as "biblical law," works on trial procedure usually refer not only to trial-related legislation and narratives but also to trial terminology and imagery in Hebrew poetry. Gemser himself devotes attention, albeit limited, to this aspect of his observations.[22] The most extensive example of this kind of study on the subject of trial procedure is Pietro Bovati's monograph *Re-Establishing Justice: Legal Terms, Concepts and Procedures in the Hebrew Bible*. Bovati draws on numerous earlier studies, among which he singles out Gemser's article on "the *rîb* pattern," together with works by Isaac Leo Seeligmann and Hans Jochen Boecker.[23]

The aim of works like Bovati's is to describe, as comprehensively as possible, trial procedure as one aspect of ancient law. While the Hebrew Bible never purports to provide a full account of how to conduct a trial, works like Bovati's mine the available materials, including prayers, to achieve scholarly aims. In the words of Bovati's own characterization of his work, "the procedural elements have been organized into a system that is not to be found—at least with the same precision and completeness—in any of the biblical texts."[24] For our purposes, then, the value of this kind of study lies in the identification of the legal-procedural concepts underlying the terminology that the prayers use. Moreover, because it

---

legal language as "a picturesque expression that stems from the common understanding of a hostile relationship as a trial" (Sigmund Mowinckel, *Psalm Studies*, trans. Marc E. Biddle, 2 vols., HBS 2 [Atlanta: SBL Press, 2014; originally published 1921–1924], 1:32; also see 1:109–10). Mowinckel's interpretation limits itself to the Israelite perception of the "hostile relationship," rather than to an understanding of prayer.

22. Gemser, "The *rîb*- or Controversy-Pattern," 122–25.

23. Bovati, *Re-Establishing Justice*, 388. See I. L. Seeligmann, "Zur Terminologie für das Gerichtsverfahren in Wortschatz des biblischen Hebräisch," in *Hebräische Wortforschung: Festschrift zum 80. Geburtstag von Walter Baumgartner*, ed. Benedikt Hartmann et al., VTSup 16 (Leiden: Brill, 1967), 251–78; and Hans Jochen Boecker, *Redeformen des Rechtslebens im Alten Testament*, WMANT 14 (Neukirchen-Vluyn: Neukirchener Verlag, 1970). For other works on the subject, see references in Bovati, *Re-Establishing Justice*, 23–26.

24. Bovati, *Re-Establishing Justice*, 21.

provides a beginning-to-end picture of the adjudicatory process, it allows us to appreciate exactly how prayer might fit into this process.

To some extent, prayer occupies a similar place in the works of both Bovati and Gemser. For both, prayer is just one source on which to draw in understanding an aspect of ancient Israelite culture. Thus, although both anticipate the work presented here, neither devotes full attention to the topic. Moreover, when we compare the two studies, we see that these authors assign different, even inverted, significance to the legal and theological information that the trial imagery provides. Bovati and other authors like him, whose task is describing ancient legal procedure, tend to avoid full consideration of their insights' theological implications in service of their main goal.[25] Gemser's study, on the other hand, relies on courtroom imagery not for its legal information but as a window into "Israel's experience of, and attitude to, the Divine."[26] For Gemser, instead of theology serving the purposes of legal inquiry, law, in effect, serves theology.

In studying Hebrew prayer, my purpose aligns more closely with that of Gemser, rather than with that of authors like Bovati. In this book, at least, law and legal terminology are not ends in themselves but rather a means toward the end of understanding Hebrew prayer. Unlike Bovati, therefore, this book does not offer a complete description of the ancient Israelite trial. Instead, it applies legal-procedural insights, including some by Bovati himself, to interpret specific aspects of prayer. I aim to explore how the courtroom furnishes a meaningful "social analogy," in Greenberg's terms, on which prayer models itself. Doing so holds the promise of greater insight into one aspect of how Hebrew prayer conceives of God.

The Value of Metaphor

So far, I have noted Gemser's rejection of Schmidt's more concrete interpretation of legal language in prayer, as well as the literary-theological aim that Gemser sets for his work. At the root of Gemser's study, however, is an even more valuable understanding of the category of metaphor. Gemser makes a crucial distinction between metaphor used "as a purely literary style-motif" and metaphor that serves as "a form of thinking and feeling, a category, a frame of mind." In prayer, metaphoric lawsuit terminology is not merely literary artifice or adornment to otherwise plain speech or even argument. Rather, the lawsuit metaphor reveals something fundamental about the religious world in the Hebrew Bible and the

---

25. See, e.g., the remarks in ibid., 27.
26. Gemser, "The rîb- or Controversy-Pattern," 136.

ancient Near East. It opens a window onto how biblical authors and their contemporaries understood their relationship to the divine.

In many respects, Gemser's brief remarks on the courtroom metaphor as "a frame of mind" anticipate current understandings of the cognitive significance of metaphoric language in general. In biblical studies, Job Jindo's more recent work on the book of Jeremiah presents a statement and analysis of what Jindo calls "the cognitive approach" to metaphors in the Hebrew Bible.[27] Drawing on advances in philosophy and literary theory since the 1970s, Jindo, quite like Gemser, distinguishes between understanding metaphor as something extrinsic to a literary work and viewing metaphor as a "mode of orientation."[28] In approaching the biblical text, Jindo advocates for the latter view of metaphor. Thus, his principles of exegesis include attention to the following two features of poetic metaphor:

> Metaphors as conceptual constructs: In poetry, metaphors may function not merely as literary ornaments but also as conceptual constructs of a poetic reality that the composition is designed to represent. For this reason, the images and motifs in literature cannot be paraphrased. Once we paraphrase them, we lose the reality of the poetic composition, which, in a sense, is the essence of poetry.
>
> Metaphors as mode of orientation: Metaphor has a cognitive value, and it thereby orients our perception of the object it describes. It presents not only a proposition but also a specific perspective, or orientation through which to perceive that proposition. In poetry, metaphors may orient, or reorient, our perception of reality through the poetic reality they represent, and we thereby come to perceive relations and distinctions that previously we never noticed.[29]

Proper attention to metaphor is vital to appreciating the reality that poetic works (in Jindo's case, biblical prophecies) create. Because metaphors express one idea in terms of another, they are fundamental to what poems have to say, or to how poems convey meaning. It is through metaphors that poems reorient perceptions or present new perceptions and, in turn, create new realities.[30]

These insights into metaphor readily inform our investigation of

---

27. Job Y. Jindo, *Biblical Metaphor Reconsidered: A Cognitive Approach to Poetic Prophecy in Jeremiah 1–24*, HSM 64 (Winona Lake, IN: Eisenbrauns, 2010). See also Lam, *Patterns of Sin*, 6–14. For a survey of earlier work on metaphor and its application to biblical studies, see Marc Zvi Brettler, *God Is King: Understanding an Israelite Metaphor*, JSOTSup 76 (Sheffield: JSOT Press, 1989), 13–28.
28. Jindo, *Biblical Metaphor Reconsidered*, 1.
29. Ibid., 44–45.
30. Compare Lam, *Patterns of Sin*, 207–8.

prayer. By their very nature, all prayers employ some form of metaphoric speech. Moreover, regardless of the metaphors they employ, prayers are sources of insights into ancient thinking about the human–divine relationship. Whenever we study ancient prayers, therefore, we must explicate metaphors. It is because metaphors have "cognitive value" and attest to "a frame of mind" that they provide an answer to our opening question, When people prayed in biblical Israel and the ancient Near East, what did they think they were doing?

By means of the courtroom metaphor, prayers from the biblical world reorient the dialogue between humans and deities. When prayers employ the language of the courtroom, they transport their original speakers and, by extension, us, as readers, into a very particular setting. While all prayers are governed by what Greenberg calls analogous "inter-human speech patterns," these prayers specify that the analogy comes from the realm of legal disputation. The language itself evokes the conventions of this particular setting; it is not just any "inter-human speech pattern" but a pattern that litigants use in their discourse between themselves and with adjudicators. In turn, the participants in the discourse of prayer play out a legal drama.[31]

This drama encompasses both what is said during prayer and what is said *about* prayer. Regarding the wording of prayer, Tzvi Abusch observes that, throughout the corpus of ancient Near Eastern religious literature, "with the introduction of legal images and courtroom metaphors, prayers for divine guidance are modified and even transformed into addresses to divine judges … and legal formulations serve as complements of and alternatives to prayer."[32] I explore examples of these legalisms in prayer in chapters 2 and 3. Closely correlated to these are terms for prayers themselves, including Hebrew təpillâ, that derive from the forensic sphere, which I address in chapter 1. Similarly, as I will argue in chapter 4, there are significant overlaps between the legal domain and what humans and their divine interlocutors are said to do during prayer.

The Problem of Metaphor

Understanding the courtroom as a meaningful "social analogy" to ancient Near Eastern prayer determines, at least in theory, a straightforward research path and method of reading. One can approach given prayers

---

31. Compare the general observations about "legal metaphors" by Finn Makela, "Metaphors and Models in Legal Theory," *Les Cahiers du Droit* 52 (2011): 397–415, here 400. I am grateful to Job Jindo for referring me to this article.

32. I. Tzvi Abusch, "*Alaktu* and *Halakhah*: Oracular Decision, Divine Revelation," *HTR* 80 (1987): 15–42, here 26.

with an eye toward connections between the language of the prayers and the language of legal argument. Similarly, when it comes to descriptions of prayer, one can observe how these descriptions evoke analogous descriptions from human courtrooms.

The approach here closely resembles that taken by Marc Brettler in his study of the "God is King" metaphor in the Hebrew Bible. In the introduction to his book by that same name, Brettler writes:

> [A]ny attempt to understand "God is king" must involve a complete depiction of human kingship in ancient Israel, the metaphor's vehicle, just as the metaphor "my love is a rose" may only be understood by someone who knows what a rose is. Since Israelite kingship encompasses a complex and very incompletely understood set of institutions, a re-examination of Israelite kingship is a necessary part of this study. The seemingly extraneous, lengthy expositions on human kingship, the vehicle of the metaphor, are however an essential prerequisite for understanding the image of God as king.[33]

Proper appreciation of any metaphoric expression requires full knowledge of what Brettler refers to as the metaphor's "vehicle," which others call its "source."[34] In Brettler's case, the vehicle or source is kingship; in our case, it is the courtroom. Only by understanding what ancient literature has to say about the human source institution can we understand the analogy being drawn to the "tenor," or "target," in the divine sphere.[35]

Knowledge of human courtrooms, then, is fundamental to demonstrating, exploring, and understanding the legal analogues in prayer. Consider again the example from the Akkadian ritual *Maqlû*, where the patient demands judgment from the gods: "judge my case, decide my decision" (*dīnī dīn purussâya purus*). Its very formulation suggests some connection to law and points to the courtroom as the root metaphor. But how deep is the connection between the terminology and the legal imagery? Is this demand simply a creative use of standard Akkadian words with overtly legal meanings, or are there more extensive connections between the vocabulary and the legal imagery? In other words, does the demand for judgment make the prayer sound like a speech that might have been made in human courts? Answering these deeper questions requires comparing the Akkadian prayer with Akkadian court records. Without this

---

33. Brettler, *God Is King*, 13–14.
34. For the language of "source" and "target," see Lam, *Patterns of Sin*, 13.
35. For the particular importance of relying on contextual information about the vehicle to explicate the metaphor, see Brettler, *God Is King*, 16, 24–25. For the more basic problem of determining how "the linguistic intuitions of the ancients" understood not only the source but also the target, see Lam, *Patterns of Sin*, 109–13.

kind of comparison, the suggestion that the speaker takes on the persona of a plaintiff loses a good deal of its force.

When it comes to the specific example of the demand for judgment in *Maqlû*, trial records in Akkadian show that human litigants would make similar demands in the presence of adjudicators.[36] The speakers in the ritual employ language that would have been current in the legal parlance of their day. More generally, with regard to Mesopotamian literature, the abundance of Akkadian legal texts, including trial-related documents, allows for fruitful comparisons.[37] Within the vast corpus of ancient writings preserved in cuneiform on clay tablets, ancient religious literature is complemented by more mundane legal documents. We can read the dialogue between humans and their deities alongside the legal discourse between humans and their fellows. We can, therefore, identify and appreciate the vehicle of the courtroom metaphor as well as its tenor.

In contrast, with regard to biblical texts, the general dearth of actual Israelite legal documents prevents this kind of inquiry.[38] This paucity reflects the nature of the available sources, in terms of both their material character and their contents. From the point of view of physical characteristics, fewer Hebrew sources survive, in part, because vellum and papyrus, the organic media often used in alphabetic writing, are more perishable than clay. In terms of content, surviving writings in the Hebrew Bible and outside it do not include actual legal documents that would furnish the most direct parallels to the abundance of texts in cuneiform.[39] The Bible does, of course, provide some evidence for "real-life" courtrooms in laws, narratives, and elsewhere. In effect, however, the biblical picture of trial procedure comes at one remove from what actually took place.

To further illustrate the problem, let us return to the example of the demand for judgment. When it comes to its occurrences in *Maqlû*, we stand on justifiable ground when we say that it represents a legalism incorporated into prayer. Can we say the same for Hebrew analogues?

---

36. Shalom E. Holtz, "Praying as a Plaintiff," *VT* 61 (2011): 258–79; Holtz, "Maqlû I.73–121 and Trial Procedure," *JANER* 17 (2017): 140–48.

37. For examples, see Jean Bottéro, "Symptômes, signes, écritures," in *Divination et rationalité*, ed. J. P. Vernant et al., Recherches anthropologiques (Paris: Seuil, 1974), 140–41; Ivan Starr, *The Rituals of the Diviner*, BMes12 (Malibu, CA: Undena, 1983), 58; and Tzvi Abusch, *Mesopotamian Witchcraft: Toward a History and Understanding of Babylonian Witchcraft Beliefs and Literature*, AMD 5 (Leiden: Brill, 2002), 236–45.

38. See Magdalene, *Scales of Righteousness*, 3–4; and Bruce Wells, *The Law of Testimony in the Pentateuchal Codes*, BZABR 4 (Wiesbaden: Harrassowitz, 2004), 3–4.

39. The justifiably celebrated exception is the Yavneh Yam, or Meṣad Ḥashavyahu, inscription. For the interpretation of this text as a legal record, see F. W. Dobbs-Allsopp, "The Genre of the Meṣad Ḥashavyahu Ostracon," *BASOR* 295 (1994): 49–55. Even this, however, represents only one side's plea to another, rather than a record of an entire trial from beginning to end. Thus, it goes only so far in overcoming both the quantitative and qualitative imbalance with the cuneiform corpus.

When psalms include a similar demand for judgment, are these simply artful incorporations of legal words, or do they, too, make prayers out of courtroom speech? In making the latter claim, the absence of Hebrew trial records stands as a serious impediment. The Hebrew evidence, at best, allows only an indirect glimpse of what might have been said during an actual trial. Identifying the courtroom origins of any locution thus requires some reconstruction based on an assumption that the literary reality accurately reflects the legal reality. This assumption is not, in itself, unwarranted,[40] but it does raise the risk of engaging in circular logic: one secondhand glimpse of courtroom speech proves that another, equally secondhand glimpse, is also a courtroom form of speech.[41]

Moreover, even this kind of extrapolation faces the additional problem of the overlap between legal and general vocabularies.[42] The example of the demand for judgment, with its overt use of the verb "to judge," alleviates this particular concern. But other terms, such as verbs for hearing and seeing, or locutions such as questions to God are not as overtly rooted in the courtroom. Without knowing how these terms and locutions function in actual courtrooms, we might never detect their legal nuances. On the other hand, without additional evidence, we risk misinterpreting prayers by burdening otherwise simple terminology with technical legal meanings it may not actually have. Just because the terminology can have forensic nuances does not mean that it must.

The problems just raised here are comparable to those that F. Rachel Magdalene has raised in her important, comprehensive study *On the Scales of Righteousness: Neo-Babylonian Trial Law and the Book of Job*. As with Hebrew prayer, the courtroom has long been seen as a key to understanding the book of Job.[43] And, as with Hebrew prayer, this legal analysis has suffered from limiting itself to the biblical evidence. Magdalene breaks new ground by turning to the corpus of Neo-Babylonian trial documents,

---

40. See Magdalene, *Scales of Righteousness*, 27–53.

41. For comparable observations on courtroom imagery in prophecy, see Meindert Dijkstra, "Lawsuit, Debate and Wisdom Discourse in Second Isaiah," in *Studies in the Book of Isaiah: Festschrift Willem A. M. Beuken*, ed. Jacques Van Ruiten and Marc Vervenne, BETL 132 (Leuven: Leuven University Press, 1997), 251–71, here 254.

42. See Martin Buss, "The Idea of the Sitz im Leben—History and Critique," ZAW 90 (1978): 157–70, here 168; and additional discussion of Buss's observation in Yael Avrahami, *The Senses of Scripture: Sensory Perception in the Hebrew Bible*, LHBOTS 545 (New York: T&T Clark International, 2012), 226. Raymond Westbrook has characterized the effects of a legal context on otherwise regular vocabulary as "provid[ing] a new set of clothes, so to speak, for the naked phrase" ["A Matter of Life and Death," in *Law from the Tigris to the Tiber: The Writings of Raymond Westbrook*, ed. Bruce Wells and F. Rachel Magdalene, 2 vols. (Winona Lake, IN: Eisenbrauns, 2009), 2:251–64, here 255]. Compare the similar observation by Seeligmann in "Zur Terminologie," 253–54.

43. For a summary of this scholarship, with references, see Magdalene, *Scales of Righteousness*, 1–2.

in particular, as the basis for reconstructing the legal reality behind Job's metaphoric lawsuit. Using the trial procedure that emerges from her analysis of the Akkadian texts, Magdalene demonstrates that the book of Job's "legal metaphors track a very complicated and procedurally complete trial,"[44] and that it "mimics to an important degree ancient Near Eastern legal documents of practice."[45]

This book aims to do for Hebrew prayer what Magdalene's *On the Scales of Righteousness* has done for the book of Job. Like Magdalene, I view the available Akkadian evidence as a crucial supplement to what the Hebrew Bible tells us about Israelite trial procedure and courtroom language. To identify the "inter-human speech patterns," in Greenberg's terms, on which prayer in Hebrew models itself, I rely on the firsthand picture of interhuman litigation available from Mesopotamian courtrooms. More broadly, the Akkadian materials give us a picture of the legal world out of which the idea of praying legally emerges. They allow us to anchor prayer's courtroom metaphors in legal reality.

This approach's validity rests on the well-established relationship between law in the Hebrew Bible and the cuneiform legal sources. Comparisons between the two legal cultures have long shown commonalities between legislation, legal practice, and legal terminology. While the precise contours and causes of these commonalities remain open to debate, I agree with Magdalene's assessment near the outset of her work:

> [T]here is a legal meta-tradition that is operating across vast time periods and geographic expanses of the ancient Near East. In order to understand any of its legal systems, one must see that system within the broader legal meta-tradition. This is especially important given the gaps in our legal sources from the ancient world and the highly cryptic nature of the legal materials that we possess. Reading across legal systems of similar philosophy and structures will assist us in filling in those lacunae.[46]

It is on the basis of this "legal meta-tradition" that we, following Magdalene (and many, many others), use Akkadian legal writings to fill in the gaps left in Hebrew. Because the adjudicatory process is an aspect of this meta-tradition, I imagine that trials in biblical Israel would have resembled the trials attested throughout the long history of Mesopotamian legal

---

44. Ibid., 8.
45. Ibid., 264.
46. Ibid., 31. Compare Pamela Barmash, *Homicide in the Biblical World* (Cambridge: Cambridge University Press, 2005), 140–47, 204–5; and Bruce Wells, "Introduction: The Idea of a Shared Tradition," in Wells and Magdalene, *Law from the Tigris to the Tiber*, xi–xviii. For the debates on this topic, see the literature cited in Magdalene, *Scales of Righteousness*, 31 n. 16; and in David P. Wright, *Inventing God's Law: How the Covenant Code of the Bible Used and Revised the Laws of Hammurabi* (Oxford: Oxford University Press, 2009), 3–28.

writings. In this way, the cuneiform sources inform our interpretation of Hebrew prayer's legal background.

Thus, in this book, comparative methodology serves us in two ways, each of which requires reading prayers together with different primary sources. In light of the concerns just elaborated, I read Akkadian and Hebrew prayers together with records from human courtrooms, mostly in Akkadian. This allows us to show, for example, that the demand for judgment occurs both in prayer and in the vocabulary of human litigation. Evidence like this proves that the prayer–courtroom connection extends well beneath the surface of the prayers' literary formulations. In addition, I compare Hebrew prayers and terminology of prayer to similarly worded prayers and terms in Akkadian. To continue with the example of the demand for judgment, the occurrence of these demands in Akkadian and Hebrew religious literature attests to the extent, across both cultures and historical time, of prayer's "social analogy" to the courtroom.

As a concluding observation, before the main exposition, I note that neither of these applications of the comparative method indicates direct influence of one culture on another. Thus, for example, when comparison allows us to demonstrate, based on the Akkadian, that a demand for judgment probably occurred in Hebrew legal parlance, we should not conclude that the Hebrew legalese is borrowed from the Akkadian. Nor should we understand the occurrence of demands for judgment in both Hebrew and Akkadian prayers as evidence that the idea of praying legally migrated into Hebrew prayer from a foreign source.

Rather, instead of direct influence, we can invoke and expand the concept of the meta-tradition to explain the parallels we will explore in the chapters that follow. The shared legal vocabulary and its appearance in religious literature both stem from a cultural heritage that extends beyond this or that particular parallel. We might properly apply the term meta-tradition to characterize this broader common culture, of which law and religious thought are but two aspects. In other words, alongside the ancient Near Eastern legal meta-tradition, the source of the manifest overlaps between Hebrew and Akkadian legal writings, stand other shared features of common Near Eastern culture. Just as this common culture, or meta-tradition (as we suggest applying this term), has given rise to similar thought and writing about law, so has it also given rise to shared ways of thinking about the relationship between humans and the divine realm.

We can, therefore, characterize our task in this book as using one aspect of the common Near Eastern culture to illuminate another. By studying the shared legal tradition, we gain insight into the shared religious worldview. Reading prayers together with trial records allows us to pursue the "social analogy" between the discourse conventions of human adjudication in the ancient Near East and the conventions of human–divine communication.

1

The Idea of Praying Legally

The basic Hebrew terms for prayer are the noun *təpillâ* and the related verb *hitpallēl* ("to pray"). Scholarship has long observed a connection between the courtroom and these basic words.[1] Fundamentally, the noun means "plea" or "petition," from which emerged the specialized meaning "prayer." This semantic overlap reflects the concept of prayer as "making one's case" before God, the judge. Along similar lines, the related verb means something like "to make a plea for oneself."

The prayer–courtroom connection inherent in this basic Hebrew term for prayer, as well as in others, offers a glimpse into what might be called an ancient theory of prayer. As is often the case, ancient authors rarely, if ever, make explicit theological statements. Instead, the forensic theology of prayer must be recovered from ancient terminology for prayer and from narratives about prayer. Doing so is the purpose of this chapter.

Our sources in this chapter, therefore, differ from the sources for this book's other chapters. Rather than considering prayers themselves, this chapter analyzes descriptions of prayer, mostly terminology but also some later ancient narratives. This "theoretical" evidence indicates an ancient awareness of the prayer–courtroom connection that underlies its manifestations in the prayers themselves.

Law and the Terminology of Prayer: Hebrew *təpillâ*

In seeking to establish a connection between the quintessential Hebrew terms for prayer, *təpillâ* and *hitpallēl*, etymology—that is, the study of the words themselves, without regard for context—proves to be of only limited use. The precise meaning of the root *p-l-l*, from which the noun and the verb derive, remains elusive. This is because, as a glance at the relevant sections of a concordance shows, the root's usages pertaining to prayer greatly overwhelm other usages in Hebrew.[2] Moreover,

---

1. Greenberg, *Biblical Prose Prayer*, 21–22, with references to earlier literature.
2. The noun *təpillâ* occurs, in various forms, seventy-seven times. The plural noun

the connections between these other usages—some of which do, in one way or another, pertain to law—and the most common one, "prayer," are not readily apparent.³ Attempts, at times creative, at tracing the semantic history of the Hebrew terminology for prayer only demonstrate the uncertainties inherent in this line of inquiry.⁴

Widening the etymological field to include other Semitic languages does not advance the case. For example, the Akkadian verbal cognate of Hebrew *p-l-l* occurs in Old Assyrian legal texts, but its meaning remains open to debate, as evidenced by the comment "(meaning uncertain)" in the *Chicago Assyrian Dictionary*.⁵ Chaim Cohen has observed that, in the texts themselves, the verb refers to an action that often leads to an oath as a response. Based on this, he proposes the meaning "to sue, to make a legal claim for punitive damages."⁶ If Cohen is correct, then there is reasonable semantic proximity between the Akkadian and the Hebrew, without the connection to prayer.⁷ Earlier readings of the Assyrian texts, however, take the verb to denote a process of surveying or overseeing the management of goods used in commerce, a meaning that cannot be excluded, despite Cohen's suggestion.⁸ Of course, this administrative meaning has little to do with the courtroom, much less with prayer. In short, Akkadian provides, at best, only shaky support for a connection between prayer and the courtroom and may, in fact, be entirely irrelevant.⁹

---

pəlîlîm, the next most frequently attested nominal derivative of *p-l-l*, occurs just three times, with other words (*pəlîlâ*, *pəlîliyyâ* and *pəlîlî*) occurring only one time each. The verb *hitpallēl* occurs eighty times, while related D-stem forms occur only four times.

3. For example, the noun *pəlîlîm* occurs in the law in Exod 21:22. See, however, the sobering observation by Amos Ḥakham, on Job 31:11, another place in which the noun *pəlîlîm* occurs: "the meaning of *pəlîlîm* is probably not the same in all these verses" (*The Bible: Job with the Jerusalem Commentary* [Jerusalem: Mosad Harav Kook, 2009], 314).

4. For an example of the kind of creative but ultimately unconvincing semantic speculation that the root *p-l-l* and its connections to prayer have spawned, see D. R. Ap-Thomas, "Notes on Some Terms Relating to Prayer," *VT* 6 (1956): 230–39. A more disciplined argument can be found in Adele Berlin, "On the Meaning of *pll* in the Bible," *RB* 96 (1989): 345–51.

5. *CAD* P, 51 (*palālu* B).

6. Chaim Cohen, "The Ancient Critical Misunderstanding of Exodus 21:22–25 and Its Implications for the Current Debate on Abortion," in *Mishneh Todah: Studies in Deuteronomy and Its Cultural Environment in Honor of Jeffrey H. Tigay*, ed. Nili Sacher Fox, David A. Glatt-Gilad, and Michael J. Williams (Winona Lake, IN: Eisenbrauns, 2009), 437–58, here 457.

7. Ibid., 457–58.

8. Cécile Michel, "Règlement des comptes du défunt Huraṣānum," *RA* 88 (1994): 121–28, here 124; and Michel, "Hommes et femmes prêtent serment à l'époque paléo-assyrienne," in *Jurer et maudire: Pratiques politiques et usages juridiques du serment dans le Proche-Orient ancien; Actes de la table ronde organisée le samedi 5 octobre 1996 à l'université de Paris, X-Nanterre*, ed. Francis Joannès and Sophie Lafont, Méditeraneés 10–11 (Paris: L'Harmattan, 1996), 105–23, here 112.

9. Connections to Arabic require even greater philological contortions than the Akkadian. See Ap-Thomas, "Notes on Some Terms Relating to Prayer," 230–39. For critiques of

Much as the words for prayer, on their own, tell us little about the concept of prayer that underlies them, their usage in Hebrew obscures a good deal, too. In the Hebrew Bible, the terms *təpillâ* and *hitpallēl* refer to prayer, that is, to communication along the human–divine axis, almost exclusively. Numerous locutions regularly describe communication between humans as well as prayers of humans to deities, but *təpillâ* and *hitpallēl* are reserved for prayer.[10] As a result, locating the human-to-human analogue for *təpillâ* proves a difficult task.

Nevertheless, an important exception to this nearly exclusive, specialized usage occurs in Ps 109:7:

> When he sues, may he come out in the wrong; and may his *təpillâ* miss its mark [*tihyeh laḥăṭāʾâ*].

This verse is part of a longer set of imprecations against an enemy (Ps 109:6–20).[11] Who utters these imprecations against whom—whether the main speaker in the psalm against the enemy or, the other way around, the enemies against the main speaker—remains a question.[12] Either way, someone wishes for someone else to have a bad day in court: "When he sues, may he come out in the wrong." This lawsuit is the immediate context for the *təpillâ* of the victim of the imprecation, either the speaker's enemy or the speaker himself.

In this case, however, context can obscure as much as it can illuminate. Overall, because this verse occurs in a psalm addressed to God, it is possible to situate it along the human–divine axis, rather than along the human–human one. Interpreting along the human–divine axis exploits not only the verse's overall context in an address to God but also the verse's charged vocabulary. Thus, the NRSV renders the verse:

> When he is tried, let him come forth guilty;
> let his prayer be counted as sin!

---

the etymological approach, see J. F. A. Sawyer, "Types of Prayer in the Old Testament: Some Semantic Observations on Hitpallel, Hithannen, etc." *Semitics* 7 (1980): 131–43.

10. In the case of the verb, the clearest exception occurs in Isa 45:14. For the noun, see the discussion of Ps 109:7 below. For a convenient chart of the distribution of addressees of various prayer terms in Biblical Hebrew, see Sawyer, "Types of Prayer," 140.

11. On technical grammatical grounds, the second verbal form in Ps 109:7 is clearly indicative, not jussive, so this verse itself may not contain an actual imprecation. Nevertheless, context supports the jussive translation, if only because the verse, construed as indicative, still describes the anticipated result of the imperative in the previous verse. See John Goldingay, *Psalms*, 3 vols., BCOTWP (Grand Rapids: Baker Academic, 2008), 3:280 n. 37.

12. See Stephen C. Egwim, *A Contextual and Cross-Cultural Study of Psalm 109*, BTS 12 (Leuven: Peeters, 2011), 59–65, with additional references to earlier literature. Also see Frank-Lothar Hossfeld and Erich Zenger, *Psalms 3: A Commentary on Psalms 101–150*, trans. Linda M. Maloney, Hermeneia (Minneapolis: Fortress, 2011), 126–27.

According to this rendering, the verse expresses a speaker's hope for an opponent to be judged as guilty and for the opponent's unsuccessful, even counterproductively sinful, prayer. The word *təpillâ* has its usual meaning, "prayer," as does the word *ḥăṭāʾâ*, which usually refers to sin. Moreover, the word describing the opponent's action is understood as passive ("when he is tried"), which allows for, and even suggests, that the "trial" imagined here takes place before God, rather than in a human venue.[13] In this situation, "coming forth guilty" would, quite naturally, lead to prayer, which, in turn, God might "count as sin," in the typical sense of that last word.

The main flaw in the NRSV's translation lies in its misinterpretation of the verse's opening word. The word is the infinitive form of the root *š-p-ṭ*, meaning "to judge," conjugated in a stem (the N-stem) that often serves to make active verbs passive. Thus, a passive translation, "when he is judged," is grammatically possible. This stem, however, can also have a reciprocal meaning that reflects "mutual action."[14] Throughout the Hebrew Bible, when the particular root *š-p-ṭ* appears in this stem, it has the reciprocal, rather than the passive, meaning. This is the basis for translating "when he sues," rather than "when he is judged." The verb refers to the human object of the imprecation engaging another human litigant in a lawsuit; nobody is "being judged," passively. Correctly translating the part of the verse that refers to judgment precludes interpreting the verse along the human–divine axis. The verse implies nothing about a judgment before or by God; judgment here occurs only before a human authority.

Once it is clear that the first half of Ps 109:7 refers to the human courtroom, then this is the likely context for the verse's second half, too. Thus, this verse establishes a clear connection between the human courtroom and the word *təpillâ* and so provides the crucial Hebrew evidence for a forensic conception of prayer. Here the word *təpillâ* is likely to mean something other than the usual "prayer," because this usual meaning is specific to the human–divine relationship.[15] In other words, in Ps 109:7 we have a unique case of a "prayer" (*təpillâ*) directed to a human, rather than to God.

What is this *təpillâ*? Sheldon Blank suggests "a defense plea," and

---

13. For this interpretation, see, among medieval Jewish interpreters, Rashi, and, among moderns, Mitchell Dahood, *Psalms: Introduction, Translation, and Notes*, 3 vols., AB 16–17A (Garden City, NY: Doubleday, 1966–1970), 3:102.

14. GKC §51.

15. Similarly, the word *ḥăṭāʾâ*, which usually refers to sin, should be reinterpreted along the lines suggested by our translation "miss its mark." For support of this interpretation, see Judg 20:16 and literature cited in Lam, *Patterns of Sin*, 221 n. 12, with Lam's own discussion on 158–60. The connection to Judg 20:16 is raised already by Qimḥi, in his commentary on this verse. For a similar translation, see Norbert Lohfink, *In the Shadow of Your Wings: New Readings of Great Texts from the Bible*, trans. Linda M. Maloney (Collegeville, MN: Liturgical Press, 2003), 120.

other scholars, earlier and later, adopt similar suggestions.[16] In the context of Ps 109:7, this meaning makes good sense. The verse begins (7a) with a general description of failure to win a lawsuit, and then (7b) specifies that an unsuccessful plea is this failure's cause. Furthermore, this meaning also takes advantage of the word's much more common meaning, "prayer." The word *təpillâ* refers to a plea, usually to God and, in the unique case of Ps 109:7, to a human adjudicator.[17]

Psalm 109:7 provides the word *təpillâ* with meaning outside the realm of prayer. Other biblical examples show the word's legal connections even when it refers to prayer. Twice in his great dedicatory prayer, Solomon describes how God will answer the distressed nation when they pray (1 Kgs 8:45, 49):[18]

> From heaven, You will hear their prayer and supplication and render their judgment [*wəʿāśîtā mišpāṭām*].

> From heaven, Your abode, You will hear their prayer and supplication and render their judgment [*wəʿāśîtā mišpāṭām*].

In these verses, the description of God's response to prayer demonstrates the blending of prayer and the courtroom. The word *təpillâ* must refer to a prayer directed to God that God hears, but God's reaction after hearing is to "render their judgment" (*ʿ-ś-y mišpāṭām*). The Hebrew phrase consists of the verb "to do" (*ʿ-ś-y*) with the noun "judgment" or "justice" (*mišpāṭ*) as its object. Similar usages elsewhere refer to the actions of human adjudicators.[19] Here, then, in responding to prayer, God acts as a just judge.[20]

In the two verses, there is a clear connection between prayer and judgment. Attention to the broader context of Solomon's prayer, however, exposes a certain difficulty in a strictly adjudicatory interpretation of the phrase here translated "and render their judgment." The preceding verses show that the nation prays because it faces war (1 Kgs 8:44) or captivity (1 Kgs 8:46–48), not because it seeks legal adjudication. A legal response is

---

16. Sheldon H. Blank, "The Confessions of Jeremiah and the Meaning of Prayer," *HUCA* 21 (1948): 331–54, here 337–38 n. 12, with references to earlier literature. See also E. A. Speiser, "The Stem *PLL* in Hebrew," *JBL* 82 (1963): 301–6, here 306; Dahood, *Psalms*, 3:102; Leslie C. Allen, *Psalms 101–150*, WBC 21 (Waco, TX: Word Books, 1983), 70, 72.

17. The arguments in this paragraph, especially consideration of the word's usual meaning, are grounds for rejecting the suggestion that the word *təpillâ* in Ps 109:7 means "judgment" (see Greenberg, *Biblical Prose Prayer*, 22; and NJPS).

18. These verses are repeated with only minor variation in 2 Chr 6:35, 39. For a similar conceptual collocation of prayer and judgment, without the specific noun *təpillâ*, see 1 Kgs 8:59.

19. See, e.g., 1 Kgs 3:28; Jer 7:5; Ezek 18:8.

20. For discussion of hearing as a forensic term, see chapter 4 below.

not what the nation needs, nor is it what the nation gets, when God "forgive[s] ... and grants[s] them mercy in the sight of their captors" (1 Kgs 8:50). Elsewhere in the Hebrew Bible, the legal-sounding collocation here translated as "to render their judgment" has a broader meaning, along the lines of "to do justice" or "to act justly." This broader understanding makes good sense of the situation Solomon describes. In response to prayer, God acts not so much by judging as by doing what is right on the nation's behalf.

Nevertheless, we should not dismiss the narrower, adjudicatory understanding of God's response to prayer in these verses. While the Hebrew collocation tolerates the broader interpretation, there is here an important difference that supports the narrower one. In Solomon's prayer, the possessive suffix (-ām, "their") on the noun "judgment" points toward the specifically legal interpretation "render their judgment." The broader interpretation "to do justice," or the like, best fits instances in which this collocation occurs without a possessive suffix or another, similar indicator of "whose" judgment is being "rendered." This grammatical consideration keeps the legal understanding in play, even as other, contextual factors point elsewhere.

Rather than resolve this tension by adopting one interpretation and rejecting the other, we can build on it. In 1 Kgs 8, the Hebrew collocation that describes God's response to prayer points to a meaningful ambiguity. While the grammar requires the narrow, adjudicatory interpretation "to render their judgment," the broader meaning still applies. To render proper judgment is, after all, one way to act justly. The context of prayer draws out this blurry line between "rendering judgment" and "doing justice." God responds by "judging" petitioners' cases, but also by doing what is right and just on their behalf.[21]

In sum, the Hebrew word *təpillâ* encapsulates an idea of praying legally. The very word for prayer reveals an underlying connection to the courtroom. To pray is to plead before God the judge as a litigant might in a human courtroom. Consistent with this idea, adjudicatory terminology characterizes God's response to prayer.

The Courtroom and *təpillâ*: Some Rabbinic Examples

Later rabbinic tradition preserves and refracts the association between *təpillâ* and the legal process. In particular, *təpillâ* is construed as the antidote to a divine decree—*gəzar dîn* or *gəzērâ*. Thus, Genesis Rabbah, in one brief

---

21. See Jan Assmann, Bernd Janowski, and Michael Welker, "Richten und Retten: Zur Aktualität der altorientalischen und biblischen Gerechtigkeitskonzeption," in *Die rettende Gerechtigkeit*, vol. 2 of *Beiträge zur Theologie des Alten Testaments*, ed. Bernd Janowski (Neukirchen-Vluyn: Neukirchener Verlag, 1999), 220–46, here 237–38.

formulation (44:12), lists *təpillâ*, along with repentance (*təšûbâ*) and almsgiving (*ṣədāqâ*), as something that cancels evil decrees.²²

This connection, and particularly its legal nuances, comes into full view in the majestically moving Hebrew *piyyuṭ* (prayer-poem) known by its incipit *Untannê Tōqep Qəduššat Hayyôm* ("Let us proclaim the sacred power of the day"), originally recited during the New Year (Rosh Hashana) prayers.²³ Strictly speaking, this poem's main liturgical purpose is to introduce the *Qəduššâ*, the recitation of biblical verses (Isa 6:3 and Ezek 3:12b) in imitation of angelic prayer. Thus, the prayer culminates, after contrasting human evanescence and divine permanence, with the *Qəduššâ* themes. However, consistent with its place in the liturgy for the High Holiday also known as "the Day of Judgment," this prayer begins with a sustained evocation of the divine courtroom on that very day:²⁴

> Let us proclaim the power of the day's holiness,
> For it is an awe- and fear-filled day.
> On it Your sovereignty is exalted,
> Your throne is established with love,
> And You sit upon it in truth.
> Truly, You are Judge and Prosecutor,
> Expert and Witness,
> Writer and Signatory,
> Recorder and Recounter.
> You recall all that is forgotten.
> You open the book of remembrance,
> It speaks for itself,
> And every human's hand has signed it.
>
> A great ram's horn is sounded,
> And a still small voice is heard.
> Angels are alarmed, gripped in terror and trembling,
> They say, "Behold, the Day of Judgment!"
> An accounting of the hosts of heaven in judgment!
> For even they are not found innocent before You in judgment!

---

22. See Menahem Schmelzer, "Penitence, Prayer and (Charity?)," in *Minḥah le-Naḥum: Biblical and Other Studies Presented to Nahum M. Sarna in Honour of His 70th Birthday*, ed. Marc Brettler and Michael Fishbane, JSOTSup 154 (Sheffield: JSOT Press, 1993), 291–99. Similarly, some rabbinic texts refer to prayers, particularly those of intercession, with the term *sanigoryāʾ*, derived from a Greek forensic term that denotes speeches in court. For discussion and examples, see Meira Z. Kensky, *Trying Man, Trying God: The Divine Courtroom in Early Jewish and Christian Literature*, WUNT 2/289 (Tübingen: Mohr Siebeck, 2010), 303–15.

23. Goldschmidt, ed., מחזור לימים הנוראים, 1:169–72. For scholarly analysis of this prayer, as well as contemporary theological reflections on it, see Lawrence A. Hoffman, ed., *Who By Fire, Who By Water: Un'taneh Tokef* (Woodstock, VT: Jewish Lights, 2010).

24. For an annotated translation, see Joel M. Hoffman, "*Un'taneh Tokef*: Behind the Translation," in Hoffman, *Who by Fire*, 29–48.

> And all that live on Earth pass before You like a flock of sheep.[25]
> Like a shepherd inspecting his flock, passing his sheep under his staff,
> So do You pass, number, count and judge every living soul,
> Apportioning the lot of every creature,
> And writing their verdict.
>
> On Rosh Hashana they are inscribed,
> And on the Fast of Yom Kippur they are sealed:
> How many shall pass away and how many shall be created;
> Who shall live and who shall die—
> Who at a proper time and who not at a proper time,
> Who by fire, who by water,
> Who by starvation, who by thirst,
> Who by earthquake, who by plague,
> Who by strangling, who by stoning.
> Who shall find rest, and who shall wander about;
> Who shall be serene, and who shall be troubled;
> Who shall be tranquil, and who shall be tormented;
> Who shall be impoverished, and who shall be enriched;
> Who will be lowered and who will be raised.
>
> But repentance, prayer and charity cancel the stern verdict.

This part of the poem makes prayer out of the details of trial procedure. It assigns God not only the role of judge but also other functions, too, including, based on Jer 29:23, "expert and witness" (*yôdēaʿ wāʿēd*). Using a combination of shepherding and courtroom imagery, it describes how God passes judgment on all earthly creatures. God's verdict (*gəzar dîn*) occupies a central place in the prayer, which describes not only how God writes and seals the verdict but also its possible contents (in starkest detail), as well as how humans might avert its worst outcomes.

The poem's close connection between the trial scene, the divine decree, and prayer is critical for our purposes here. Together, these elements demonstrate some of the thinking behind the legal conception of prayer. So conceived, prayer is the human response to adverse rulings issued by God, the judge. In effect, then, the rabbinic example mirrors the evidence from 1 Kgs 8. In the biblical verses, the connection between prayer and litigation occurs in the judgment terminology that characterizes God's response to prayer. In contrast, the rabbinic text elaborates, at least implicitly, on the role of humans as petitioners or litigants. Prayer gives humans their day in the divine courtroom, so to speak, or the opportunity to change God's judgment.

---

25. On the problems of the phrase *kibnê mārôn*, see Hoffman, "Behind the Translation," 38–39.

It is easy to understand this connection between prayer and divine judgment as an abstract theological idea without much specific application. In some rabbinic examples, however, the general connection between prayer and divine judgment takes on very precise legal-procedural attributes.[26] Consider, for instance, the following scene from Deuteronomy Rabbah's long retelling of the death of Moses:

> When Moses saw that the decree had been sealed against him, he began a fast, drew a small circle, stood inside, and said: "I am not moving from here until You rescind that decree!" At that time, what did Moses do? He wore sackcloth and wallowed in ashes, and stood in prayer and supplication before God, so that Heaven and earth—the entire order of creation, shook! ... What did God do? At that time, He declared, at each and every gate of each and every firmament, at each and every court of law, that they must not accept Moses's prayer, and not bring it before Him, for the decree against Moses had been sealed. (11)

The quoted selection begins at the end of the judicial process, when Moses realizes that the decree (or the legal decision; *gəzar dîn*) against him has been sealed. In response, Moses takes his stand, first in protest, then in prayer, *təpillâ*. Here, then, is a narrative expression of the idea stated briefly in the earlier quotation from Genesis Rabbah and illustrated more fully in the poem *Untannê Tōqep Qeduššat Hayyôm*. For Moses, as for Genesis Rabbah and *Untannê Tōqep*, prayer has the potential to overturn the decree. Thus, for Moses to pray is a most natural response to the situation he faces.

God's reaction in this midrash shows that a court of law is the natural place for *təpillâ*. In order to prevent Moses from praying, God has to shut down the courts. Under normal circumstances, if the tribunals at every gate of heaven would have remained open, Moses's *təpillâ* would have made it through. This narrative detail exposes the rather concrete conception of prayer's connection to the divine courtroom. In heaven, as on earth, the machinery of justice can slow down the legal process. If the courts are not in session, pleas are not heard.[27]

---

26. Compare Chaya Halberstam's observation about the depictions of the divine courtroom, more generally, in Sipre Deuteronomy, where the rabbis discover "in heaven an adherence to formal and even bureaucratic procedures" ("Justice without Judgment: Pure Procedural Justice and the Divine Courtroom in *Sifre Deuteronomy*," in *The Divine Courtroom in Comparative Perspective*, ed. Ari Mermelstein and Shalom E. Holtz, BibInt 132 [Leiden: Brill, 2014], 49–68, here 49).

27. God's apparent subversion of justice fits Meira Kensky's observation that the divine courtroom "is used as a way of interrogating the issue of God's justice ... to beg the question of whether God is just at all, by bringing up the parallels to the human courtroom, not notable for their abilities faithfully and consistently to execute justice" (*Trying Man, Trying God*, 331).

In addition to this concretization of the prayer–courtroom connection, the midrash also situates prayer at a rather specific point within the adjudicatory process. Moses prays only after God has sealed the decision. In modern legal terms, it is an appeal, an attempt to overturn an adverse decision. A successful təpillâ convinces the judge to reverse the ruling.

While this rabbinic narrative has Moses using prayer to appeal God's ruling, the question of prayer's proper place in relation to the divine decree is actually a matter of debate among Tannaim. The debate, recorded in the Babylonian Talmud, takes up the topic of failed prayer:

> Rabbi Meir said, "Two take ill of the same disease or two ascend the scaffold to be punished for the same offense—one recovers and one does not recover, one is saved and the other is not saved. Why did one recover and one not recover? Why was one saved and the other not saved? One prayed and was answered, one prayed and was not answered. Why was one answered and one not answered? One prayed a perfect prayer, and was answered. One did not pray a perfect prayer, and was not answered." Rabbi Eleazar said, "One prayed prior to the divine decree, the other prayed after the divine decree." Rabbi Isaac said, "Calling out [ṣaʿāqâ] is beneficial to Man, whether prior to the divine decree or after the divine decree." (Roš Haš. 17b–18a)

Must prayer precede the divine decree, or can prayer be effective even after God has reached a decision? For Rabbi Eleazar, prayer can be effective only before the issuance of the divine decree. Timing is key; praying too late yields unsuccessful results.[28] According to Rabbi Meir, on the other hand, unsuccessful outcomes stem from some imperfection in the prayer itself, perhaps in its content or the manner in which it is offered. Rabbi Isaac formulates an explicit rejection of Rabbi Eleazar, possibly as an explanation in support of Rabbi Meir. Timing, for him too, is irrelevant. In the face of a divine decree, prayer is always effective.

Overall, the terms of this debate accept a connection between prayer and the divine decree, in general. In one way or another, all three rabbis accept the idea that prayer is humanity's way of effecting change in the divine courtroom by overturning the divine ruling. Rabbi Eleazar takes this general idea one step further and assigns prayer a specific place in the adjudicatory process: prayer is a plea or an argument, rather than an appeal. As such, it must come while the divine court is still in session and the case remains open. This contrasts with Deuteronomy Rabbah, which depicts Moses's prayer as an appeal. In terms of Deuteronomy Rabbah's narrative, Moses should not have waited to begin praying until the decree was sealed.

---

28. For similar positions, see Sipre Num 42.

These rabbinic discussions of prayer's proper timing open a window onto the biblical materials, too. Specifically, in 1 Kgs 8, təpillâ comes before mišpāṭ, which implies that it precedes divine adjudication rather than responds to it. Thus, it would align with the idea of prayer as a plea or argument, rather than as an appeal. Nevertheless, the fact that prayer precedes judgment in 1 Kgs 8 need not exclude the idea of prayer as an appeal: God's mišpāṭ in response to the people's təpillâ could be the reversal of an original, unmentioned judgment against them. Similarly, in the realm of human justice, the təpillâ in Ps 109:7 could easily be construed as an appeal, rather than simply a plea. In all these sources, adversity stems from a divine decree that requires action in court, in the form of prayer, for the decree to be reversed. Successful prayer results in a new judgment that undoes the original harsh decree.

Two Semantic Analogues

As we have already seen, etymological comparisons do little to illuminate the idea of praying legally that stands behind the Hebrew word təpillâ. Based on cognate roots in other Semitic languages, it is practically impossible to trace a clear path to the common Hebrew usage. Nevertheless, a semantic overlap between prayer and the courtroom does occur in prayer terminology from other ancient Near Eastern cultures. Presented here are two examples of analogues to the prayer–courtroom connection inherent in Hebrew təpillâ. The first, from Akkadian, is rather limited in scope. The second, from Hittite, is more extensive.

In Akkadian, the verb and the noun sullû are among the terms denoting "prayer."[29] Unlike the Hebrew terms təpillâ and hitpallēl, which overwhelmingly take divinities as their objects, this Akkadian term can occur with objects other than deities. In Akkadian, one "prays" (sullû) to humans, too. Thus, the *Chicago Assyrian Dictionary* offers the following definitions for the verb sullû: "1. to pray to, to implore (gods), 2. to beseech, to appeal to (kings), 3. to plead with, petition (other persons)."[30] In some late instances, the verb even loses its prayerlike connotations and becomes a "polite form used when addressing the king," entirely equivalent to more standard verbs of speech.[31]

In this respect, at least, the Akkadian verb sullû is different from Hebrew təpillâ, because the Akkadian term has a much broader range of usage that does not connect specifically to the courtroom. In three Late

---

29. For a full overview, see Takayoshi Oshima, *Babylonian Prayers to Marduk*, ORA 7 (Tübingen: Mohr Siebeck, 2011), 9–14.
30. *CAD* S, 366 (sullû A). For the noun, see CAD S, 365–66 (sullû A).
31. *CAD* S, 368 (sullû A2b).

Babylonian contracts, however, the occurrence of *sullû* hints at the kind of legal conception of prayer we are exploring here. These contracts establish farming partnerships and stipulate, among other things, that the partners will interact with the crown as equals. The stipulation incorporates the verb *sullû*, as follows:

> mim-ma ma-la ina lib$_3$-bi il-la-' LUGAL KI a-ḫa-meš u$_2$-sal-lu-u$_2$

> Whatever should arise [*il-la-'*] concerning (the field), together, they shall petition [*u$_2$-sal-lu-u$_2$*] the king.[32]

The formulation of this line suggests, without explicitly stating, that litigation is the reason that the partners will have to petition (*sullû*) the king. In similar clauses elsewhere in Akkadian legal texts, the verb "to arise" (*elû*) can refer specifically to legal claimants or claims that might undermine the validity of a particular transaction.[33] Our admittedly vaguer clause could, therefore, anticipate a similar legal situation "arising," in the wake of which the partners, as litigants in a trial, would "petition" the king.

If the terse, general formulation of this clause has been correctly unpacked, then the use of *sullû* here reflects the kind of overlap between prayer and the courtroom that is inherent in Hebrew *təpillâ*. In Akkadian, as in Hebrew, a term that denotes "prayer," can, in rare instances, refer to the presentation of a legal claim in court.

It is important not to overstate the case here. The broader use of *sullû* outside the context of prayer, especially in reference to the king, distinguishes it from Hebrew *təpillâ*. Even the examples of *sullû* that we have interpreted in the context of legal claims mention the king. Thus, even these rare occurrences may not indicate anything inherently legal about the verb *sullû*; they may simply be examples of speech directed to the king. Concerning prayer, then, Akkadian *sullû* may reflect nothing more than a concept of the deity as a king. Still, the evidence allows us to note that legal contexts did not preclude the use of the term *sullû*. At the very least, we can say that a term for speech to kings and gods has a place, however limited, in the realm of law, too.

Hittite prayer terminology offers a much deeper conceptual and semantic parallel to the idea of praying legally that is inherent in Hebrew *təpillâ*. In Hittite, the word *arkuwar*, cognate of English "argument," denotes "prayer" and "is a juridical term, referring to the presentation of a plea, an argumentation, or a defense against an accusation."[34] According

---

32. *BE* 10, 55:10–11. Also see *BE* 9, 60:10 and *BE* 10, 44:8. All are cited in *CAD* S, 268 (*sullû* A2b).

33. *CAD* E, 123–24 (*elû* 2d'2').

34. Itamar Singer, *Hittite Prayers*, WAW 11 (Atlanta: Society of Biblical Literature, 2002),

to Yitzhaq Feder, the words *təpillâ* and *arkuwar* reflect a shared conception of prayer:

> A semantic development from pleading one's case in court to prayer finds direct corroboration in the Hittite term for prayer, *arkuwar*.... In fact, the Hittite conception of prayer, as reflected in its structure and content, is modeled directly after a court proceeding, in which the defendant (the king) must convince the interceding gods to present his case before the divine assembly. Thus, the function of *arkuwar* is to persuade the gods through moral arguments, self-justification and cultic promises. This unambiguous Hittite evidence provides solid proof for the process of semantic development from legal intercession to prayer underlying Biblical Hebrew *təpillâ*.[35]

Although they are not cognate words, Hebrew *təpillâ* and Hittite *arkuwar* are conceptually related. Thus, Hittite provides what other ancient languages do not: a terminological bridge between the courtroom and prayer, parallel to the one we find in Hebrew.

Moreover, Hittite prayers are legal in more than name alone. Court proceedings shape the "structure and content" of prayer in Hittite. Prayers regularly contain phrases such as "I hereby plead my case," and "O gods, set my case down before yourselves and investigate it."[36] These show that the legal valences of the term *arkuwar* accurately reflect the Hittite conception of prayer as legal proceeding.[37] In Hittite, one not only speaks legally about prayer; one prays legally, too.

At the Royal Court of Last Appeal: Seeking Favor and Calling Out

As we have seen above, Ps 109:7 is a critical source for eliciting the meaning of the word *təpillâ* on the human-to-human axis. This very psalm also opens a broader window into the forensic theology that underlies prayer

---

5. Also see René Lebrun, "Observations sur la prière Hittite," in *L'expérience de la prière dans les grandes religions*, ed. Henri Limet and Julien Ries, Homo Religiosus 5 (Louvain-la-Neuve: Centre d'Histoire des Religions, 1980), 31–57, here 48–49.

35. Yitzhaq Feder, "Pleading One's Case before God: A Hittite Analogy for תפלה," *ZAW* 125 (2013): 650–53, here 652–53.

36. These two examples occur in *CTH* 378.III (Singer, *Hittite Prayers*, 56–57 [No. 10]) and *CTH* 71 (Singer, *Hittite Prayers*, 77–78 [No. 18]). Other, similar examples can be found throughout Singer, *Hittite Prayers*.

37. For a statement of some of the theological implications, see Lebrun, "Observations sur la prière Hittite," 54–55.

in its usual sense, that is, in the context of communication from humans to God. Verse 4 of the psalm is the entry point:

In response to my love, they accuse me,
But I pray.

This verse presents the contrast, well-known throughout the Psalms, between the individual speaker and a group of adversaries. "They" are set against the speaker, who says, *waʾănî təpillâ*, most literally, "but I prayer." While a grammatical explanation of this phrase remains a bit elusive, its sense is plain enough.[38] Grammar aside, the following question remains: should *təpillâ* be construed here along the human–divine axis, as it might anywhere else, or, in light of verse 7, is the specifically human-to-human interpretation preferable? To state it somewhat simply: in this verse, is the audience of the speaker's *təpillâ* God or a human judge?

Here both options are possible. One could pursue the human-to-human direction, as in the later verse. In this reading, the speaker and the speaker's opponents are adversaries in a lawsuit. To the claims of these opponents, the speaker responds with a *təpillâ*, a plea to a human judge. Unlike in verse 7, however, nothing here compels this reading. It is just as likely that, in the face of adversaries, perhaps legal ones, our speaker turns directly to God, with a prayer. In context, this latter possibility suggests a rather elegant, self-referential aspect to the psalm's opening verses. With the phrase *waʾănî təpillâ*, the speaker refers to the immediately surrounding verses (1–5), in which God is directly addressed.

Rather than choose, one might, instead, retain aspects of both interpretations. To make this argument, it is probably best to consider the psalm as a whole. Twentieth-century scholarship's quest for *Sitze im Leben* fueled the identification of our speaker as a defendant in a trial. This position is based not only on the reference to a legal matter in verse 7a ("when he sues") but also on other legal-sounding features. Prominent among these is the root *ś-ṭ-n*, which describes the speaker's opponents (vv. 20 and 29), the opponents' actions (v. 4), and "an accuser" (v. 6) who will stand to the right of the object of the imprecations (the same person who will offer a failed *təpillâ* in v. 7). Features like these led Hans Schmidt, mentioned in the introduction, to consider this psalm a "prayer of the defendant" (*Gebet der Angeklagten*) in his 1928 study that bears that title. According to Schmidt, our speaker must be an actual defendant standing before a temple tribunal, facing an accusation of murder.[39]

---

38. By way of paraphrase, one can supply an English verb, either to express the noun's relationship to the pronoun *waʾănî* [along the lines of "I (stand in) prayer"] or to substitute for the noun *təpillâ* itself ("I pray," instead of "I prayer").

39. See Schmidt, *Das Gebet der Angeklagten*, 40–45.

Schmidt's confident and specific reconstruction of Ps 109's setting is difficult to defend. The psalm's legal terminology does not attest to the speaker's legal status any more than the use of poverty terms evidences the speaker's low financial status. Instead, just as the speaker assumes a posture of poverty, our speaker takes on the persona of a defendant or an accused individual. Because prayer/*təpillâ* is perceived as making one's case, one presents oneself to God as a litigant. The opponents are "accusers," and the prayed-for outcome is imagined in legal terms: salvation in Psalm 109 is set as a courtroom scene, complete with stage directions. According to verse 31, God "will stand to the right" of the speaker. God steps in to act as legal defense, and assumes the position that, according to verse 6, might otherwise be occupied by an "accuser" (*śāṭān*).

All of this impacts our understanding of the word *təpillâ* in verse 4. It means "prayer," and it refers specifically to the communication that the speaker directs to God in the psalm itself. At the same time, however, it also contributes to the speaker's rhetorical casting of prayer in legal terms. Thus, verse 4 itself presents *təpillâ* as an appropriate response to the speaker's adversaries and their accusations. Adversaries who, by accusing, act, as it were, in the legal realm, prompt *təpillâ*, a plea or an appeal.

This interpretation of verse 4 aligns well with biblical and broader ancient Near Eastern theologies of prayer. Humans' suffering, conceived of as judgment by the gods, prompts appeals for relief. In particular, one seeks divine intervention when suffering comes about because of other humans, and no solution presents itself in the intrahuman domain. In prayer, people turn to deities as courts of last resort, as a way of being heard when human means of achieving justice have been exhausted.

The word *təpillâ* in verse 4 expresses precisely this idea. The speaker, whom human justice has failed, turns to God with a plea. The enemies present their accusations, and the speaker has not found a forum in which to lodge a successful response, but for God. In the world of this psalm and its speaker, God is the ultimate arbiter, who hears the speaker's side of the story and who will administer justice on the speaker's behalf.

In this conceptual framework, *təpillâ* is the perfect term to describe the speaker's communication with God. Certainly, *təpillâ* is prayer—what the speaker has to say to God. At the same time, for the speaker in Ps 109, *təpillâ* is very much a matter of law. Through *təpillâ*, the speaker gets a day in court, so to speak, or the opportunity to make a case against the others who have lodged their accusations.

This concept of prayer as ultimate appeal also underlies two other sets of Hebrew prayer terms: those derived from the root *ḥ-n-n*, which pertains to requests for favor, and those derived from the roots *z-ʿ-q*, *ṣ-ʿ-q*, and *q-r-ʾ*, all of which belong to the semantic domain of "calling." In certain human-to-human contexts, all of these terms can describe someone's last-ditch effort to obtain justice.

Both sets of terms are used more diversely than the quintessentially prayer-related *təpillâ*; they regularly describe communication along the human-to-human axis, and not just between humans and gods. Thus, it is easier to locate the human analogue to prayer that these terms reflect. We cannot, however, argue that these terms, in and of themselves, mark prayer as courtroom speech. While their semantic range is broader than that of *təpillâ*, these terms are hardly restricted to the realm of the courtroom. Nevertheless, these other terms do occasionally occur in legal contexts in a manner that fits well with, and even enriches, the legal conception of prayer. Put otherwise, the idea of praying legally cannot rest on these terms alone, but these terms certainly have a place alongside stronger evidence.

The Hebrew word *təḥinnâ* regularly occurs as a synonymous parallel to the word *təpillâ*, and the legal conception of prayer is one manifestation of this pairing. This can be seen in the verses from Solomon's prayer that we considered above (1 Kgs 8:45, 49), where the collocation of the two nouns demonstrates that the legal conception of prayer applies equally well to both terms. Both *təpillâ* and *təḥinnâ* can elicit God's response through judgment. Similarly, Solomon includes the following wish in his blessing to the people after the conclusion of his longer prayer (1 Kgs 8:59):

> And may these words of mine, which I have offered in supplication [*hithannantî*] before YHWH, be close to YHWH our God, day and night, to render the judgment [*laʿăśôt mišpaṭ*] of his servant and the judgment of his people, Israel, according to each day's need.

Here, instead of the noun *təḥinnâ*, Solomon employs the related verb *hithannēn* in reference to the prayer he has offered in the preceding verses. As in the two verses from the prayer itself, this verse also describes God's response in terms of "rendering judgment" (*ʿ-ś-y mišpāṭ*). And, as in the earlier verses, the wording here encompasses the ambiguity between the narrower, adjudicatory understanding of God's response ("to render judgment") and the broader understanding ("to do justice").

Outside of prayer, the noun *təḥinnâ* and the verbs related to it often describe communication from a person of lower status toward a person in power.[40] The subject of the verb *hithannēn*, usually the person of lower status, implores the person of higher status for compassion or favor. Other derivatives of the root *ḥ-n-n* are an important part of the vocabulary of

---

40. Karl Wilhelm Neubauer, "Der Stamm Ch N N im Sprachgebrauch des Alten Testaments" (Th.D. diss., Kirchlichen Hochschule Berlin, 1964). Throughout his study, Neubauer emphasizes the significance of the root in the context of vassal–overlord relationships. Also see D. R. Ap-Thomas, "Some Aspects of the Root HNN in the Old Testament," *JSS* 2 (1957): 128–48.

pardon, in which an anticipated punishment (usually by God) is suspended by an act of mercy.⁴¹ Thus, this root fits into the domain of resolving human disputes and naturally collocates with recognizable legal terminology. For example, near the end of the book of Judges, the community elders anticipate saying *honnûnû ʾôtām* ("grant them to us in mercy") when the families of the brides captured by the Benjaminites come to the elders with a dispute (*lārîb*) (Judg 21:22). Similarly, Job declares *limšōpəṭî ʾetḥannān* ("I would plead for mercy with my judge" NJPS) (Job 9:15).⁴²

Two narratives about the prophet Jeremiah's encounters with King Zedekiah (Jer 37:12–21 and Jer 38:14–28) illustrate the use of the noun *təḥinnâ* in the specific context of the law. Both stories depict Jeremiah imploring the king to be removed from imprisonment in the house of Jonathan the scribe.⁴³ The language used to describe this appeal for clemency is "let my supplication [*təḥinnâ*] fall before you" (Jer 37:20) and "I am casting my supplication [*təḥinnâ*] before the king" (Jer 38:26).⁴⁴ While neither story contains a formal trial scene or overt legal terminology, the law, in general, certainly pertains to Jeremiah's situation as a prisoner. We can, therefore, read Jeremiah's words to Zedekiah as appeals against the punishment that Jeremiah faces. Here Jeremiah appeals to the king as the ultimate human authority who possesses the power to change the prophet's fate by removing him from prison.

Through the lens of the law, we can understand Jeremiah's appeal to Zedekiah in two ways. For Jeremiah, Zedekiah, as king, may function as the ultimate arbiter. With this appeal, Jeremiah's case progresses through normal adjudicatory channels. Alternatively, Jeremiah turns to Zedekiah not because of the king's capacity as judge but because the king can act outside the stream of justice. In light of the place of the root *ḥ-n-n* in the vocabulary of mercy and pardon, the use of the noun *təḥinnâ* supports this latter view. Still, there is only a thin line between Zedekiah's roles as ultimate judge and granter of extralegal pardon. Jeremiah, at least, hopes for the same legal result, regardless of the authority under which it is granted.

From either of these perspectives, Jeremiah's *təḥinnâ* to Zedekiah can inform the legal understanding of prayer. The person offering a *təḥinnâ*

---

41. Bovati, *Re-Establishing Justice*, 143–61, with a specific discussion of this root on 154–55. For a specific example, see 2 Sam 12:22.

42. For additional legal analysis of this verse and Judg 21:22, see Magdalene, *Scales of Righteousness*, 193–94.

43. The two narratives may, in fact, be two versions of the same story. See Ronnie Goldstein, *The Life of Jeremiah: Tradition* [sic] *about the Prophet and Their Evolution in Biblical Times* [Hebrew], Biblical Encyclopaedia Library 30 (Jerusalem: Bialik Institute, 2013), 13–27.

44. In Jer 38, the prophet does not actually implore the king; Zedekiah tells Jeremiah to use imploring the king as an excuse, in the face of any questioning by officers, for why the king and the prophet have met. For present purposes, one may assume that, in order to be plausible, this excuse retains some connection to reality; the fact that it is, in the end, a lie is irrelevant here.

faces a desperate situation, equivalent to Jeremiah's imprisonment. God has the power and authority to remedy this situation, much as King Zedekiah could order Jeremiah released from prison. In legal terms, the speaker's distress can be understood as an adverse judgment subject to appeal before a higher court.[45] God is the ultimate court of appeal, the last address for humans seeking a just response to their cause. Alternatively, presenting a *təḥinnâ* may be a means of throwing oneself on the mercy of the court. Legal channels may, indeed, be exhausted, but the judge's powers remain.

In the context of prayer, Hebrew terms for calling on or crying to God reflect a similar conception of prayer as ultimate appeal. Most basically, of course, these terms describe the communicative action of uttering prayer as a louder, more emphatic form of address. Even so, analogies to situations outside the specific context of prayer indicate that "calling out" has an almost technical meaning, close to "raising a hue and cry" for legal relief.[46] Distressed biblical characters cry out for justice to people in power. For example, the woman whose son Elisha revived goes "to cry out [*liṣʿōq*] to the king about her house and farm" (2 Kgs 8:3, 5).[47] Like Jeremiah, who, imprisoned, begs Zedekiah to release him, this woman appeals to the highest human authority, presumably to have her land restored to her.

Confirmation of the legal overtones of the king's role as the receiver of the cry comes from two Old Babylonian letters written to Zimri-Lim, king of Mari. Both letters report a prophecy in which the god Adad demands that the king act justly with those who "call out" (Akkadian *šasû*) to him:

> Whenever a wronged man or a wronged woman calls to you, stand by and judge their judgment. That is what I desire from you.[48]

> Now hear a single word of mine: If anyone with a legal case calls out to you, saying, "I have been wronged," stand by and judge his judgment; answer him fairly. This is what I desire from you.[49]

---

45. Magdalene, *Scales of Righteousness*, 13–25.

46. Richard Neslon Boyce, *The Cry to God in the Old Testament*, SBLDS 103 (Atlanta: Scholars Press, 1988), 25–40.

47. Other examples of "crying out" to the king occur in 2 Sam 19:29; 1 Kgs 20:39; and 2 Kgs 6:26. For a similar situation before the king, with the regular verb of speech *ʾ-m-r*, rather than a verb of calling, see 2 Sam 14:12 (Boyce, *Cry to God*, 28–40). In much the same way, the widow of the prophet "calls out" (*ṣāʿăqâ*) to Elisha for relief (2 Kgs 4:1). For discussion of the legal aspects of these situations, see Bovati, *Re-Establishing Justice*, 314–28; and Magdalene, *Scales of Righteousness*, 143, 150.

48. A. 1121 + A. 2731:53–55, published recently, with translation and bibliography, in Martti Nissinen, *Prophets and Prophecy in the Ancient Near East*, WAW 12 (Atlanta: Society of Biblical Literature, 2003), 17–21 (No. 1).

49. A. 1968: 6'–11' (Nissinen, *Prophets and Prophecy*, 21–22 [No. 2]).

This prophecy imagines "wronged" people "calling out" to the king, like the woman in the Elisha story and other biblical characters. Alongside these similarities, however, the prophecy goes beyond the biblical texts by providing an expressly adjudicatory context. This is most obvious in the use of the terms for "judgment" (*dīnu*) in reference to both the "caller" and the king's response to the call. The caller is a person with a legal case (*ša dīnim*), and the king is to respond as a judge, to "judge their judgment" (*dīnšunu dīn*).

Moreover, the language that refers to the "wronged" individuals has legal overtones, as well. Both versions of the prophecy use forms of the Akkadian verb *ḫabālu* to describe the "wronged" individuals or what they claim. King Hammurabi of Babylon, a famous contemporary of Zimri-Lim of Mari, employs the very same term in his own law collection to describe a "wronged man," who, in all likelihood, has been ill-served by the legal system. It is precisely that kind of adjudicatory "wrong" that Hammurabi imagines his well-known laws to be correcting.[50] The imagined petitioners at Mari are not just men or women in general distress. They are, rather, people who have been "wronged" by the very system meant to provide justice for them.

The Mari texts' use of judgment language reflects a legal conception of the distressed people's actions. Their cry to the king is not simply one of anguish or oppression; it is a demand for legal relief from the highest authority in the land. The biblical cries to the king have similar roots in the law. Israelite petitioners, in analogous situations, expected similar legal outcomes from their king.[51]

Those who cannot find redress by calling out to human authorities can call out to God.[52] The following biblical law illustrates this point vividly:[53]

---

50. Martha T. Roth, "Hammurabi's Wronged Man," *JAOS* 122 (2002): 38–45.

51. Compare Moshe Weinfeld, *Social Justice in Ancient Israel and in the Ancient Near East* (Jerusalem: Magnes, 1995), 49, with additional literature in n. 14.

52. In one Aramaic papyrus from Elephantine "calling out to (a) god" (*mqryʾ ʿl ʾlhn*) occurs as a legal mechanism (Bezalel Porten and Ada Yardeni, *Textbook of Aramaic Documents from Ancient Egypt*, 4 vols. [Winona Lake, IN: Eisenbrauns, 1986], 2:144–145 [B7.2]). Porten and Yardeni label it a "judicial declaration" imposed by adjudicating authorities to resolve a dispute in which there is insufficient evidence (145). This is not exactly parallel to the biblical examples of "calling out" to God in prayer or, for that matter, calling to the human king, both of which are means of obtaining relief rather than evidence to resolve a dispute. Nevertheless, the Aramaic text does show that "calling out" belongs in the context of legal action. For discussion, see Bezalel Porten, *Archives from Elephantine: The Life of an Ancient Jewish Military Colony* (Berkeley: University of California Press, 1968), 156–58; and Porten and Yardeni, *Textbook of Aramaic Documents*, 145. On the question of the reading of the relevant lines, compare K. van der Toorn, "Ḥerem-Bethel and Elephantine Oath Procedure," *ZAW* 98 (1986): 282–85 with Ada Yardeni's drawing presented in Bezalel Porten, "Cowley 7 Reconsidered," *Or* NS 56 (1987): 89–92.

53. For similar reminders elsewhere in biblical legislation, see Exod 22:21–22, 26; Deut 15:9.

> You shall not abuse a needy and destitute hireling.... You must pay him his wages on the same day, before the sun sets, for he is needy and urgently depends on it; else he will call out [wəlōʾ yiqrāʾ] to YHWH against you and you will incur guilt. (Deut 24:14–15)

The impoverished worker, denied his wages, will "call out" to God, who will take up the needy man's case. Unlike the biblical characters who call out to the king, this destitute hireling bypasses human justice completely and turns instead to God. God, in a manner quite like the king in the narrative, addresses the petitioner's case and finds against the unjust Israelite employer.[54]

This law provides the crucial nexus between the human-to-human institution of "calling out" to the king for legal redress and the human-to-divine action of "calling out" to God in prayer. In prayer, humans, faced with the failings of human justice, present their cases to God, the ultimate arbiter. References to calling out to God in prayers themselves reflect this legal conception. Consider the following example, from the book of Lamentations:

> I called Your name, YHWH, from the nethermost pit.
> Hear my voice! Do not let your ear ignore my groan, my cry!
> Draw near on the day I call You, say, "Do not fear!" Champion my cause, YHWH, redeem my life.
> YHWH, see the wrong against me, judge my case! (Lam 3:55–59)

These verses trace a clear path from "calling out" to "judgment." They begin with several references to the speaker's call, and ask God to heed it. The speaker prays for God not only to take notice but also to assume the role of judge: "Judge my case!" Here the call to God amounts to a legal action in the divine courtroom, an appeal for justice from the ultimate judge.

The lament that opens the book of Habakkuk also connects the cry to God with justice, but by exposing God's failure to heed. The prophet complains:

> How long, YHWH, shall I cry and You not hear, shall I shout, "Violence," and you not save?
> Why do You make me see iniquity, and You look upon wrong?
> Raiding and violence are before me,
> Strife and contention go on!
> That is why ruling stops and justice never emerges;
> For the villain hedges in the just man—
> Therefore justice emerges twisted. (Hab 1:2–4)

---

54. Boyce, *Cry to God*, 41–42.

In an ideal situation, matters would proceed as the speaker in Lamentations describes them. God would hear humans appealing for justice and would act justly on their behalf. In Habakkuk, however, God has failed to hear the speaker's cries and shouts. The result is a complete perversion of justice. For the system to achieve its desired ends of justice and societal well-being, God must be available to hear the cries of the distressed. When God does not meet this expectation, the very rule of law fails, "justice never emerges"—or, worse yet, "emerges twisted."

In these two biblical prayers, the call to God appears alongside the overtly legal term for "justice" or "judgment" (*mišpāṭ*). This collocation underscores the idea of calling to God, through prayer, as a demand for adjudication. Thus, verbs of calling to God are, like the prayer terms *təpillâ* and *təḥinnâ*, also expressions of the idea of praying legally.

When speakers pray by "calling out" to God, they present themselves as appellants in the divine courtroom. Their situation is analogous to that of the oppressed workers in the biblical laws, who call out to God for justice. This analogy extends beyond the terminology about prayer to features of prayers themselves, specifically to speakers' self-presentation as plaintiffs. The following chapter examines how speakers incorporate legal terminology and concepts and, through prayer, demand justice from God.

2

Praying as a Plaintiff

In one Old Babylonian prayer, a speaker named Kuzullum turns to the god Nanna for assistance in pursuing a legal claim:

> O Nanna! You are king of heaven and earth.
> I trusted you, but Elali son of Girni-isa has wronged me.
> Judge my case!
>
> He did not have money, so he approached me.
> With my money he paid off his debts.
> He contracted a marriage.
> He had a son and a daughter.
> But he did not repay me.
> He did not return all of my money.
> He has wronged me ...
>
> I trusted Nanna and,
> in the orchards, facing Ekišnugal, facing Ningal of Egadi,
> before Ninšubur the ... of Kisalmah, before Alammuš, before Nanna-igidu and Nanna-adah he swore to me:
> "May I be damned if I wrong you and your sons," he swore.
> "May these gods be my witnesses," he swore.
>
> Moreover, in the orchards, facing Ekišnugal, before Nanna, before Šamaš,
> "May I, Elali, be damned if I wrong Kuzullum! Before Nanna, before Šamaš, may there be no heir for Elali!"
>
> Thus he swore!
> One cursed (for breaking the oath) by Nanna and Šamaš shall be filled with "leprosy," grow poor and not have an heir.
> Elali swore by Nanna and Šamaš but he has wronged me!
>
> May Ninšubur, king of property, step forth and
> May Nanna and Šamaš judge my case!
>
> May I witness the greatness of Nanna and Šamaš![1]

---

1. UET 6, 402. The translation here follows Benjamin R. Foster, *Before the Muses: An Anthology of Akkadian Literature*, 3rd ed. (Bethesda, MD: CDL, 2005), 215–16. See also William L. Moran, "UET 6, 402: Persuasion in the Plain Style," *JANESCU* 22 (1993): 113–20.

Kuzullum, creditor of Elali, has not received payment for the money owed to him, so he turns to Nana and Šamaš for redress. Kuzullum relates the details of the case and charges that Elali has violated oaths by the gods and has not repaid him. Apparently despairing of human means of achieving redress, Kuzullum offers his prayer to the gods, with the hope of finally being paid.

In this prayer, the forensic language comes quite naturally; Kuzullum's circumstances, as he describes them in the prayer, are cause for a legal action, a "case" against Elali. An unpaid debt warrants a legal-sounding prayer, regardless of whether one imagines prayer, in general, in legal terms. In other words, if this prayer were the only evidence for the legal conception of prayer, the case would be quite weak. Still, this prayer is important because it shows the place of the gods as the ultimate arbiters. In the world of this prayer, the legal system extends from earth to heaven, with the divine courtroom as the ultimate court of appeal.[2] As witnesses to the original oath, Nanna and Šamaš have jurisdiction over its violation.

Two elements of language, present already in the opening lines of Kuzullum's prayer, set its particularly legal tone. First, he declares that Elali has "wronged" (*ḫabālu*) him. As we have already seen, this verb, which occurs throughout the prayer, refers to perceived failures of the adjudicatory system.[3] Second, he follows this brief description with a demand for judgment: "judge my case!" (*dīnī dīn*). A similarly worded demand for divine judgment comes near the end of the prayer: "May Nanna and Šamaš judge my case!" (*dīnī lidīnū*). These nearly identical lines frame the specifics, as Kuzullum narrates them in the prayer, and transform his statements of fact into a legal claim lodged before the gods. Kuzullum tells the gods his history with Elali not just to voice his frustration but in order to achieve justice. Elali has "wronged" him, and, through prayer, Kuzullum demands that justice be served.

Both of these elements—the posture of having been "wronged" and the demand for judgment—occur also in other prayers from the ancient Near East, even those, unlike Kuzullum's prayer, that lack an overt, specific context in a human legal dispute. In Kuzullum's case, they fit the specific occasion for prayer. Elsewhere, they emerge from the deeper-seated legal conception of prayer. Just as the terminology describing prayer, which we analyzed earlier, connects prayer to the adjudicatory process, so do the speakers' assumption of the stance of having been wronged and their incorporation of demands for judgment. By means of these two elements, speakers present themselves as plaintiffs. Thus, these two

---

2. See Raymond Westbrook, "International Law in the Amarna Age," in *Law from the Tigris to the Tiber: The Writings of Raymond Westbrook*, ed. Bruce Wells and F. Rachel Magdalene, 2 vols. (Winona Lake, IN: Eisenbrauns, 2009), 2:265–84, here 270.

3. Roth, "Hammurabi's Wronged Man," 44–45.

features of prayers concretize within prayers themselves the idea of praying legally.

Justice and the Stance of Poverty

The following two Akkadian incantations, one addressed to the fire god Girra and the other to the sun god Šamaš, belong to exorcism rituals for healing possessed individuals:

> Girra, you are mighty and furious,
> You [set aright] gods and kings, you judge the case of the wronged man and woman [*tadân dēnu ša ḫabli u ḫabilti*],
> [At my case], stand by, like Šamaš, the hero,
> Judge my case, decide my decision [*dīnī dīn purussâya purus*]!
> Remove [the evil ghost] from my body, so I may proclaim the praise of your great godhead.[4]

> Šamaš, noble of the Anunnaki, lord of the Igigi, supreme leader, ruler of the people,
> Judge of heaven and earth, whose command is irrevocable,
> ......
> You judge the case of the wronged man and woman; you make their decisions go right [*dīn ḫablim u ḫabilti tadân purussêšina tušteššir*].
> I am so-and-so son of so-and so; exhausted, I kneel.
> (I) who, because of the anger of god and goddess, an obligation has bound.
> An *utukku*-demon, a *rābiṣu*-demon, a ghost, a *lilû*-demon—paralysis, twisting, numbness of flesh, dizziness,
> Stiffness, insanity have they weighed out for me and daily they cause me to twist.
> Shamash, you are the judge! I have brought you my life! In the matter of the sickness that has seized me, I kneel for judgment!
> Judge my case, decide my decision [*dīnī dīn purussâya purus*]! Until you grant a decision to my case,
> To any ot[her] case [do not] give a decision! After you grant a decision to my case,
> (and) my obligation has let me go (and) fled [from] my body, wherever I put my trust, may the gods agree with your word.
> [May the heavens be ple]ased with you; may the earth rejoice in you.[5]

---

4. *KAR* 267:27–30. A critical edition, with textual parallels, can be found in Jo Ann Scurlock, *Magico-Medical Means of Treating Ghost-Induced Illnesses in Ancient Mesopotamia*, AMD 3 (Leiden: Brill, 2006), 356–58 (No. 119).

5. Köcher *BAM* 323:19–35. A critical edition, with parallels and commentary, can be found in Scurlock, *Magico-Medical Means*, 530–35 (No. 226). See also Duane Smith, "A Ritual

Unlike Kuzzulum, whose prayer began this chapter, the speakers here are not engaged in a legal dispute with another human. The prayers themselves and the surrounding rituals make it abundantly clear that the speakers pray for relief from possessing ghosts and other elements. Significantly, though, the prayers here recall the legal terms that Kuzullum uses in his prayer. Most obviously, just like Kuzullum, the speakers demand judgment and even use one phrase that is exactly the same, "judge my case" (*dīnī dīn*), and expand it poetically with a synonymous parallel—"decide my decision" (*purussâya purus*). With this, the specific resolution to the problem at hand (removal of the ghost), becomes a matter of law and justice. The deities are asked to act as divine judges to resolve the case.

As significantly, even before the demands themselves, the speakers invoke the deities as judges who provide justice for people who have been "wronged." Here they employ two adjectival forms (*ḫabli* and *ḫabilti*) derived from the very same verb (*ḫabālu*) that Kuzullum repeatedly employs in his accusation that Elali has "wronged" him. The speakers refer to "wronged men and women," in general, without explicitly mentioning their own situation. Still, this particular invocation, especially in combination with the subsequent demand for judgment, suggests that the speakers, just like Kuzullum, have been wronged and seek redress in the divine courtroom. In that venue, the ghosts and possessing demons are as much a matter of law as is collecting a debt.

Other Akkadian prayers are slightly more explicit about the speakers' self-presentation as having been "wronged." There, instead of just invoking the deity's general capacity to protect wronged individuals and hinting thereby that they seek this protection, the speakers actually refer to themselves as having been "wronged."[6] In the Hebrew Bible, the analogues are the speakers' common description of their own situations using what Amy C. Cottrill calls "the language of self-abasement," specifically terms related to affliction, oppression, and poverty, such as *ʿānî* and *ʾebyôn*.[7] These terms bring to mind the cry of the oppressed to the king

---

Incantation-Prayer against Ghost-Induced Illness: Shamash 73," in *Reading Akkadian Prayers and Hymns: An Introduction*, ed. Alan Lenzi, ANEM 3 (Atlanta: Society of Biblical Literature, 2011), 197–215.

6. Werner Mayer, *Untersuchungen zur Formensprache der babylonischen 'Gebetsbeschwörungen,'* StPohl: Series Maior 5 (Rome: Pontifical Biblical Institute, 1976), 71–72; *CAD*, Ḫ, 16 (*ḫablu*).

7. Amy C. Cottrill, *Language, Power, and Identity in the Lament Psalms of the Individual*, LHBOTS 493 (New York: T&T Clark, 2008), 114. Cottrill collects many references from the Psalms (115, nn. 52–58). To these, add forms of the verb *d-l-l* in Pss 79:8; 116:6; 142:7; forms of the verb *ʿ-n-y* in Isa 64:11; Pss 88:8; 90:15; 102:24; 119:71, 75, 107; and constructions with the nominal form *ʿŏnî* in Pss 9:14; 25:18; 31:8; 44:25; 119:50, 92, 153; Lam 1:9; 3:1, 19. Also related are descriptions and invocations of God as savior of the oppressed and the poor, e.g., 1 Sam

or to God, discussed at the end of the previous chapter. The speakers cast themselves in a role analogous to that of the "poor or destitute hireling" of Deut 24:14–15, who seeks redress by "crying out" to God. Their prayers are, accordingly, pleas for divine justice.

Cottrill observes that the speakers' adoption of the abased stance is "part of the performance of the role of the dependent client."[8] Rather than reflecting any speaker's specific economic or personal circumstances, the language of self-abasement gives expression to the "patronage relational framework."[9] Speakers assume this stance in order to position themselves advantageously for prayer. As devoted clients or subjects of God, their divine patron, the psalmists are "simultaneously assertive and dependent"; even as they present themselves abjectly, they assume agency to request that God remedy their situation.[10]

We can refine Cottrill's patronage-based interpretation of the language of self-abasement by considering the idea of praying legally. God's role as patron (to adopt Cottrill's terminology) has a particularly legal aspect. God, as ultimate arbiter, protects the poor by "adjudicating the case [$ʿ$-$š$-y $mišpāṭ$]" of those in need.[11] In this role, God is similar to human kings, who stand at the top of the adjudicatory system and are specifically charged with providing justice for the poor.[12] As we have already seen, the conceit of prayer as crying out to God invokes this particularly legal aspect. One seeks legal redress by crying out to God just as one might do by crying out to the human king.

The legal analogy extends to the perspective of the praying individuals; the clients' abasement (again, in Cottrill's terms) is closely associated with legal difficulty. Throughout the Hebrew Bible, one of the main problems the poor face is attaining legal justice. Biblical texts caution against judging the poor unfairly and condemn people who do.[13] Given the close biblical association between poverty and the need to attain justice, the destitute typify those who might cry out for justice. Thus, people who cry out to God in prayer adopt the stance of those who would typically be the ones crying out, the poor.

2:8 (// Ps 113:7); 2 Sam 22:28 (// Ps 18:28); Jer 20:13; Pss 14:6; 34:7; 68:11; 107:41; 140:13. For observations on cognate language in Aramaic, see Jonas C. Greenfield, "The Zakir Inscription and the Danklied," in *Proceedings of the Fifth World Congress of Jewish Studies, The Hebrew University, Mount Scopus-Givat Ram, Jerusalem, 3–11 August, 1969*, ed. Pinchas Peli, vol. 1, *Ancient Near East, Bible, Archaeology, First Temple Period* (Jerusalem: World Union of Jewish Studies, 1972), 174–91, here 178–80.

8. Cottrill, *Language, Power, and Identity*, 122.
9. Ibid., 114. Compare Lambert, *Repentance*, 33–45.
10. Cottrill, *Language, Power, and Identity*, 137.
11. Deut 10:18; Pss 25:9; 103:6; 140:13 (see below); 146:7; Job 36:6.
12. E.g., Jer 22:1–17; Ps 72:2–4, 12–14; Prov 29:14.
13. E.g., Exod 23:6; Deut 24:17; Isa 1:17, 23; 10:1–2; Jer 5:28; Ezek 22:29.

In fact, just as some prayers associate crying out and the law, so do some prayers draw explicit connections between affliction and courtroom parlance. Psalms 9–10, commonly considered to be a single original poem, consistently depict God as judge and elaborate on the theme that "it is specifically as judge that the Lord recognizes and adjudicates the rights of the weak and the afflicted."[14] In this prayer, first-person speech is confined to 9:2–5 and 9:14–15, so we rarely hear the speaker's self-description. When we do, however, we find both self-abasement and adjudication. The speaker pleads as one oppressed—"See my oppression [ʿonyî] at the hands of my enemies!" (9:14). A connection to the law occurs near the beginning of the prayer (9:5), when the speaker turns to God with praise for anticipated salvation. The hoped-for relief is described in overtly judicial language: "for You have judged my case and my cause" (ʿāśîtâ mišpāṭî wədînî). For the speaker, it is specifically God's judgment that will bring about relief from oppression.[15]

Alongside these limited first-person examples, frequent third-person general descriptions of God's attention to the oppressed contribute to the speaker's own self-abasement. These descriptions suggest that the speaker finds a common cause with those who seek and have received divine aid. Here, too, we find that oppression and salvation are colored with a legal hue. The closing verses (10:16–18) present a perfect illustration of the nexus between kingship, law, crying out, and poverty:

> [16]YHWH is king forever and ever,
> Nations will perish from his land.
> [17]You hear the entreaty of the lowly [taʾăwat ʿănāwîm], O YHWH!
> You make their hearts firm,
> You incline Your ear.
> [18]To judge orphan and downtrodden [lišpōṭ yātôm wādāk],
> So that men of earth shall tyrannize no more.

The progression of these verses indicates that God's kingship (v. 16) manifests itself in God's attentiveness to "the entreaty of the lowly" (v. 17). As king, God acts as judge to make matters right for these "downtrodden"

---

14. Patrick D. Miller, "The Ruler in Zion and the Hope of the Poor: Psalms 9–10 in the Context of the Psalter," in *David and Zion: Biblical Studies in Honor of J. J. M. Roberts*, ed. Bernard F. Batto and Kathryn L. Roberts (Winona Lake, IN: Eisenbrauns, 2004), 187–97, here 194. See also Notker Füglister, "'Die Hoffnung der Armen ist nicht für immer verloren': Psalm 9/10 und die sozio-religiöse Situation der nachexilischen Gemeinde," in *Biblische Theologie und gesellschaftlicher Wandel: Für Norbert Lohfink, SJ*, ed. Georg Braulik, Walter Gross, and Sean McEvenue (Freiburg: Herder, 1993), 101–24, here 105.

15. A similar pairing of distress and legal relief occurs in Isa 38:14 and Ps 119:122. In both verses, the speaker's relief is imagined, quite specifically, as God's standing surety (ʿ-r-b) so that an oppressive (ʿ-š-q) creditor will let the speaker be.

individuals (v. 18). Significantly, the verb "to judge" (*lišpōṭ*) emphasizes the legal aspect of God's response to the poor.

These later verses echo, in language and theme, earlier verses in the prayer (9:8–10):

> ⁸YHWH shall sit (enthroned) forever,
> He established his throne for justice.
> ⁹It is he that shall judge [*yišpōṭ*] the world with righteousness,
> Adjudicate [*yādîn*] nations with justice.
> ¹⁰YHWH shall be a stronghold for the downtrodden [*laddāk*],
> A stronghold for times of trouble.

Again, the verses progress from God's kingship (by allusion to the throne in v. 8) to God's judgment (v. 9) to God's protection of the downtrodden (v. 10). Unlike in 10:18, the nations, rather than the "downtrodden," are the direct objects of judgment. Still, the juxtaposition of God's judgment in verse 9 and the downtrodden in verse 10 implies that God's protection is an aspect of God's judgment. When God judges, the poor benefit, and, to emphasize our point here, that benefit pertains to law.

We find a similar association of law and salvation for the abased near the end of Ps 140. As in Pss 9–10, the speaker in Ps 140 makes this connection as part of an expression of confidence in God's favorable response: "I know that YHWH will adjudicate [*ʿ-ś-y dîn*] the poor, render judgment [*mišpaṭ*] for the destitute" (Ps 140:13; cf. Ps 25:9). As in Pss 9–10, this generally worded, third-person description implies that the speaker makes common cause with the poor (*ʿānî*) and needy (*ʾebyōnîm*). The speaker, like all abased individuals, has turned to God for justice and is confident in God's adjudication.

In Ps 140, this verse comes closest to the speaker's own assumption of the abased stance. Unlike in Pss 9–10, there is no first-person self-reference to the speaker's own oppression or poverty, nor does the psalm refer to the speaker's own "case" that God will adjudicate. Nevertheless, the speaker's plea, like the expression of confidence at the end of the chapter, also alludes to adjudication. The speaker prays for relief from an opponent described as "an evil, lawless man" (*ʾādām rāʿ ʾîš ḥămāsîm*) (vv. 2, 5). The Hebrew term for "lawless man" (*ʾîš ḥămāsîm*) is related to the word (*ḥāmās*) that Habakkuk "shouts" (1:2; translated earlier as "violence") in the passage from Habakkuk discussed at the end of the last chapter. Other biblical characters employ the word similarly, which suggests that it is a formal utterance used when "crying out."[16] The psalmist's incorporation of this term in the plea aligns the prayer with other "cries." The speaker, like other abased individuals, seeks justice by crying out.

---

16. See Jer 20:8; Job 19:7; cf. Isa 60:18; Jer 6:6–7.

In all of the prayers surveyed here, the speakers assume the stance of individuals calling out to the deity for justice. In the Akkadian prayers, they present themselves as having been "wronged," and in Hebrew they take on an oppressed persona. Most striking in all of the examples we have seen are the legal terms that accompany the speakers' self-presentation. By pairing law and the stance of oppression or poverty, the speakers situate their diminished position squarely within the courtroom context. Prayer's rhetorical conventions transform them into the quintessential plaintiffs.

From their assumed position as oppressed plaintiffs, the speakers pray for legal relief. Their diminished situation is, in itself, an aspect of prayer's legal character. At times, however, the speakers in prayers actually demand legal justice. These demands for judgment, to which the discussion now turns, give even clearer expression to the speakers' self-perception and self-presentation as plaintiffs.

The Demand for Judgment[17]

Psalm 54 traces the typical arc of the psalms known as the "laments of the individual." The poem progresses from prayer of distress to confidence in God's salvation. The main body of the psalm reads:

> ³O God, by Your name, deliver me,
> And with Your might, judge me [*tədînēnî*]!
> ⁴O God, hear my petition [*təpillātî*], give ear to the words of my mouth.
> ⁵For strangers have risen against me, and ruthless men seek my life,
> They do not imagine God before them—*Selah*.
> ⁶God is my aid! YHWH is among my supporters!
> ⁷He will turn back the evil to those who stare me down;
> With Your truth, destroy them!
> ⁸With a freewill offering, I will sacrifice to You,
> I will praise Your name, YHWH, for it is good!
> ⁹For it has rescued me from all trouble,
> And my eye can gaze (triumphant) upon my enemies.

The middle verses of the psalm, verses 5–7, indicate the speaker's main topic: asking for God's help in the face of enemies. These verses convey the speaker's reason for prayer and what the speaker expects to achieve. But there is more to the psalm than just this main point, more than begging for salvation in times of trouble. As the use of the verb *d-y-n* ("to judge") in verse 3 makes plain, the speaker wants God to act as judge.

---

17. This section develops material already discussed in Holtz, "Praying as a Plaintiff."

In light of this, the word *təpillâ* in verse 4 straddles the by-now-familiar line between "prayer" and "petition." Together, these features color what follows in a legal hue. They transform the description of the speaker's distress—"for strangers have risen against me, and ruthless men seek my life" (v. 5)—into a complaint lodged before God the judge. In the same vein, the prayed-for outcome becomes a statement of the petitioner's "remedy sought."[18]

The speaker's demand, "judge me!" (*tədînēnî*) is significant not only for its legal overtones but also because of its position near the beginning of the psalm. So placed, it announces, practically from the outset, the speaker's self-positioning as a plaintiff. The speakers in two other psalms also make their demands for judgment near the beginnings of their prayers, to similar effect. The first two words in Ps 26:1, following the one-word superscription, are "Judge me, O YHWH!" (*šopṭēnî* YHWH). So also in Ps 17:2, where the speaker says, "From before You, let my judgment emerge!" (*milləpānêkā mišpāṭî yēṣēʾ*). Here the only element that precedes the demand for judgment is a demand to be heard that even includes the word *təpîllâ* (17:1). Exactly this kind of pairing occurs in Ps 54, but in the reverse order, with the demand to be heard (v. 4) after, rather than before, the demand for judgment (v. 3).[19] In all three psalms (17, 26, and 54), the overall effect is the same: the prayers' legal tone confronts us, as readers, from the very beginning. As (or perhaps more) importantly, from the internal perspective of these psalms, the speakers leave no ambiguity regarding the roles they cast for themselves and for God: they are plaintiffs and God is judge.

A number of Akkadian *namburbi* prayers contain a demand for judgment in a similarly prominent, opening position. These prayers were recited as part of rituals conducted to dispel the portents of an observed evil omen, such as a lunar eclipse or any number of wild animals.[20] Here is one such prayer, in this case for averting the evil prompted by a wildcat "that persistently wails, moan and hisses in a man's house":[21]

---

18. For this legal concept and its application to the results of a different prayer, see Raymond Westbrook, "Witchcraft and the Law in the Ancient Near East," in *Law from the Tigris to the Tiber*, 1:289–300, here 291.

19. For more on the legal significance of the demand to be heard, see the discussion in chapter 4 below.

20. For an overview of these texts, with additional bibliography, see Alan Lenzi, ed., *Reading Akkadian Prayers and Hymns: An Introduction*, ANEM 3 (Atlanta: Society of Biblical Literature, 2011), 36–40.

21. Stefan M. Maul, *Zukunftsbewältigung: Eine Untersuchung altorientalischen Denkens anhand der babylonisch-assyrischen Löserituale (Namburbi)*, BaF 18 (Mainz: Philipp von Zabern, 1994), 332–35 (VIII.6.2):15–33. Similarly positioned demands also occur in ibid., 256–64 (VIII.6.1):10–2', and 278–82 (VIII.2.2):2"–15". See also the text published in Scurlock, *Magico-Medical Means*, 208–10 (No. 15):5–8.

> Incantation: Ea and Marduk, merciful gods,
> Who free the bound, who raise the weak,
> Who love mankind—
> Ea and Marduk, on this day
> Stand by me in my trial [*ina dīnīya izizzānimma*]!
> Judge my case, decide my decision [*dīnī dīnā purussâya pursā*]!
> The evil of this wildcat which wails (and) moans in my house, day and night, terrifies me. Whether (due to) an offense against my god or an offense against my goddess,
> Ea and Marduk, resplendent gods,
> Avert from me the evil of evil signs (and) portents, which have taken place in my house! May it not approach, may it not come near, may it not press upon (me), may it not affect me!
> May it cross the river! May it go over the mountain!
> May it be 3600 miles distant from my person!
> Like smoke may it rise to heaven!
> Like an uprooted tamarisk may it not return to its place! (my translation)

This prayer progresses from an invocation of the two gods, Marduk and Ea, to a brief statement of the speaker's problem (fear of the evil that the cat's wail portends) and ends with an elaborated request for the gods to remove the evil. As in the psalms just discussed, the demand for judgment introduces the specific occasion for the prayer, here the wailing cat, there the speakers' more generic enemies. The effect of this organization is similar in the Akkadian and in the Hebrew prayers. In both, the speakers do more than seek divine assistance for pressing problems. Rather, by calling on the gods to "judge the case" before reporting fear of a wailing cat, the speaker in the *namburbi*, like the speakers in the psalms, presents a cause to the gods as a matter of law for them to decide. In the case at hand, the speaker seeks relief from the deities in their adjudicatory capacity.[22]

In the psalms and the *namburbi* prayers, the very formulation of the demand for judgment links the prayers to the courtroom. Addressing the deities with imperative forms of verbs meaning "judge" (Hebrew *š-p-ṭ* or *d-y-n*; Akkadian *dânu* and *parāsu*) unequivocally evokes the realm of adjudication. The Akkadian formulation, which occurs in many other prayers and not just here, also includes nouns for "case" (*dīnu*) and "decision"

---

22. This much can be said based on the prayer itself, without taking a stand on the degree to which the *namburbi* ritual as a whole reflects a trial. On this broader issue, see Stefan M. Maul, "How the Babylonians Protected Themselves against Calamities Announced by Omens," in *Mesopotamian Magic: Textual, Historical, and Interpretive Perspectives*, ed. Tzvi Abusch and Karel van der Toorn, AMD 1 (Groningen: Styx, 1999), 126–27; and Niek Veldhuis, "On Interpreting Mesopotamian Namburbis," *AfO* 42/43 (1995/1996): 145–54, here 150–51.

(*purussû*).²³ All of these are terms quite at home in the realm of human-to-human adjudication, so their presence in prayers signals an overlap between the earthly and the divine courtrooms.

Apart from the overtly legal resonances of its constituent elements, the demand for judgment itself formed a part of ancient Near Eastern legal parlance. Plaintiffs would address demands for judgment, which F. Rachel Magdalene characterizes as "an early form of prosecutorial language," to human adjudicators.²⁴ In Neo-Babylonian trial records, plaintiffs end their statements with a direct address to the judges: "Render our decision!" (*purussâni šuknā*) or "Judge my case against [the named defendant]!" (*itti* PN *ipšā dīnī*).²⁵ In the Hebrew Bible, which lacks trial records as such, we still find an equivalent statement in Isaiah's vineyard parable (Isa 5:1–7). There the prophet presents the metaphoric case of *Vintner* (symbolizing God) *v. Vineyard* (symbolizing Judah). After narrating the vintner's devoted care and the vineyard's disappointing output, the prophet addresses his audience, casting them in the role of judges, with the imperative: "Now then, residents of Jerusalem and people of Judah, judge [*šipṭû-nāʾ*] between me and my vineyard!" (Isa 5:3). Elsewhere, even in the absence of a formally (or at least metaphorically) constituted tribunal, biblical characters conclude accusations against each other by invoking God as judge. Thus, the enslaved Israelites begin their complaint to Moses and Aaron, "May YHWH look upon you and judge (*wəyišpōṭ*)!" (Exod 5:21) and Sarai ends her complaint to Abram, "May YHWH judge between me and you!" (Gen 16:5).²⁶ Despite surface differences in formulation, these Akkadian and Hebrew demands are, for all intents and purposes, equivalent to the ones that occur in prayers. They show that, in the prayers, the speakers' self-presentation as plaintiffs relies on conventions of legal speech.

In terms of position, there is a difference between the placement of the demand for judgment in Pss 17, 26, and 54 and its placement in the Neo-Babylonian legal texts, in Isaiah's parable, and in Sarai's speech. In the psalms considered thus far, the demand comes at the beginning, while in the other texts the demand for judgment comes at the end of the complaint. In this later position, it marks a climactic conclusion to the complaint itself, rather than an introduction. This is readily apparent in the following example, from a Neo-Babylonian trial record:

---

23. Mayer, *Untersuchungen zur Formensprache*, 221–22.
24. Magdalene, *Scales of Righteousness*, 74–75.
25. Shalom E. Holtz, *Neo-Babylonian Court Procedure*, CM 38 (Leiden: Brill, 2009), 27–35, 41–44 (Summary Table 1.1).
26. Holtz, "Praying as a Plaintiff," 272–74.

50   *Praying Legally*

> Arad-Innin son of Šākin-šumi, Kalbaya son of Silim-Bēl, Šamaš-iddin son of Bēl-iddin, grandsons of Bēl-aḫḫē-iddin descendant of Gimil-Nanaya said thus to Nabû-aḫḫē-bulliṭ, the provincial governor:
> "In year 4 of Nebuchandezzar, king of Babylon, Bēl-aḫḫē-iddin, our father's father, paid 5 1/2 mina of silver for expenses to Bēl-aḫḫē-iddin son of Gudādu descendant of Sîn-lēqi-unninnī. In the debt-note, he took his house which is at the grand gate of the Eanna (temple) as pledge. Until now, the former *qīpu*-officials of the Eanna have control over that house; they have not released the house into our possession. Render our decision against the *qīpu*-officials of the Eanna! (*purussâni šukun*)."[27]

The legalities of the case, a dispute stretching back three generations over seized mortgaged property that has not been made available to the creditor's heirs, need not detain us here. Instead, we focus on the formulation of the plaintiff's statement. The demand for judgment, an imperative, stands in contrast to the rest of the statement, which employs first-person and third-person forms. This change in voice transforms the plaintiff's statement from the narration of facts into a plea for justice to be served. As it is presented, the plaintiff's speech in court ends with a rhetorical flourish designed to command the judges' attention and to move them to action.[28]

Apart from its very formulation, the demand for judgment also occupies a pivotal position within the trial records' overall structure. At the end of the plaintiff's statement, the demand comes just prior to the notices of the judges' actions in the case (summoning the defendant, consideration of evidence, etc.).[29] This juxtaposition indicates that the plaintiff's demand has indeed achieved the desired result; it has convinced the judges to try the case. Furthermore, the section detailing the judicial actions, which directly follows the demand for judgment, often begins with a notice that "the judges heard their arguments" (*dibbīšunu išmû*).[30] Thus, it almost seems as if the judges are moved to action with the demand for judgment still ringing in their ears.[31]

Isaiah deploys the demand for judgment similarly. His speech follows the outline of the plaintiff's statement in the Neo-Babylonian texts, beginning with narration of the case and reaching a climax with the demand for judgment. Like the Neo-Babylonian examples, the biblical text contains an imperative, spoken by the plaintiff and addressed to the judges, to

---

27. BIN 2, 134:1–11. For edition, discussion, and additional bibliography, see Shalom E. Holtz, *Neo-Babylonian Trial Records*, WAW 35 (Atlanta: Society of Biblical Literature, 2014), 102–6 (No. 26).

28. This is true of the speeches as recorded by the documents, regardless of what was actually spoken in the judges' presence. See Holtz, "Praying as a Plaintiff," 266–67; and Holtz, *Trial Records*, 6–7.

29. Holtz, *Court Procedure*, 32–37.

30. Ibid., 36.

31. Holtz, "Praying as a Plaintiff," 265–66.

adjudicate the case (Isa 5:3b). And, like its Neo-Babylonian counterparts, the demand for judgment comes at the end of the narration of the case itself in the previous verses. It marks a turning point in the speech, both grammatically, with a shift to imperative voice, and rhetorically, with the transition from telling the story to demanding action.[32]

Thus far, we have considered the climactic and pivotal position of the demand for judgment outside the realm of prayers, in legal (or, in Isaiah's case, quasi-legal) texts. When we return to prayers, we find a similar patterning in several examples from the ancient Near East. The first example comes from the opening incantation in the Babylonian anti-witchcraft ritual, *Maqlû* (I.1–36).[33]

> I call you, gods of the night,
> With you, I call Night, the veiled bride;
> I call Twilight, Midnight, and Dawn.
> Because a witch has bewitched me,
> (5) (Because) a deceitful woman has accused me,
> (because) she has caused my god and my goddess to be estranged from me,
> I have become sickening to those who see me;
> I am unable to rest night or day.
> Threads continually fill my mouth,
> (10) They kept food [lit., flour] away from my mouth,
> They diminished the water from where I drink.
> My joyful song is wailing, my rejoicing is mourning.
> Stand by me, O great gods, hear my suit!
> Judge my case [*di-ni di-na*], grant me a decision [*a-lak-ti lim-da*]!

---

32. Hubert Irsigler, "Speech Acts and Intention in the 'Song of the Vineyard' Isaiah 5:1–7," *OTE* 10 (1997): 39–68, here 52–53. This transitional sense is reinforced by the word *waʿattâ* and the vocative mention of the audience in verse 3a. Compare the use of Akkadian *inanna* in a similar position in the decision records in Raymond Philip Dougherty, *Records from Erech, Time of Nabonidus (555–538 B.C.)*, YOS 6 (New Haven: Yale University Press, 1920), 92:20; and Paul-Alain Beaulieu, *Legal and Administrative Texts from the Reign of Nabohidus*, YOS 19 (New Haven: Yale University Press, 2000), 101:24. The first-person possessive suffix at the end of the verse marks an additional shift that occurs here, in which the speaker, rather than the speaker's friend, turns out to be the vineyard's owner. This change is probably a feature of parabolic speech, as proposed by Yair Hoffman, "The Song of Vineyard" [Hebrew], in הצבי ישראל: *Studies in Bible Dedicated to the Memory of Israel and Zvi Broide*, ed. Jacob Licht and Gershon Brin (Tel Aviv: Tel Aviv University, 1976), 69–82, here 75–81. Although unparalleled in Akkadian legal documents, the "juridical parable" has been identified as a feature of biblical forensic discourse (see Bovati, *Re-Establishing Justice*, 82–83 with literature cited in n. 48).

33. Translation here follows those in Abusch, *Witchcraft Series Maqlû*, 44–47; and in Daniel Schwemer, "Empowering the Patient: The Opening Section of the Ritual *Maqlû*," in *Pax Hethitica: Studies on the Hittites and the Neighbours in Honour of Itamar Singer*, ed. Yoram Cohen, Amir Gilan, and Jared L. Miller, StBoT 51 (Wiesbaden: Harrassowitz, 2010), 311–39, here 314–16.

(15) I have fashioned the image of my (enemy) wizard and witch,
Of my (enemy) sorcerer and sorceress,
I have placed (them) beneath you and I hereby argue my case [*a-dib-bu-ub di-ni*].
Because she has done evil, she has plotted misdeeds,
Let her die, let me live!
(20) May her witchcraft, her magic, her sorcery be undone!
May the tamarisk, whose crown is luxuriant, cleanse me,
May the date-palm, which withstands all winds, release me,
May the soapwort, which fills the earth, purify me,
May the pinecone, which is filled with seed, release me!
(25) Before you, I have become as clean as *sassatu*-grass,
I have become pure, I have become clear as *lardu*-grass.
Her spell is that of an evil witch,
(but) her word is returned to her mouth, her tongue is tied.
On account of her witchcraft, may the gods of the night strike her,
(30) May the night's three watches release her evil sorceries.
May her mouth be tallow, may her tongue be salt:
May that (mouth) which spoke evil against me drip away like tallow,
May that (tongue) which performed witchcraft dissolve like salt.
Her knots are untied, her sorceries are wiped away,
(35) all her words fill the steppe—
by the command spoken by the gods of the night.

The beginning of this incantation (lines 1–14) follows the form of the plaintiff's speech in the decision records. After the opening invocation (lines 1–3), the speaker states the complaint, which reaches a climax in the demand for judgment (line 14). The purpose of this rhetorical strategy is clear; as Tzvi Abusch writes, "It is intended … to explain and justify the plaintiff's request to the divine court that it convene and hear his case."[34] In the legal texts, as in the incantation, the demand for judgment is the rhetorical note that moves, or is meant to move, the court to action.

But the incantation does not end with the demand for judgment. In lines 20–36, the speaker continues by describing how the gods of the night should rule in the case of the petitioner versus the witch. Here, alongside references to ritual purification, is the statement of the "remedy sought," or, in Daniel Schwemer's formulation, "a confident announcement of the desired verdict."[35] With the demand for judgment, the incantation moves from plea to action.

We see a similar structure in two Hebrew prayers embedded in prose sources: the prayer of the Judean king Jehoshaphat, narrated in 2 Chr 20, and Abram's prayer as it is narrated in column 20 of the Genesis Apocryphon. Both prayers incorporate a demand for judgment for climactic,

---

34. Abusch, *Mesopotamian Witchcraft*, 9.
35. Schwemer, "Empowering the Patient," 317.

concluding effect, rather than as an opening. And, in both, this courtroom connection sheds light on the surrounding narratives, beyond the prayers themselves.

Jehoshaphat, faced with the threat of war against a "great multitude" of Moabites and Ammonites encamped at Ein Gedi, declares a national fast. The nation gathers at the Jerusalem temple and the king leads them in prayer (2 Chr 20:1–5). He begins by invoking Solomon's prayer and reminding God of his promise to save the nation whenever it calls out in distress (20:6–9). Following this, he turns to the specific matter at hand:

> Now, the Ammonites, Moabites and the people of Mt. Seir—in whose territories you forbade the Israelites to enter as they were coming from the Land of Egypt, and from whom they turned away without destroying them—they repay us by coming to drive us from Your possession which You have given us to possess. Our God, shall you not judge them [tišpoṭ-bām]? For we have no strength in the face of this great multitude that comes against us, and we know not what we must do! Our eyes are upon You! (20:10–13)

This part of the prayer reports the specific threat that the nation faces from the treacherous invaders and then makes a final, desperate plea for divine aid. God is the nation's only hope, their only source of strength.

Jehoshaphat's desperate concluding plea begins with the question, "Our God, shall you not judge them [tišpoṭ-bām]?" (v. 12). The use of the judgment verb š-p-ṭ marks this rhetorical question as a demand for judgment, expanded with the expressions of desperation in the remaining part of the prayer. According to Sara Japhet, the verb itself "is well chosen to carry the whole burden of the plea."[36] When all is said and done, King Jehoshaphat and his nation need God to "judge" in their favor and save them. They make their case through prayer.

In terms of its structure, this part of Jehoshaphat's prayer parallels the plaintiffs' speeches in the Neo-Babylonian decision records. Like the Neo-Babylonian plaintiffs, Jehoshaphat ends his presentation of the case climactically, with a demand for judgment. In fact, in the prayer, the sense of climax is further heightened by the expressions of desperation that expand the demand itself.

The parallel between Jehoshaphat's prayer and the Neo-Babylonian records extends beyond the climactic placement of the demand

---

36. Sara Japhet, *I and II Chronicles: A Commentary*, OTL (Louisville: Westminster John Knox, 1993), 792. See also Rimon Kasher, "The Saving of Jehoshaphat" [Hebrew], *Beth Miqra* 31 (1985–86): 242–51, here 250; and Gary N. Knoppers, "Jerusalem at War in Chronicles," in *Zion, City of Our God*, ed. Richard S. Hess and Gordon J. Wenham (Grand Rapids: Eerdmans, 1999), 57–76, here 69. The observation on the verb holds true even though the verb occurs here in unique combination with the preposition bə-.

for judgment. The overall structure of the records, not just the plaintiffs' speeches, affords an interpretive insight into the surrounding narrative, too. In the legal records, the plaintiffs' speeches are embedded in a recognizable structure, between a brief introductory sentence ("[PLAINTIFF] said thus to [AUTHORITY]") and the record of the adjudicators' response.[37] Basically, the Jehoshaphat narrative follows this order. The opening verses (2 Chr 20:1–5, esp. 5) introduce Jehoshaphat, and his prayer that follows corresponds to the plaintiffs' statements. In the Bible, the equivalent of the adjudicatory response comes in the subsequent speech by the prophet Jahaziel (20:14–17).[38] The prophet's encouraging words promise the nation victory. Without saying so explicitly, the narrative indicates that, like the human judges in the Neo-Babylonian records, God has heard the plaintiff Jehoshaphat's plea and will take action. In light of this, one might wish to read even the narration of the prophecy's fulfillment (vv. 19–24) as equivalent to notices of compliance with judicial decisions present in trial records from throughout the long history of cuneiform law.[39]

Abram's prayer in the Genesis Apocryphon, part of the extensive Aramaic renarration of the patriarch's descent to Egypt, is occasioned by Sarai's abduction by the pharaoh. On his first night without his wife, Abram, distressed by the loss, and with "flowing tears," prays:

> Blessed are You, God Most High, my Lord for all ages. As You are Lord and Ruler of all, and as You rule over all kings on the earth, to do justice over them all, I hereby lodge my complaint to you [qbltk] regarding Pharaoh Zoan, king of Egypt, who has taken my wife from me by force. Do justice for me against him [ʿbd ly dyn mnh], and show Your great arm against him and all his household! This night, may he not be able to defile my wife, (separated) from me, so that it be known about You, my Lord, that You are Lord of all kings on the earth. (1QapGen ar XX, 12–16; my translation)

Abram's complaint itself, in which he specifies what Pharaoh has done to Sarai, comes enveloped in legal language, preceded by the phrase "I lodge my complaint to you [qbltk]"[40] and followed by a demand for judgment, "Do justice for me against him [ʿbd ly dyn mnh]." Both of these

---

37. Holtz, *Court Procedure*, 27–46.

38. See Mark A. Throntveit, *When Kings Speak: Royal Speech and Royal Prayer in Chronicles*, SBLDS 93 (Atlanta: Scholars Press, 1987), 71–72; and Pancratius C. Beentjes, "King Jehoshaphat's Prayer: Some Remarks on 2 Chronicles 20,6–13," *BZ* 38 (1994): 264–70, here 270.

39. See Holtz, *Court Procedure*, 69–74, 307; and Eva Dombradi, *Die Darstellung des Rechtsaustrags in den altbabylonischen Prozessurkunden*, 2 vols., FAOS 20 (Stuttgart: Steiner, 1996), 1:106–12.

40. See Michael Sokoloff, *A Dictionary of Jewish Palestinian Aramaic of the Byzantine Period* (Ramat-Gan: Bar-Ilan University Press, 2002), 2# קבל (473).

elements underscore the prayer–courtroom connection, in general. More specifically, like Jehoshaphat and the Neo-Babylonian plaintiffs, Abram demands judgment only after he reports what Pharaoh has done against him.

Unlike Jehoshaphat and his Neo-Babylonian counterparts from the legal records, however, Abram goes beyond complaint. His prayer does not end with the demand for judgment. Instead, Abram continues with a statement of the "remedy sought" in his case against Pharaoh. Thus, rather than coming as a climactic ending, the demand for judgment marks a pivotal point between the complaint to God against Pharaoh and Abram's prayer for God to take action. Here the demand serves as a fitting conclusion to the complaint that precedes it and as the opening to the requests that follow. As an ending to the complaint, the demand plays the role familiar to us from the Neo-Babylonian plaintiffs' speeches; it turns a complaint into a call for adjudication. At the same time, Abram's demand for judgment moves the prayer into the general mode of demand, a call for God to take action in this case.

This pivotal positioning of the demand for judgment in Abram's prayer recalls the similar placement of the demand for judgment in the overall structure of the Neo-Babylonian trial records. As we have already mentioned, in the legal texts, the demand for judgment marks the transition to the notices of the judicial actions in the case. Abram's demand for judgment marks a similar transition, to the actions he expects God, as judge, to take. In essence, then, the demand comes at the same point between the plaintiff's role in the case and the adjudicator's, once we allow for the difference between the future-looking mode of prayer and the past-looking perspective of the legal record. In the legal records, the judges' part in the case is noted as fact, while the prayer incorporates God's part as fact-to-be.

Moreover, the legal tone of Abram's prayer suggests a legal interpretation of the narrative that follows it. Immediately after Abram prays, on the very same night, God takes action against Pharaoh by visiting a "chastising spirit" upon him and preventing him from approaching Sarai. In light of the prayer, God's response is equivalent to the adjudicators' responses in the trial records. Like a human judge, God hears Abram-the-plaintiff's petition, including its explicit demand for judgment, and is moved to act. God decides in Abram's favor and against Pharaoh. In a sense, then, the narrative can be read as a trial record of sorts, a notice of Abram's successful day in the divine court of law.

When we turn our attention from narrative contexts to biblical poetic prayers, we also find examples of demands for judgment in pivotal positions. As in Abram's prayer, these demands mark the transition from the complaint to the statement of the "remedy sought." Here we consider two examples: Pss 42–43 and Lam 3. Psalms 42–43, like other psalms of lament, progress from despair to hope, from the speaker's tears as daily bread (42:4) to the speaker's promised praise on the lyre (43:4). In this particular poem, two elements accompany the progression. First, the speaker's longing for being in God's presence mirrors the longing for salvation and gives it a spatial dimension; the temple, where God is said to be present, is the place of hope. This theme is encapsulated in the speaker's question: "When shall I come to appear before God?" (42:3). Furthermore, a repeated verse (42:6, 12; 43:5) expresses the speaker's continued confidence and highlights the poem's ultimately positive direction. Even at the most perilous moments, the speaker, through the refrain, remembers that God is ever present.

The repeated verse divides the poem into three parts: (1) 42:1–5; (2) 42:7–11; and (3) 43:1–4. Part 1 announces the speaker's longing, and briefly alludes to the critical confrontation between the speaker and taunting enemies (42:4). Part 2 consists mainly of the speaker's complaint. It is here that we read the fullest description of the speaker's predicament (42:10–11):

> [10]I say to God, my rock,
> "Why have You forgotten me?
> Why must I walk gloomily,
> Under enemy oppression?"
> [11]Crushing my bones,
> My foes revile me,
> Always saying to me, "Where is your God?"

After the refrain (42:12), part 3 opens with the demand for judgment, reprises the question to God, and prays for the speaker's return to the temple:

> [1]Judge me [*šopṭēnî*], O God,
> Champion my cause
> Against faithless people,
> Rescue me from a treacherous, corrupt man.
> [2]For You are my God, my stronghold,
> Why have You abandoned me?
> Why must I walk gloomily,
> Under enemy oppression?
> [3]Send forth Your light and Your truth;
> They will guide me;
> They will bring me to Your holy mountain, and to Your dwelling,
> [4]That I may come to God's altar,
> To the God, delight of my joy;
> That I may praise you with the lyre,
> O God, my God!

It is in this final part of the poem that we observe the speaker's change of heart, accompanied by the spatial shift to the temple. Here the speaker envisions a triumphant arrival at the temple, after God has acted against the enemy.

In this last part of the prayer, a change in the way the speaker addresses God accompanies the speaker's change of attitude. Earlier parts of the poem (Ps 42) present God with the speaker's emotions and predicament but avoid direct requests. Hints of the prayer's purpose come from the speaker's questions to God, but the speaker never explicitly asks God to do anything. All of this changes at the beginning of Ps 43, with the demand for judgment. For the first time, the speaker tells God what to do by means of imperative verbal forms. As the prayer continues, the speaker makes specific requests from God—"Rescue me from a treacherous, corrupt man" (43:1); "Send forth Your light and Your truth; they will guide me" (43:3)—regarding how to remedy the problem. The speaker has gained the confidence to move beyond a simple complaint to actually expecting a resolution from God.

Something similar occurs in Lam 3. In broadest strokes, the chapter's first fifty-four verses describe the speaker's troubles and even accuse God of being their root cause. When this part of the prayer addresses God (and at times it does not even do that), it avoids volitional verbal forms, those used to express requests or demands, in favor of verbs in the indicative mood, that state facts. Then, the speaker declares, "I have called Your name, YHWH" (v. 55), and the tone of the poem changes. Just after this "call," we find the first overtly volitional form: "Do not let Your ear ignore my groan, my cry" (v. 56).[41] Others follow, including the demand for judgment, in the imperative ("judge my case," v. 59).[42] With these, the speaker advances from complaint to action, from despair to hope. The speaker's purpose, it turns out, is not just to report the problem to God. The speaker wants God to take action against the enemies by destroying them (vv. 64–66).

In addition to introducing the volitional forms, these last twelve verses of Lam 3 (55–66) move the poem away from pure desperation by taking up two themes: commanding God's attention and getting God to take action. They call on God to hear (v. 56) and see (v. 63); God can no longer ignore the speaker's plight.[43] As a result, God must punish the speaker's enemies

---

41. The lament's concluding verses include a number of perfect forms, normally construed as indicative, but which can, at times, be interpreted as volitional, or precative. If that is the case here, then the volitional mood is intensified throughout this part of the lament. See Iain W. Provan, "Past, Present and Future in Lamentations III 52–66: The Case for a Precative Perfect Re-Examined," *VT* 41 (1991): 164–75.

42. I accept the MT *šopṭâ*, rather than the forms of the LXX and the Peshitta, which reflect a perfect, *šāpaṭṭā* (see Provan, "Past, Present, and Future," 169 n. 17).

43. Compare Lam 3:50, which hints at the speaker's desperation. See also 3:36. In light of this motive, one might interpret the perfect forms in 3:56, 59a, 60, 61 as indicative perfect

(vv. 64–66). The demand for judgment (v. 59b) straddles these two themes. It specifies that the speaker seeks judicial attention from God, and, at the same time, it indicates the speaker's expectation for action. Thus, it epitomizes the movement within the poem's final verses and, as a result, within the lament as a whole. As the poem ends, the speaker imagines a path toward resolving the crisis. God's judgment is the first step.

In both of these examples (Pss 42–43; Lam 3), the demand for judgment marks the pivotal point of the prayer's progress. The Neo-Babylonian trial records afford insight into this positioning and expose how the legal conception of prayer affects these prayers' formulations. Plaintiffs before God demand judgment just as they do when they stand before human adjudicators. Their grievances build up to their demands for judgment, which, as in Abram's prayer, close the speaker-plaintiff's part in the case and indicate that God-the-adjudicator is to take action.

In the prayers, this literary-structural observation has further theological implications. It is significant that anticipation or expectation of God's judgment occurs precisely where the speakers begin to express the resolution to their crises. At this pivotal point, the demand for judgment reflects more than a religious-poetic appropriation of conventional courtroom speech and rhetoric. Not only do these speakers pray as plaintiffs by adopting the language of the court, but they also adopt the mind-set of plaintiffs, who pin their hopes on the adjudicatory process. They, like plaintiffs anywhere, expect adjudication to resolve their grievances. God's judgment is what will bring about the "remedy sought," the undoing of their lamentable situations.

Consequently, a close link emerges between judgment and relief. In fact, some have suggested that the Hebrew verb "to judge," in these and similar contexts, has little to do with the adjudicatory process and more to do with the act of relief or salvation.[44] Thus, for example, instead of "judge me," in Ps 43:1, the NJPS renders the verb as "vindicate me," and, instead of "judge my case" in Lam 3:59, it translates as "vindicate my right." Despite the conceptual arguments in their favor, these translations disregard the obvious overlap with the language of the courtroom, where "judgment" must refer to something legal. Even if, in the end, the speakers in prayers expect more than a ruling, when they demand judgment they allude to God's adjudicatory authority. In prayer, judgment is a step toward the "remedy sought," not the remedy itself. To fail to grasp this

---

forms, rather than precatives, that refer, in a sort of summary, to the troubles that the speaker has reported earlier in the poem. The perfect forms put God on notice, as it were, that God has "heard" (vv. 56, 61) and "seen" (vv. 59a; 60) and that, as a result, God cannot claim to be unaware.

44. For discussion and literature, see Alec Basson, *Divine Metaphors in Selected Hebrew Psalms of Lamentation*, FAT 2/15 (Tübingen: Mohr Siebeck, 2006), 80.

distinction is to misunderstand the speakers' position as plaintiffs, and, more broadly, to ignore the idea of praying legally.

Plaintiffs or Appellants?

Throughout this chapter, I have used the term *plaintiff* to describe the legal self-presentation of speakers in prayers. For the most part, this terminological choice is meant to reflect the prayer–courtroom connection, in general, as opposed to assigning the speaker a more specific role within the imagined courtroom drama. While this ambiguous use of English may not rise to the standards of today's courtrooms, where the term *plaintiff* refers specifically to the party who initiates the lawsuit,[45] it does nevertheless serve the purposes of understanding ancient prayers. The English word *plaintiff* conveys the point that speakers in prayers do more than simply recount their woes before a deity. When speakers pray, they make their case.

Our sources themselves usually require us to rely on the ambiguously broad, rather than technically specific, usage of the word *plaintiff*. To justify retaining some measure of ambiguity, we can point to the rabbinic debate, quoted in the previous chapter, about when prayer is most effective. The very fact that there is a debate at all, that not everyone situates effective prayer at the same moment in the adjudicatory process, attests to the uncertainty entailed in applying strict legal-procedural categories to this aspect of the prayer–courtroom connection.

The specifics of that debate are instructive too. To recall, Rabbi Eleazar holds that prayer must precede the divine decree. For him, prayers cannot be appeals of God's adjudicatory rulings. Rather, they must occur earlier in the adjudicatory process. According to Rabbi Eleazar, then, the technical sense of the term *plaintiff* could, in fact, apply. On the other hand, Rabbi Meir and Rabbi Isaac agree that prayers uttered after divine decrees remain effective. Technically, then, speakers of prayers are closer to appellants than plaintiffs. A similar role for the speakers as appellants emerges from other sources, such as the climactic line in *Untannê Tōqep Qəduššat Hayyôm*, that view prayer as a means of canceling a divine decree.

Ancient legal sources do, in fact, attest to a procedure of appeal.[46] While the documentation allows us to reconstruct this process, it does not give us a full record of what might have been said during the proceedings.[47] For the purposes of comparison with prayers, then, the available

---

45. Bryan A. Garner, ed., *Black's Law Dictionary*, 9th ed. (Saint Paul, MN: Thomson Reuters, 2009), 1267, s.v. "plaintiff."
46. Magdalene, *Scales of Righteousness*, 64–65.
47. See the example of Arch Tremayne, *Records of Erech, Time of Cyrus and Cambyses*

texts are of only limited value; they afford us procedural knowledge about appeals, but not much insight into the spoken words that might connect to the wording of prayers. Conversely, the kinds of trial records that do quote speeches (such as the Neo-Babylonian example cited above) give no clear indication that they reflect an initial trial or an appeal. In terms of the inquiry in this chapter, we know that the demand for judgment was a feature of courtroom speech, but not much beyond that. Thus, in prayers, the presence of a demand for judgment does not tell us if speakers are appellants or plaintiffs, in the technical senses of these two terms.

At the same time, though, we should consider the possibility that prayers, in concept if not in formulation, reflect an appeal. When speakers in prayers present themselves as oppressed or wronged, as we have seen, they call attention to the similarity between their situation and that of others seeking redress for legal injustice. Through prayer, they bring their case to a higher court, just as the oppressed, having exhausted more local legal channels, might call out to the king. In prayer, the divine courtroom becomes the ultimate court of appeal. We see this quite clearly in the narrative situation of Abram's prayer in the Genesis Apocryphon. There Abram, wronged by Pharaoh, the highest human authority, turns to the only higher authority, God, with an appeal for justice.[48]

Moreover, if, in the ancient mind-set, adverse divine decrees or judgments are the root causes of situations that bring about the need for prayer, then by praying one is appealing these decrees or judgments.[49] This is evident in the *namburbi* prayer quoted earlier. There the speaker explicitly attributes the evil, portended by the wailing cat, to a possible offense against a personal god or goddess. The *namburbi* prayer is a turn to Ea and Marduk, more prominent deities, to issue a ruling that will avert the evil. In the speaker's mind then, the possible offense against the personal deity has led to an unfavorable judgment, which the speaker now seeks to overturn by appealing to Ea and Marduk, divine adjudicators with wider jurisdiction and higher authority.[50] Similarly, speakers in biblical prayers may attribute their own desperate situations to adverse divine rulings. Thus, the remedy they seek may, in fact, require a new ruling that will nullify the earlier ones.[51] In this understanding, their demands for judgment are actually expressions of appeals.

(538–521 B.C.), YOS 7 (New Haven: Yale University Press, 1925), 31, quoted in chapter 4 below and discussed in Holtz, *Trial Records*, 163–65 (No. 39). For another example, see Holtz, *Trial Records*, 55–56 (No. 15).

    48. I am grateful to the anonymous referee from Brown Judaic Studies for this suggestion.

    49. Magdalene, *Scales of Righteousness*, 23–24.

    50. Ibid., 23.

    51. Because the biblical context, unlike the religious view in the *namburbi*s, precludes

The next chapter will introduce yet another possible role for the speakers in prayers—that of defendants. We will study a number of biblical psalms that, when read through the lens of the prayer–courtroom connection, suggest that they convey the speakers' responses to accusations. Mainly for simplicity's sake, I will discuss these responses as if they occurred during an initial round of adjudication, rather than as part of an appeal of a guilty verdict. Still, it is possible that these prayers, too, invoke the appeals process.

Let me illustrate by considering the oath of innocence, one of the legal responses that we will examine more closely in the following chapter. The presence of this kind of oath in a prayer indicates that the speakers seek to clear themselves of some negative charge or accusation. Do they swear this oath as defendants standing trial for the first time, or might they do so as appellants seeking to overturn a ruling that they are guilty? Here, as with the demand for judgment, the texts do not point clearly in one direction, and our overall purpose remains simply to establish and explore the general connection between prayer and procedure. Nevertheless, we should remain open to the possibility that these prayers evoke appeals proceedings.

---

appeal to higher divine authorities, this ruling must come from the same adjudicatory source as any earlier rulings now being overturned on appeal.

3

Prayer, Procedure, and Protest

Toward the end of the previous chapter, our analysis demonstrated not only that the demand for judgment is anchored in courtroom parlance but also that, in some cases, it marks a pivotal moment in the prayers themselves. When speakers in prayers demand judgment, they begin to see a way out of their situations; their hoped-for outcomes are "remedies sought," in the technical legal sense of that expression. Speakers have a certain expectation that God's adjudicatory process will yield favorable results. Even though the final outcome remains unknown, praying legally allows distressed speakers to pray confidently.

The present chapter will expand this insight by exposing three other connections between prayer and the adjudicatory process: confession, denial of wrongdoing, and counteraccusation. When these occur in prayers, especially in the Hebrew laments, they suggest that the speakers are praying in response to an accusation; in terms of the prayer–courtroom connection, some preliminary actions have taken place. While the actual accusation may be absent from the prayer, the speakers imply that they are aware of something that requires them to respond. Thus, we consider the possibility that, alongside their possible roles as plaintiffs or appellants, the speakers are defendants.

Identifying our three subjects with legal-sounding terms is, in part, informed by our own legal conception of prayer, rather than by what the speakers themselves say they are doing. One purpose of this chapter can, therefore, be said to be the justification of applying these categories to what we see in the prayers. When speakers declare or deny that they have done something wrong, or when they "turn the tables" and implicate God, to what extent do their words reflect a particularly legal notion of prayer? Do their words and actions align with how human courts operated?

As with the demand for judgment, ancient Near Eastern trial records allow us to establish analogies between prayers and trial procedures. Thus, they confirm the prayer–courtroom connection. In addition, the particular examples we consider here show that the speakers' attitudes during prayer are similar to the confidence that we have detected in the demand for judgment. The wording of the prayers to be analyzed indicates that the speakers stand accused. At the same time, though, their confessions, denials of wrongdoing, or accusations to God register to varying degrees their dissatisfaction with the workings of divine justice. By invoking trial procedures, prayer becomes a form of protest.

Confession's Legal Functions

The book of Jeremiah records the following two prayers (14:2–9, 19–22), offered, according to an introductory verse (14:1), "concerning the droughts":

> ²Judah mourns,
> Her gates languish, bowed to the ground,
> While the outcry of Jerusalem rises.
> ³Their nobles sent their youths for water;
> They came to cisterns, they did not find water,
> They returned, their vessels empty,
> Ashamed and humiliated, they covered their heads.
> ⁴Because the ground cracked,
> For there was no rain on the land.
> Plowmen are ashamed, they covered their heads.
> ⁵Even the hind in the field gave birth and abandoned (her fawn),
> For there was no grass.
> ⁶And the wild asses stood on the bare heights,
> Snuffed air like jackals,
> Their eyes pined,
> For there is no herbage.
> ⁷Though our iniquities testify against us,
> O YHWH, act for the sake of Your name;
> Our rebellions are many;
> We have sinned against You.
> ⁸O Hope of Israel,
> Its deliverer in time of trouble,
> Why are you like a stranger in the land,
> Like a traveler who stops only for the night?
> ⁹Why are You like a man stunned,
> Like a warrior who cannot deliver?
> Yet You are in our midst, O YHWH,
> And Your name is attached to us—
> Do not forsake us!
>
> ¹⁹Have You rejected Judah?
> Have You spurned Zion?
> Why have You smitten us, so that we have no cure?
> (Why do we) hope for peace but there is no good,

For a time of healing, but (meet) terror instead?
²⁰We acknowledge, O YHWH, our wickedness, the iniquity of our fathers,
For we have sinned against You.
²¹For Your name's sake, do not disavow (us),
Do not disgrace Your glorious throne!
Remember, do not annul Your covenant with us.
²²Can any of the false gods of the nations make rain?
Can the skies (on their own) give showers?
Only You, O YHWH, our God!
We hope in You,
For it was You who made all these things!

Confession is one feature common to both of these prayers. In the first prayer, the nation declares, "Our rebellions are many; we have sinned against You." In the second, they say, "We acknowledge, O YHWH, our wickedness, the iniquity of our fathers, For we have sinned against You." In the context of these prayers, and others like them, what is the purpose of this confession? What does the nation's confession contribute to its plea?

A first step toward an answer comes from two legal images, one in each of the prayers. In the first prayer, the nation refers to its sins as "testifying against" them (14:7). The locution they employ is the same locution (Hebrew ʿ-n-y + bə) that denotes the activities of witnesses or accusers in human courtrooms. For example, it is this locution that describes the action prohibited by the ninth of the Ten Commandments: "you shall not bear false witness against your fellow [taʿănê bərēʿăkā]" (Exod 20:13). By means of this same legalism, the prayer personifies sins as accusatory witnesses. The point of this verse is to undercut, if not discredit, damaging evidence that these sins-as-witnesses furnish.

In the second prayer, the legal image derives from the understanding of the covenant as a binding agreement between God and the nation. The nation builds its case by reminding God of this contractual obligation: "Remember, do not annul Your covenant with us" (14:21). Here we might compare a similar strategy by Moses in his intercessory prayer following Israel's sin of the golden calf, where he invokes the promise to the patriarchs in order to convince God to relent (Exod 32:13).[1] There, as here, the speakers present God with a legal argument in their favor.

Both of these legal images—the personification of the sins as witnesses

---

1. Yochanan Muffs, *Love and Joy: Law, Language, and Religion in Ancient Israel* (New York: Jewish Theological Seminary of America, 1992), 13. For a similar suggestion regarding the first prayer (14:7), see David Elgavish, "'Concerning the Droughts': Jeremiah 14:1–15:9—Structure and Significance," in *"My Spirit at Rest in the North Country" (Zechariah 6.8): Collected Communications to the XXth Congress of the International Organization for the Study of the Old Testament, Helsinki 2010*, ed. Hermann Michael Niemann and Matthias Augustin, BEATAJ 57 (Frankfurt am Main: P. Lang, 2011), 51–64, here 58.

and the legal argument based on the covenant—situate the prayer in the conceptual world of the courtroom. It follows, then, that the nation's confession might also serve some legal purpose. This makes good sense, given our modern association between confession and the legal domain of prosecuting wrongdoings. Once prayer invokes the courtroom, then confession is something we might expect to find too.

In pursuing this angle, a broader consideration of confession is in order. Recently, scholarship has observed that confession in the biblical and ancient Near Eastern contexts (and, perhaps, unlike modern understandings) is different from contrition or penitence. When biblical characters, including speakers in prayers, confess, they "articulate sin" but do not express regret.[2] Therefore, David Lambert argues that confession must play some other, nonpenitential role. He proposes that we "comprehend articulating sin as effecting material states, enmeshed in social relations, and shaped according to the needs of communication."[3] Confession, as far as we can tell from the biblical and ancient Near Eastern corpus, has a concrete function that can be identified in the social realm. To appreciate this function, we must look beyond confessing individuals' mental states and toward the effects of their confessions on their relationships to their interlocutors. Only by appreciating confession as a social act can we understand what confession is meant to achieve.

According to Lambert, law, especially adjudication, provides a meaningful context for a proper understanding of confession. He refers to "confession's judicial and relational dimensions" and characterizes "confession as a constructive practice, determining legal status and defining power relations."[4] As legal acts, confessions addressed to God can achieve two ends, both of which affirm God's power over the individual making the confession. In one of its legal purposes, "confession figures as the equivalent to judgment—as condemnation of the self."[5] For example, by confessing after the Bathsheba incident, King David in effect issues a legal ruling against himself that "goes a long way toward restoring and, indeed, generating the deity's power." As a result, the king's confession-as-ruling leads directly to the remission of his sin and the mitigation of his sentence.[6]

The other purpose of confession brings it into the orbit of "the ordeal, whereby truth is imposed through the exercise of power, through the successful production of pain."[7] Pharaoh's confession, "I am guilty this time; YHWH is in the right, and I and my people are in the wrong" (Exod 9:27), typifies this purpose of confession. It comes on the heels of affliction by

---

2. Lambert, *Repentance*, 51–67.
3. Ibid., 67.
4. Ibid., 59, 63.
5. Ibid., 64.
6. Ibid., 64. Compare Magdalene, *Scales of Righteousness*, 132–33 n. 18.
7. Lambert, *Repentance*, 56.

God, and, once uttered, ends it (at least temporarily). Rather than constituting an act of self-judgment or self-condemnation, confession comes "closer to an act of submission, surrender" to the authority of the law.[8]

Lambert identifies these legal aspects of confession in biblical narratives. When it comes to confessions in prayers, however, he does not raise the possibility that law is relevant there too. Instead, Lambert emphasizes confession's general, relational dimensions, without specific reference to the law. In prayers of lament, confession "spells out the power structure" that allows God to relieve the petitioner's distress and serves to identify the sin, "thus paving the way for its successful removal."[9] Conspicuously absent is any suggestion that these purposes of confession in prayer might stem from the underlying idea of praying legally.

Despite this absence from Lambert's analysis, there is a case to be made for confession as an aspect of the legal conception of prayer. To make this case, I begin with Lambert's own literary observation on the occurrences of confession in prayers. He identifies a "sequence from suffering to sin," where the confession is closely tied to describing the speakers' woes.[10] We see this in the first of the two communal prayers above, where confession (14:7) follows descriptions of drought's effects on humans and animals (14:2–6). Similarly, the communal lament in Lam 5 vividly describes the people's suffering (vv. 1–16a) as the lead-in to their confession, "Woe to us, for we have sinned" (v. 16b).

In individual prayers, too, confession and suffering go hand in hand, as Lambert himself notes.[11] Psalm 41:5–11 illustrates this:

> [5]I have said, "YHWH, have mercy upon me!
> Heal me, for I have sinned against You."
> [6]My enemies say evil against me,
> "When will he die and his name perish?"
> [7]If one comes to see (me), his heart speaks falsehood,
> He gathers to himself evil thoughts;
> When he goes outside, he speaks.
> [8]Together, against me, all my enemies whisper,
> Against me they plot evil.
> [9]"Something baneful has settled in him,
> Having taken to bed, he will not rise again."
> [10]Even my ally, in whom I have trusted—he who shares my bread—
> Has turned his heel against me.
> [11]But You, O YHWH, have mercy upon me;
> Raise me, so I can repay them!

---

8. Ibid.
9. Ibid., 62.
10. Ibid.
11. Ibid.

Here, the speaker's confession, "for I have sinned against you" (41:5b), precedes, rather than follows, the description of suffering, but the close link between the two remains. And, with Lambert, I observe that the confessions in all of these prayers are limited to statements that the speakers have sinned; contrition goes unexpressed.

The co-occurrence of confession and suffering also characterizes the following Akkadian prayer, which belongs to a class of prayers designated as *eršaḫunga* by ancient scribes. This Sumerian term means "lament for appeasing the (deity's) heart," and, accordingly, these prayers aim for reconciliation of a perceived rupture between the speaker and the gods. In this example, confession is part of the speaker's strategy:[12]

> I broke my god's taboo in ignorance.
> I crossed my goddess's bounds in ignorance.
> O lord, my wrongs are many, great are my sins.
> O my god, my wrongs are many, great are my sins.
> O my goddess, my wrongs are many, great are my sins.
> O whichever god, my wrongs are many, great are my sins.
> O whichever goddess, my wrongs are many, great are my sins.
> The wrong which I did, I do not know.
> The sin which I committed, I do not know.
> The taboo which I broke, I do not know.
> The bounds I crossed, I do not know.
> A lord glowered at me in the rage of his heart.
> A god has made me confront the anger of his heart.
> A goddess has become angry with me and has made me sick.
> Whichever god has caused me to burn.
> Whichever goddess has set down affliction (upon me).
> I would constantly seek (for help) but no one would help me.
> I cried but they [i.e., no one] did not approach me.
> I would give a lament but no one would hear me.
> I am distressed; I am alone; I cannot see.
> I search constantly for my merciful god (and) I utter a petition.
> I kiss the feet of my goddess, I keep crawling before you.
> To whichever god, return to me, I implore you [lit., I speak a petition]!
> To whichever goddess, return to me, I implore you!
> O lord, return to me, I implore you!

As in Ps 41, the speaker's confession comes before, rather than after, the description of suffering. Still the sense of the prayer is that the suffering—the sickness, the loneliness, the distress—has prompted the confession. This is not only a logical interpretation of the speaker's unstated reasoning, but it also emerges from the speaker's explicit statements of uncertainty. The

---

12. For an edition, with complete bibliography and discussion, see Charles Halton, "An Eršaḫunga to Any God," in *Reading Akkadian Prayers and Hymns: An Introduction*, ed. Alan Lenzi, ANEM 3 (Atlanta: Society of Biblical Literature, 2011), 447–64.

speaker has no clear idea of the wrongdoing committed nor even of the deity that has been wronged. The speaker's suffering is the only certainty, and confession—to anything!—is the response.[13]

In the context of prayers, the close connection between suffering and confession indicates that confession serves as a means toward ending the suffering. This is why speakers incorporate confessions into their prayers; they believe that by confessing they can achieve relief. For Lambert, as seen above, this belief stems from an underlying code of behavior, an etiquette of sorts that governs the communication between humans and the divine sphere. For prayer to be effective, it must reaffirm the power of the divine to absolve sin and relieve suffering. It is to that expressive, rather than specifically legal, end that prayers include confession.

Yet Lambert's two observations on the legal function of confession in narratives apply also to the situation of prayer. In theory at least, the two legal functions of confession can explain its connection to suffering in prayers. As in the incident of David and Bathsheba, we might conceive of the speakers' confessions in prayers as self-condemnations. In this understanding, confession's legal purpose is to mitigate the sentence. Mentioning the suffering during prayer reminds the divine judge that punishment has, in fact, already begun. Prayers that include confessions are, in effect, a motion to end suffering on the grounds that earlier suffering constitutes "time served."

This legal understanding of confession's connection to suffering relies on a punitive understanding of suffering: suffering arises as divine punishment for some wrongdoing.[14] Human adversity, in this view, results naturally from an adverse judgment; just as convicted criminals face penalties, so do humans convicted by the divine court experience suffering. Confession ends suffering by mitigating the need for punishment.

This possibility makes sense in theory and explains the biblical examples in which characters like King David are "on trial" in the divine courtroom. There God, as the ultimate legal authority, can mitigate the punishment based on confession. In human courtrooms, however, at least as far as ancient Near Eastern records show, confession did not actually mitigate punishment. This is best seen in the abundant documentation from the tribunals that took place in the Neo-Babylonian Eanna temple in Uruk. These tribunals adjudicated cases of offenses against temple property, often embezzlement, for which offenders had to restore the misappropriated goods as well as pay a thirtyfold penalty. For reasons discussed below, suspects often confessed before these tribunals. At this point, it is crucial to note that their confessions did not change

---

13. Compare the similar, much longer catalogue of misdeeds in Šurpu, II.5–103 (Erica Reiner, *Šurpu: Collection of Sumerian and Akkadian Incantations*, AfO Beiheft 11 [Graz: E. Weidner, 1958], 13–16).

14. See Magdalene, *Scales of Righteousness*, 13–25.

the expected outcome of their cases; they still had to pay the penalties. For example, one particularly well-documented offender, named Gimillu, stands trial and is convicted for twelve different criminal acts committed in the year 539–538 BCE.[15] According to the long record of the proceedings, in seven of the cases, the basis for conviction is Gimillu's own confession, on its own or in combination with others' testimony.[16] In all of these, Gimillu is obligated to pay thirtyfold for the misappropriated items.[17]

In light of this evidence, we turn to Lambert's other legal understanding of confession, whereby confession constitutes "an act of submission." This understanding suggests a non- or pre-punitive purpose for suffering. More ordeal than punishment, suffering is meant to bring about this confession-as-submission. By confessing in prayer, speakers express their submission to divine authority. Their prayers demonstrate that suffering has achieved its end and that, therefore, it should cease.

This second legal understanding of suffering's connection to confession aligns well with Rachel Magdalene's legal interpretation of Job's suffering. According to Magdalene, Job "believes that he is in the midst of an extremely arduous, even torturous, divine trial investigation. This investigation looks very much like one to which an accused might be subject in the ancient Near East, whether in a human or divine court."[18] In other words, Job's suffering is directly connected to the legal process, just not to its punitive stages. Rather, it belongs to the investigative phase of the trial. Though Job's suffering is punishing, it is not, strictly speaking, punishment.

Magdalene identifies the earthly analogue to Job's "arduous, even torturous divine trial investigation" in records of investigative procedures in the Neo-Babylonian Eanna temple at Uruk. There, we find a set of records that bear the designation "interrogation" (*maš'altu*). The following example comes from a record that belongs to a dossier of texts that document an extensive investigation into corruption among the temple's metalworkers. This particular text records the results of an interrogation by a leading temple official and the temple scribes:[19]

---

15. On Gimillu, see Michael Kozuh, *The Sacrificial Economy: Assessors, Contractors, and Thieves in the Management of Sacrificial Sheep at the Eanna Temple of Uruk (ca. 625–520 B.C.)*, EANEC 2 (Winona Lake, IN: Eisenbrauns, 2014), 159–76.

16. YOS 7, 7:43–50, 77–87, 96–146. For discussion of this text, see Holtz, *Trial Records*, 151–62 (No. 38).

17. A comparable example from the Eanna at Uruk involving the thirtyfold penalty is the text published by H. H. Figulla, "Lawsuit concerning a Sacrilegious Theft at Erech," *Iraq* 13 (1951): 95–101. See also V. Scheil, "La libération judiciaire d'un fils donné en gage sous Neriglissor en 558 av. J.-C.," *RA* 12 (1915): 1–13.

18. Magdalene, *Scales of Righteousness*, 130.

19. YOS 6, 223:1–7. For discussion of this text, see Holtz, *Trial Records*, 31–33 (No. 6).

Interrogation [*maš²altu*] of Iddin-Ištar son of Ibni-Ištar, who said as follows:
"8 ½ shekels and 1 *girû* of gold—I purchased from people for silver, and I sold to people for silver."
The *šatammu* and the scribes of Eanna said thus to Iddin-Ištar:
"Report to us, in detail, whatever (amounts of) gold you purchased from people and sold to people."

In the text that follows, Iddin-Ištar, the subject of the interrogation, provides an itemized account that includes the specific amounts of gold that passed through his hands and the names of the people with whom he has had dealings. Study of this record, together with other, similarly labeled "interrogations," indicates that the process of interrogation usually yielded confession to some wrongdoing.[20] In addition, records of confessions note that the suspects speak "without interrogation"[21] or that the suspect "testified against himself."[22] In the aggregate, these Neo-Babylonian legal records point to the likely possibility that temple authorities could resort to torture as part of their investigative procedures. The strongest evidence for this comes from a later, Seleucid-period text that describes the apprehension and conviction of thieves as follows:

> The thieves ... were caught, held and taken into the temple courthouse ... the thieves were interrogated [*ša₂-a-lu-u²*] in the temple courthouse in front of the representative of the temple administrator and the temple judges by means of the ladder of interrogation [*sim-mil-tu₂ maš-a-a-al-tu₂*] and were convicted. That day, they were burned by fire.[23]

Interrogation, according to this text, involved a device called the "ladder of interrogation." Despite the absence of earlier references to this device, there is good reason to believe that, even earlier in the Eanna's history, interrogation included inflicting physical pain. This would explain the regular correlation between "interrogation" and confession. Fear of the rigors of torture would also explain why suspects might confess "without interrogation."

Discussion of the investigation is found in Johannes Renger, "Notes on the Goldsmiths, Jewelers and Carpenters of Neo-Babylonian Eanna," *JAOS* 91 (1971): 494–503.

20. Mariano San Nicolò, "Parerga Babylonica XI: Die *maš²altu*-Urkunden im neubabylonische Strafverfahren," *ArOr* 5 (1933): 287–302. Additional literature on this subject can be found in Magdalene, *Scales of Righteousness*, 76–77 n. 95.

21. E.g., Alfred Pohl, *Neubabylonische Rechtsurkunden aus den Berliner Staatlichen Museen*, AnOr 8 (Rome: Pontifical Biblical Institute, 1933), No. 27:4–5; YOS 7, 10:1–5.

22. Examples are collected in *CAD* R, 125 (*ramanu* f3').

23. Abraham J. Sachs and Hermann Hunger, *Diaries from 261 B.C. to 165 B.C.*, vol. 2 of *Astronomical Diaries and Related Texts from Babylonia*, DÖAW.PH 210 (Vienna: Österreichische Akademie de Wissenschaften, 1989), 168:A15′–A18′.

Magdalene's interpretation of Job's suffering draws the theological connections between the likelihood of torture as part of the Eanna's investigative procedures and the religious world of the ancient Near East.[24] Job, according to Magdalene, sees himself in a position equivalent to that of Iddin-Ištar, the employee "interrogated" by the Eanna. We might draw on Job's speeches to imagine the personal experience of Iddin-Ištar or his fellow suspects under investigation.[25]

We can extend Magdalene's legal analogy to include not just the investigation itself but also the typical outcome of the investigation: the confession. If, indeed, in the ancient worldview, suffering is analogous to physically painful investigative procedures, then it is natural to find confessions of guilt alongside descriptions of suffering. Job famously resists the typical course of proceedings and refuses to confess.[26] In prayers, however, we do find the expected correlation between suffering and confession. The speakers in prayers, like Job, understand their suffering as God's equivalent of the Eanna's "ladder of interrogation." They, unlike Job, do not, or cannot, maintain their innocence in the face of the ardors to which they are subjected. Instead, they confess. By doing so, they engage in the act that should end the investigation to the satisfaction of the divine court. Thus, they expect the investigation's painful procedures to end, too.

The implications of this interpretation of confessions in prayers are worth dwelling on. If, indeed, confession is a way of ending a painful investigation, this raises the question of the speakers' sincerity when they confess. Could it be that, by confessing, the speakers in prayers aim to "get God off their back," as it were, by uttering the words they think God needs to hear without actually meaning them? In modern terms, could these speakers' confessions be unreliable because they are made under the duress of torture? Lambert himself cautions that the speakers' interior thoughts during their confessions remain "off the texts' plane of representation."[27] For all we know, the process of divine investigation yields a true confession of an actual misdeed.

Still, the unanswerable problem of sincerity exposes the deeper, more troubling question of why a confession makes effective prayer. Given the process that leads to it, why should confession find a receptive ear in the divine courtroom? From God's perspective, as it were, the answer stems from the speakers' submissiveness. When speakers state to God that they

---

24. Magdalene, *Scales of Righteousness*, 129–36.

25. A key difference, of course, between the situations is that, rather than confess, as Iddin-Ištar and other suspects do, Job seeks to defend himself. See Magdalene, *Scales of Righteousness*, 136–98.

26. Job's case is unique not only for this reason. The circumstances of Job's investigation also make its purpose different, because the goal is an act of blasphemy, rather than a confession of guilt (Magdalene, *Scales of Righteousness*, 132 n. 18).

27. Lambert, *Repentance*, 66.

are wrong, they place God in the right. Thus, confession reaffirms God's authoritative position as the judge. The speaker in Ps 51 explicitly says so:

> ⁵For I recognize my transgressions,
> My sin is before me always,
> ⁶To You alone have I sinned,
> I have done what is evil in Your eyes;
> So You are justified in Your sentence [tiṣdaq bədobrekā],
> Right in Your judgment [tizkê bəšopṭekā].

These lines explicitly juxtapose confession (vv. 5–6a) with justification of God's judgment (v. 6b). Here, with Lambert, I see confession as an act of submission to God's judicial authority.[28]

From the speakers' perspective, submissive confessions, by justifying God's authority, offer a way to understand, and perhaps also reconcile with, their own situations. Nowhere is this more apparent than in the group of postexilic texts commonly labeled "penitential prayers." Confession figures prominently in these prayers and, as Lambert notes, "is used to ground the very conditions that make prayer possible in a world after exile."[29] By confessing, the nation takes first steps on "a pathway for continuing to conceptualize the possibilities of divine presence."[30] Without confession, the nation's troubled reality would be difficult to explain. Confession, which attributes suffering to sin, paves the way forward with God.

At the same time, however, even when the speakers confess, they are hardly reticent about the suffering that brings about their confession. This is true in the laments of the individual and the community, as we have seen. Even the "penitential prayers," for all their emphasis on submission and justification of God's ways, still recall the national suffering that, however justified, has led to the nation's collective confession. By way of example, consider the following section of Nehemiah's "penitential prayer" (9:32–37).[31]

> ³²Now, our God, the great, mighty and awesome God, who keeps faith with the covenant, let not the suffering that has befallen us—our kings, our officers, our priests, our prophets, our ancestors, and all Your nation—since the days of the kings of Assyria to this day, seem little before You. ³³You are in the right, with respect to all that has come upon us, for You have acted faithfully, and we have acted wickedly. ³⁴Our

---

28. Ibid., 65.
29. Ibid., 67.
30. Ibid., 7.
31. For other direct and implicit references to the nation's suffering in similar prayers in the Hebrew Bible, compare Ps 106:47; Dan 9:16; and Ezra 9:7.

> kings, our officers, our priests and our ancestors did not follow Your teaching and did not obey Your commandments or warnings that You gave them. ³⁵When they had their own kingdom, and enjoyed Your great good that You had given them, in the broad and rich land You had placed before them, they did not serve You, and did not turn from their wicked deeds. ³⁶Today we are slaves, and the land that You gave our ancestors, to enjoy its produce and bounty—here we are slaves upon it! ³⁷On account of our sins, it increases its crops for the kings You have placed upon us; they rule over our bodies and our cattle, as they will. So we are in great distress!

The nation's confession expressly puts God "in the right" and thus justifies "all that has come upon" them (v. 33). At the same time, though, this prayer retains confession's connection to suffering. It mentions the nation's "great distress" at its enslavement to foreign powers (vv. 36–37). Confession, in other words, can explain and even justify the suffering, but it cannot remove the pain completely. The nation's hardships, their very reasons for prayer, cast a shadow over the "pathway" to reconciliation with God. Even as it accepts responsibility for its misdeeds, the nation can hardly ignore that God is the ultimate agent of the suffering, too.

The nation's stance here can be explained by invoking the suggestion that the link between suffering and confession derives from an understanding of suffering as God's equivalent to a torturous investigation. Confessions in prayer, coupled as they are with descriptions of suffering, also remind God of the duress that has brought them about. The speakers confess but do not give up their positions as sufferers. In a sense, then, confessions as we find them in prayer are not just a means of justifying God but are also a form of muted protest.[32]

In sum, for the speakers, confessions in prayer play a dual role. By confessing, the speakers hope to end God's investigation and, with that, their suffering. At the same time, the conventions of prayer allow the speakers to leave a record of their pain, even as they admit wrongdoing.

---

32. See Robert Williamson Jr., "Lament and the Arts of Resistance: Public and Hidden Transcripts in Lamentations 5," in *Lamentations in Ancient and Contemporary Cultural Contexts*, ed. Nancy C. Lee and Carleen Mandolfo, SBLSymS 43 (Atlanta: Society of Biblical Literature, 2008), 67–80, here 76; Walter Harrelson, "'Why, O Lord, Do You Harden Our Heart?' A Plea for Help from a Hiding God," in *Shall Not the Judge of All the Earth Do What Is Right? Studies on the Nature of God in Tribute to James L. Crenshaw*, ed. David Penchansky and Paul L. Redditt (Winona Lake, IN: Eisenbrauns, 2000), 163–74, here 171–72; Richard J. Bautch, "Lament Regained in Trito-Isaiah's Penitential Prayer," in *The Origins of Penitential Prayer in Second Temple Judaism*, vol. 1 of *Seeking the Favor of God*, ed. Mark J. Boda, Daniel K. Falk, and Rodney A. Werline, EJL 21 (Atlanta: Society of Biblical Literature, 2006), 83–99, here 93–95. On the particularly muted nature of the protest in Nehemiah 9, as compared to communal laments, see, in the same volume, Dalit Rom-Shiloni, "Socio-Ideological *Setting* or *Settings* for Penitential Prayers?," 51–68, here 66–67.

Thus, they give voice to their anger, or at least ambivalence, about the process that has led them to confess.

Denying Wrongdoing and the Oath of Innocence

In contrast to the speakers who confess, some speakers in prayers deny that they have done anything wrong. One extended example of this sort of denial occurs in Ps 26.

> ¹Judge me, O YHWH, for I have walked in my innocence,
> And I have trusted in YHWH, I do not falter.
> ²Probe me, O YHWH, and try me,
> Assay my kidneys and heart!
> ³For Your lovingkindness is before my eyes,
> And I have always walked on Your true path.
> ⁴I have not consorted with scoundrels,
> Or entered among hypocrites.
> ⁵I detest the assembly of evildoers,
> I do not consort with the wicked.
> ⁶In innocence, may I wash my hands,
> And circle Your altar, O YHWH,
> ⁷to proclaim aloud thanksgiving,
> and to recount all of Your wonders.
> ⁸O YHWH, I love the abode of Your home,
> And the resting place of Your glory!
> ⁹Do not gather my life-breath up with sinners,
> Nor with blood-guilty men my life,
> ¹⁰in whose hands is plotting, whose right hand is full of bribery.
> ¹¹But I shall walk in my innocence.
> Redeem me, have mercy on me!
> ¹²My foot stands on level ground.
> In assemblies I shall bless YHWH.

The word "my innocence" (*bətummî*) frames this prayer at the beginning (v. 1) and near the end (v. 11) and indicates the prayer's main theme: maintaining innocence. The speaker declares innocence at the very beginning and complements this positive declaration with a series of negative statements in denial of any association with the guilty (vv. 4–5). Likewise, innocence and a complete dissociation from the guilty characterize the desired outcome of the prayer. The prayer will succeed if the speaker can "walk in innocence" (v. 11) because God does not count the speaker among the sinners (v. 10).

The prayer's opening demand for judgment colors the focus on innocence in legal tones. The speaker's innocence will emerge by means of a legal process, culminating in God's judgment. This process will, according to verse 2, include God's investigation: "probing" (b-ḥ-n), "trying" (n-s-y) and "assaying" (ṣ-r-p). All three of these terms, especially when they occur together with terms denoting judgment, as they do here, contribute to the psalm's legal motif.[33]

The speaker's reference to the adjudicatory process, and particularly to God's investigation, gives explicit expression to a mind-set shared with the speakers who, in other psalms, confess. Like those other speakers, the speaker in Ps 26 imagines an investigative process that might uncover guilty actions. It is the necessarily uncertain outcome of this process that prompts the speaker to pray.

This shared concept of a divine investigation, however, also exposes the differences between Ps 26 and the prayers of confession. We can frame this difference in terms of the progress of the imagined process. For the speakers who confess, the suffering they experience proves to them that the process is already under way. For the speaker in Ps 26, on the other hand, the process has not yet begun. This procedural difference translates into the prayers' different tones. Prayers of confession approach God from a submissive position brought on by the ongoing suffering. We have interpreted these prayers' mentions of the suffering as muted expressions of protest—but it is important to remember that the protest is muted.[34] By contrast, in Ps 26, the speaker invites God's investigation, in confident imperatives. The speaker's confidence, rooted as it is in a sense of innocence, overshadows the fear of any impending investigation. Rather than expressing muted protest at the painful process, the speaker comes very close to challenging, even daring, God.

The interpretation of the speaker's imperatives as challenges emerges in full relief when we compare Ps 26 with Ps 131. The main body of this short psalm consists of the following two verses:

> [1]... O Yhwh! My heart has not been haughty, nor have my eyes looked too high, nor have I walked (on paths) too great or wondrous for me.
> [2]Indeed, I have imagined and quieted myself like a weaned child to his mother,
> Like a weaned child, I am, to myself.

As in Ps 26, the speaker in Ps 131 approaches God with a denial of wrongdoing. One difference between the two psalms, however, is the absence

---

33. For similar co-occurrences of b-ḥ-n and š-p-ṭ, see Jer 11:20; 12:1–3; Pss 7:9–10; 17:2–3; and Job 23:4–11. Compare Bovati, *Re-Establishing Justice*, 244–45; and Magdalene, *Scales of Righteousness*, 107–8.

34. On Neh 9, discussed earlier, see Dalit Rom-Shiloni, "Between Protest and Theodicy: The Dialogue between Communal Laments and Penitential Prayers in Biblical Prayers" [Hebrew], *Shnaton* 16 (2005–2006): 71–96, here 84.

of any demand for judgment or investigation. As a result, the speaker in Ps 131 seems much less confident than the speaker in Ps 26. In Ps 131, the speaker's tone is entirely humble.[35] The explicit denial of haughtiness (v. 1) is matched by refraining from anything, such as demanding judgment or investigation, that might be construed as bordering on the irreverent.

While Ps 131 does not contain any explicit imperatives for legal action, it does evoke the idea of praying legally. Specifically, the psalm's second verse is phrased as an oath, a truncated conditional sentence with only a protasis ("if") but without an apodosis ("then"). The truncated part of the sentence is an unstated self-curse, invoked upon the speaker if the condition proves true. Literally, then, the best rendering of the verse would be, "If I have not imagined and quieted myself like a weaned child to his mother ..." It is as if the speaker says, "May I be cursed if I have not imagined and quieted myself like a weaned child to his mother." The implication (reflected in the use of "indeed" in the English translation) is that the speaker has actually behaved in this humble manner.

The oath bears on the comparison of Pss 26 and 131 and returns us to the motif of the divine investigation. In Ps 26, the speaker confidently invites the investigation; God will not find anything incriminating. The speaker in Ps 131, by contrast, seems to be already under investigation of some sort, at least under suspicion. This explains the humbler tone, in general, and, more specifically, why the speaker takes an oath. Both the humble tone and the oath are natural responses to an (implicit) accusation.

The use of an oath formulation, rather than a simply worded affirmation, brings Ps 131 into the courtroom, where oaths are common, even today. We can, therefore, appreciate this psalm against the background of the use of oaths in human courtrooms in the ancient Near East. In that legal world, the oath, because of its concomitant self-curse, was not taken lightly. In fact, at certain points in Mesopotamian legal history, oaths were considered sufficient to dispose of a case; adjudicatory authorities would resolve legal disputes by imposing an oath on one of the parties. The sworn statement was automatically deemed true; unwillingness to swear indicated fear of the oath's consequences and that the party could not truthfully make the claim.[36]

Separate from this court-imposed oath, ancient Near Eastern court records also attest to "weakened" oaths that accompany litigants' statements but are not sufficient to settle the case.[37] Instead, litigants, of their

---

35. See Davida H. Charney, *Persuading God: Rhetorical Studies of the First-Person Psalms*, Hebrew Bible Monographs 73 (Sheffield: Sheffield Phoenix Press, 2015), 32–38.
36. Bruce Wells, F. Rachel Magdalene, and Cornelia Wunsch, "The Assertory Oath in Neo-Babylonian and Persian Administrative Texts," *RIDA* 57 (2010): 13–29, here 13–15.
37. Ibid., 17–20; and Magdalene, *Scales of Righteousness*, 78–84.

own volition, use these oaths to strengthen their claim; their willingness to incur potential harm for perjury, while not sufficient to carry the day, still "increased the efficacy of the testimony in meeting a party's burden of proof."[38] For example, the following Neo-Babylonian preliminary record from the Eanna temple documents a suspect's responses to a series of questions from temple officials:[39]

> Bēl-iddin, the *šatammu* of the Eanna, son of Sîn-ēreš descendant of Ibni-il, and Bariki-ili, the royal administrator of the Eanna, said thus to Iddinaya son of Innina-šuma-ibni, oblate of Ištar of Uruk:
> "Are there any debt-notes for dates or fragments for the estimated-yield of the fields of the Lady-of-Uruk and Nanaya in your possession? If so, do you know where they are? [...] debt notes and fragments of the treasury which Andiya, your wife, deposited in the house of Kudurrānu, whose are they?"
> In the assembly of the freemen, Iddinaya swore by Bēl, Nabû and Darius, king of Babylon, king of the lands:
> "Indeed, among the ... of debt-notes which Andiya, my wife deposited in the house of Kudurrānu, there was nothing belonging to the Lady-of-Uruk! Indeed, those debt-notes are my own!"[40]

The Eanna administration suspects that Iddinaya and Andiya, his wife, have mishandled documents belonging to the temple. Faced with the questions about these documents' whereabouts, Iddinaya denies, under oath, any wrongdoing. Still, nothing in the text indicates that this oath is imposed by the authorities; Iddinaya apparently swears of his own volition. Furthermore, the remainder of the text indicates that the oath does not end the investigation. The authorities continue with an additional question, which Iddinaya answers without an oath. A record of how this matter ends does not survive.[41]

It is this kind of nondispositive oath that the speaker in Ps 131 seems to employ. Both Iddinaya and the speaker take the oath on their own initiative, and, as far as we can tell, neither can be certain that the oath will

---

38. Wells, Magdalene, and Wunsch, "Assertory Oath," 17.

39. TCL 13, 181. For discussion of this text, see Francis Joannès, *Rendre la justice en Mésopotamie: Archives judiciaires du Proche-Orient ancien (IIIe-Ier millénaires avant J.-C.)*, Temps et espaces (Saint Denis: Presses universitaires de Vincennes, 2000), 227 (No. 168). Other Neo-Babylonian examples with clear adjudicatory contexts are listed in Wells, Magdalene, and Wunsch, "Assertory Oath," 18 n. 22.

40. Iddinaya's oaths, like the oath in Ps 131, are formulated as truncated conditional sentences, and imply that he has actually *not* performed the stated hypothetical action. The use of "indeed" in our translation reflects this.

41. The record pertains to the widely attested "Gimillu affair," about which see Holtz, *Trial Records*, 147–71, with additional literature cited there.

end the investigation.⁴² The purpose of the oath, in both cases, is to give additional force to the swearer's claim. Thus, as an evocation of the courtroom in the context of prayer, the attenuated oath fits perfectly. It both intensifies the speaker's denial and, at the same time, underscores the speaker's uncertainty about the prayer's outcome.

In the psalm, the oath's rhetorical-legal force also creates a certain, perhaps paradoxical, tension with the theme of humility. An oath is an effective legal device precisely because the speaker is confident enough to take it. Therefore, to swear that one has always been humble requires at least a modicum of belief in one's own worth. In other words, Ps 131's submissively sworn denial of haughtiness is, in and of itself, something akin to the confident imperatives inviting investigation in Ps 26. The oath, with its implicit self-curse, challenges God to act against the speaker, if indeed God can find the speaker's claim to be false.

Two other examples of oaths in prayer, in Pss 7 and 44, illustrate the function of the oath as a challenge to God. In both, as in Ps 131, the oaths support speakers' claims of innocence, of having done nothing wrong. We begin with Ps 44, a "communal lament," in which the nation supports its call for God's redemptive intervention (vv. 25–27) by contrasting God's beneficence in the past (vv. 2–9) with the nation's troubles in the present (vv. 10–17). The nation protests its innocence, even in the face of oppression by treacherous enemies:

¹⁸All of this has come upon us,
Yet we have not forgotten You, nor have we been false to Your covenant.
¹⁹Our heart has not turned back,
Nor have our feet swerved from Your path,
²⁰though You crushed us down in a place of jackals,
And covered us with deep darkness.
²¹Indeed, we have not forgotten the name of our God, nor spread our hands towards a foreign god!
²²Surely, God may investigate [$yaḥăqor$-] this,
For He knows the secrets of the heart!

In the first three verses in this section, the nation expresses its innocence in terms of its continued faithfulness to God's covenant. Despite the hardships, the nation denies any breach of the covenant—"forgetting" or "being false" (v. 18), "turning back" or "swerving" (v. 19). In the perspective of the psalm, God, rather than the nation, bears responsibility here.⁴³

---

42. Compare the remarks on the oath in Ps 7 by Bernd Janowski, *Arguing with God: A Theological Anthropology of the Psalms*, trans. Armin Siedlecki (Louisville: Westminster John Knox, 2009), 140.

43. Dalit Rom-Shiloni, "Psalm 44: The Power of Protest," *CBQ* 70 (2008): 683–98, here 686–88.

The translation of verses 21 and 22 reflects an understanding of these verses as an oath (reflected in the English word "Indeed") followed by a challenge to God. This requires some comment, because the Hebrew allows other interpretations. Specifically, the overlap between the conditional formulation, in general, and its specific usage in oaths raises the possibility that these two verses are simply an extended conditional sentence. Thus, for example, NJPS renders these verses: "If we forgot the name of our God and spread forth our hands to a foreign god, God would surely search it out, for He knows the secrets of the heart."[44] This rendering, however, makes for a weak, even contradictory, conclusion to the nation's otherwise vigorous denial of wrongdoing. Why would the people veer from their protestation of steadfast faith to describe what God would do if they actually had "forgotten"?[45]

According to this translation and interpretation, verses 21 and 22 build on and continue the momentum of the nation's denial of wrongdoing. To bolster its claim of unwavering fidelity, the nation swears an oath using the truncated conditional formulation, with the self-curse left implicit: "If we have forgotten ..." (v. 21). Following this, the nation concludes its protestation by invoking the investigative process. Like the individual speaker in Ps 26, it challenges the all-knowing God to conduct an investigation (v. 22).[46] The oath and the subsequent challenge both express the nation's confidence in its own innocence. So certain is the nation, that it flouts not only the risk of the implicit punishment for swearing falsely but also any risk that God's investigation might yield damning results.

In Ps 7, the other psalm that incorporates an oath, the speaker swears as follows:

⁴O YHWH, my God, if I have done this,
If I there is corruption in my hands,
⁵If I have dealt badly with my ally,
Or stripped my foe clean,[47]

---

44. NRSV and KJV are similar.

45. Two other possible interpretations should also be excluded: (1) that the two verses constitute a claim of innocence, because, had the nation actually done wrong, then God should have investigated; and (2) that these verses actually constitute an oath, with the self-curse made explicit in verse 22. Interpretation 1, to be effective in context, requires us to read beyond what the verse states and imagine not only the investigation but also what God's investigation should have yielded, such as a warning (so Charney, *Persuading God*, 69), or God's "grounds for a peeve against Israel" (so Loren D. Crowe, "The Rhetoric of Psalm 44," *ZAW* 104 [1992]: 394–401, here 398). Interpretation 2 suffers because (based on examples like Ps 7:4–6, discussed below, or Ps 137:5–6) in a self-curse, we expect more overtly punitive consequences than simply an investigation.

46. Compare also Jer 12:3.

47. I follow the note in NJPS. On the problems with this clause and proposed solutions, see Jeffrey H. Tigay, "Psalm 7:5 and Ancient Near Eastern Treaties," *JBL* 89 (1970): 178–86;

> ⁶ then let an enemy pursue and overtake me;
> let him trample my life to the ground,
> set my body in the dust.

Here, the formulation of the oath is particularly explicit. Instead of the more typical truncated hypothetical that we have already seen, these verses record an entire conditional statement—the hypothetical, denied action together with the consequences incumbent on the speaker. Thus, these verses give us the complete picture of the oath as a self-curse.[48]

The oath's explicit, more complete formulation goes beyond the overt purpose of adding weight to the speaker's denial of wrongdoing. The invocation of a punishment by an enemy (v. 6) derives directly from the speaker's situation: according to the psalm's opening verses (vv. 2–3), the speaker has turned to God for salvation from enemies in pursuit.[49] The oath introduces a hypothetical, but also slightly sarcastic or bitter, justification for the speaker's distress. The persecution would have been justified if, indeed, the speaker had actually done wrong (vv. 4–5). In the context of an oath, however, the speaker's point is to deny any wrongdoing and, consequently, to undercut this justification. Thus, the oath confronts God with an injustice and protests against it.

The psalm's overall structure furthers this point. The oath, as the reflex of a legal action, opens what we might call the psalm's courtroom section, consisting of verses 4–9. After the oath, this section continues with a "cry for verdict,"[50] comprising a call for God to progress toward the heavenly tribunal (vv. 7–8)[51] followed by a demand for judgment, "Judge me, YHWH, in accordance with my righteousness and my innocence" (v. 9). The remainder of the psalm takes up the theme of the punishment of the wicked (vv. 10–17) and expresses the outcome for which the speaker prays. We can, therefore, interpret Ps 7 along the lines laid out in the previous chapter: the demand for judgment marks the transition to the speaker's statement of the "remedy sought."

---

and, more recently, Yitzhak Berger, "The David–Benjaminite Conflict and the Intertextual Field of Psalm 7," *JSOT* 38 (2014): 279–96, here 286–88. All agree that this clause should be considered part of the oath's protasis.

48. Sheldon H. Blank, "The Curse, Blasphemy, the Spell, and the Oath," *HUCA* 23 (1950–1951): 73–95, here 90–91; and Blank, "An Effective Literary Device in Job 31," *JJS* 2 (1950–1951):105–7, here 107. Yitzhak Berger compares the explicit formulation here with David's conditional statement in 1 Chr 12:18 ("David–Benjaminite Conflict," 285).

49. See Peter C. Craigie and Marvin Tate, *Psalms 1–50*, 2nd ed., WBC 19 (Nashville: Thomas Nelson, 2004), 100–101.

50. R. L. Hubbard, "Dynamistic and Legal Processes in Psalm 7," *ZAW* 94 (1982): 267–79, here 268.

51. See Janowski, *Arguing with God*, 141–42. For the image of God "arising" (ʿ-w-r) for judgment, compare Ps 35:23.

The previous chapter suggested that this transition from grievance to solution by means of the demand for judgment reflects not only what might have been heard in a courtroom but also, more fundamentally, the plaintiff's mind-set. Praying plaintiffs expect the adjudicatory process to resolve the crises that led them to prayer. Confidently, they call on God to judge their case. In Ps 7, the oath adds a further dimension to this understanding of the demand for judgment's pivotal placement. Between verses 4–6 and 7–9, the psalm moves from the oath to the demand for judgment. This transition suggests that the oath plays a role in bringing the speaker to making the demand. In other words, it is the speaker's certainty, reflected in willingness to pronounce an oath of innocence, that leads the speaker to demand adjudication from God.

In light of this, the demand for judgment, at least in Ps 7, takes on a more confrontational tone. The oath, connected as it is to the speaker's own predicament, expresses not only the speaker's innocence but also the speaker's protest against an unjust situation. The demand for judgment continues this protest. A less-confident speaker might wish to avoid exposure to the machinery of divine adjudication.[52] Not so the speaker in Ps 7, who believes that the process will, without much doubt, lead to vindication. By acting as a judge, God must rectify the injustice with which God is presented.

Accusing God

The discussion of the oath of innocence in Ps 44 observed in passing that the nation blames God for the troubles that prompt it to pray. Just prior to swearing the oath, the nation contrasts its own steadfast faith with God's abandonment. The nation declares that it has remained faithful, "though You crushed us down in a place of jackals, and covered us with deep darkness" (v. 20). In a six-verse passage earlier in the same psalm, the nation addresses God with similar accusations (vv. 10–15):

> [10]You neglected and shamed us,
> And do not go forth with our armies.
> [11]You turn us back before our foe,
> Our enemies plunder at will.
> [12]You turn us, like sheep, into prey,
> And disperse us among the nations.
> [13]You sell off Your people for no fortune,
> You do not set high their price.

---

52. Compare the speaker in Ps 143:2, who specifically asks God, "Do not enter into judgment with [*b-w-ʾ bəmišpāṭ*] your servant."

¹⁴You make us a mockery among our neighbors,
The scorn and derision of those around us.
¹⁵You make us a byword among the nations,
A (source of) head-wagging among the peoples.

This extended accusatory section confirms our earlier sense of the psalm's confrontational tone. Not only is the nation convinced of its own innocence; it is also confident enough to blame God.

This series of accusations leads up to the nation's oath and challenge to God, discussed in the previous section. The confrontation continues, too, when the nation calls on God to "wake up" (v. 24a) and "arise" (v. 24b) to act on their behalf. It combines these demands with accusatory questions to God, "Why do You sleep, O YHWH?" (v. 24), and "Why do You hide your face, (and) forget our affliction and oppression?" (v. 25). These questions carry the nation's complaint against God one step further.[53] Not only has God caused the nation's oppression, as verses 10–15 charge, but, by "sleeping," "hiding face," and "forgetting," God also willfully ignores the nation's plight. Unlike its ancestors, who could count on God's support (vv. 2–3), the nation has come to view God as unreliable at best or, at worst, an enemy.

These two features of Ps 44, the direct accusation to God and the accusatory question, exemplify what Claus Westermann has called "the heart of the lament of the people in ancient Israel."[54] Accusations and questions like these, occurring together or separately, characterize other prayers in which the community complains against God (Westermann's "lament of the people").[55] Individual supplicants, too, use declarative and interrogative statements to accuse God. Thus, for example, the speaker in Ps 22 begins by combining these two accusatory forms, as follows:[56]

²My God, my God, why have You abandoned me?
(Why) so far from delivering me, from my anguished roaring?
³My God, I cry by day, but You do not answer,
And by night, no stillness for me.

---

53. On the relationship between this concluding part of Ps 44 and the earlier oath of innocence and accusations, see Barbara M. Leung Lai, "Psalm 44 and the Function of Lament and Protest," *OTE* 20 (2007): 418–31, here 425–27; and Leonard P. Maré, "Psalm 44: When God Is Responsible for Suffering," *Journal of Semitics* 21 (2012): 52–65, here 62–63.

54. Claus Westermann, *Praise and Lament in the Psalms*, trans. Keith R. Crim and Richard N. Soulen (Atlanta: John Knox, 1965), 177.

55. See Isa 63:17–64:4, 11; Pss 60:3–6, 12 // 108:12; 74:1, 10–11; 80:5–6, 13; 89:39–50; Lam 5:20, 22. These examples are drawn from the table in William S. Morrow, *Protest against God: The Eclipse of a Biblical Tradition*, Hebrew Bible Monographs 4 (Sheffield: Sheffield Phoenix Press, 2006), 79. To these, add Jer 14:8–9, 19, discussed in Morrow, *Protest against God*, 21–22.

56. See also Pss 10:1; 35:17; 39:11–12; 43:2; 88:8–9, 16–19; 102:11. Some of these examples are collected in Morrow, *Protest against God*, 49. Also Compare Jer 15:18; 20:7.

Like the community in Ps 44, the speaker here accuses God of abandonment. The opening questions (v. 2) and the direct accusation ("You do not answer," v. 3) reenforce each other to send God a clear message: God bears some measure of responsibility for the speaker's suffering.

In prose narratives, too, speakers incorporate questions in prayers to convey their complaints against God. William Morrow, who has studied prayers that protest against God, notes the examples of Abraham's opening petition at the negotiations over Sodom (Gen 18:23–25) and Moses's intercession at the incident of the golden calf (Exod 32:11–13).[57] Abraham's petition includes three questions, altogether. It begins with a question, "Will You indeed destroy the innocent along with the guilty?" (Gen 18:23), which Abraham repeats with some modification in the following verse, "Will You indeed destroy and not forgive the place?" (18:24) and concludes, "Shall the Judge of all the Earth not do justice?!" (18:25). Although Moses's prayer includes two questions (Exod 32:11, 12), Morrow correctly singles out the firs—"Why, YHWH, should Your anger burn against Your people, whom you have brought out of Egypt with great might and a strong arm?"—to exemplify the "protest prayer."[58]

These declarative and interrogative accusations to God change the roles played in the courtroom scenes that the prayers evoke. Until now, we have imagined the speakers in the roles of plaintiffs who present a case against others or of accused individuals standing trial, and God in the role of judge. When speakers accuse God, they turn the tables completely. To emphasize the courtroom analogy, we might say that part of the speakers' legal defense is the presentation of a counterclaim or counteraccusation.[59] The declarative and interrogative accusations put God on the other side of the bench, as it were. Now, it is God, rather than the speakers, who stands accused at trial.

For seasoned readers of the Hebrew Bible, the idea of putting God on trial, in prayer or otherwise, is not all that surprising. The prophet Jeremiah recognizes the possibility, even if he admits that it might be futile: "You would be in the right, YHWH, if I litigate against you [ʾārîb ʾēlêkā]. Yet I would present a case [mišpāṭim ʾădabbēr] against You" (12:1).[60] The book of Job is an extensive, elaborate example of one character's effort to sue God.[61]

Despite this general possibility, though, we must still justify our view of accusations to God in prayers through the lens of the courtroom. What, if anything, indicates that we have, in these "protest prayers" (to borrow

---

57. Morrow, *Protest against God*, 20–21.
58. Ibid., 21. The second question (Exod 32:12) does not express protest as much as it provides a motivation for God to "relent."
59. Bovati, *Re-Establishing Justice*, 115 (on Ps 44).
60. Magdalene, *Scales of Righteousness*, 139.
61. Ibid., with additional literature cited throughout.

Morrow's term), something akin to Job's litigation against God? The very presence of an argument or accusation against God suggests this, certainly in the context of prayer, which, as we understand it throughout this study, evokes the courtroom by its very nature.

Moreover, other explicit legalisms that occur alongside declarative and interrogative accusations strengthen our case. Here I can point to the verse from Jeremiah quoted just above, because, immediately after mentioning his suit, the prophet presents its substance, in the form of a question: "Why does the way of the wicked succeed, (why do) the unfaithful prosper" (Jer 12:1).[62] Likewise, Habakkuk, in his opening lament, refers to the cry for justice in his questions: "How long, YHWH, shall I cry and You not hear, shall I shout, 'Violence,' and you not save? Why do You make me see iniquity, and You look upon wrong?" (Hab 1:2–3). These prophets' questions bring to mind other "why questions," like those in Pss 44 and 22, usually interpreted as accusatory.[63] Similarly, in Ps 44, the combination of the oath of innocence, a feature of legal speech, with the accusatory statements and questions points us toward a forensic interpretation. Together, these features of Ps 44 transform the nation's role from accused to accuser.[64]

Beyond contextual clues, we can expand our discussion by reading these prayers, as we have throughout, together with ancient courtroom records. Do these accusations find meaningful legal analogues that confirm, or at least allow, the understanding that they open litigation against God? Pietro Bovati's discussion of accusations identifies three aspects that warrant consideration: the legal-procedural strategy of lodging a defensive counteraccusation, the presentation of this counteraccusation in a direct, second-person address to God, and, separately, the presentation of an accusation in the form of questions.[65] Based on Bovati, we can break down our general question into three more specific ones: Would ancient defendants lodge counteraccusations as part of their claims? Would accusers, in the context of adjudication, address their accusations directly to

---

62. Compare also Jer 11:20, where the prophet refers to God as a judge, and Jer 20:8, where, like Habakkuk (1:2), the prophet refers to "crying violence." On the legal aspects of Jeremiah's prayers, see Magdalene, *Scales of Righteousness*, 159–60.

63. See Westermann, *Praise and Lament*, 172, 176–77; Harrelson, "'Why, O Lord, Do You Harden Our Heart?,'" 169–70; Maré, "Psalm 44," 62; Bovati, *Re-Establishing Justice*, 75–80; James Barr, "Why? In Biblical Hebrew," *JTS* 36 (1985): 1–33, here 33; Francis I. Andersen, *Habakkuk: A New Translation with Introduction and Commentary*, AB 25 (New York: Doubleday, 2001), 108–9; Phil J. Botha, "Psalm 108 and the Quest for Closure to the Exile," *OTE* 23 (2010): 574–96, here 588. Despite Botha's observation, the accusatory force of the nearly identical question in Pss 60:12 and 108:12 remains.

64. Bovati, *Re-Establishing Justice*, 115.

65. Ibid., 71–83, 114–17, 299–305. Bovati's notes throughout refer to important earlier literature.

their opponents? And would accusations take the form of questions? The discussion that follows will take up each question in turn and consider the relevant biblical and ancient Near Eastern analogues.

To answer the procedural question, we can draw on Magdalene's study of the book of Job in light of Neo-Babylonian trial procedure. There Magdalene demonstrates that courts in Mesopotamia did, in fact, allow "impleader (or joinder) accusation, whereby the defendant asserted that a third party was actually responsible to the plaintiff on the claim rather than the defendant."[66] One example occurs in the record of proceedings against a shepherd named Kīnaya, who has been accused of unauthorized possession of five sheep marked with a star-shaped brand as temple property. Regarding three of these sheep, Kīnaya is found guilty. The record, however, continues as follows:[67]

> And (as for) the 2 sheep, the remainder of the 5 sheep branded with a star, about which Kīnaya said thus:
> "Since the month of Addaru, year 7, Sūqaya, the shepherd, deposited them in my flock" —
> He shall bring Sūqaya and hand (him) over to Nabû-šarra-uṣur, the royal official in charge of the Eanna, and (to) the administrators of the Eanna.
> If he does not bring Sūqaya and does not hand (him) over, he shall pay 60 sheep together with those (other) sheep, thirtyfold (for the two sheep) to the Lady of Uruk.

We learn what is at stake here from the end of the text: payment of the thirtyfold penalty for the two sheep. Under normal circumstances, Kīnaya would owe the Eanna this payment because he should not have had the two sheep in question. Kīnaya, however, seeks to avoid the penalty by accusing another shepherd, Sūqaya, of placing these two sheep in Kīnaya's flock. Kīnaya claims to have received the branded sheep innocently; it was Sūqaya who mishandled the livestock. For his claim to be successful, Kīnaya must remand Sūqaya to the authorities in the Eanna.

According to Magdalene, Kīnaya's accusation against Sūqaya and other examples like it in the Neo-Babylonian cuneiform legal corpus bear on Job's lawsuit against God. Specifically, "Job believes that God has brought him to trial unjustly, and he consequently threatens to countersue God for this act and other acts that manifest God's abusive use of divine judicial authority."[68] Job's defense, like Kīnaya's, includes a counter-

---

66. Magdalene, *Scales of Righteousness*, 69–71 (quotation from 71), with examples in nn. 60, 63, and 66.
67. YOS 6, 123:8–17. For discussion, see Holtz, *Trial Records*, 52–54 (No. 14). This example should be added to those cited in Magdalene's discussion of the joinder accusation.
68. Magdalene, *Scales of Righteousness*, 127, with ensuing discussion throughout the chapter entitled "Job's Counteraccusation" (127–76).

accusation. Similarly, in the context of prayer, Kīnaya's accusation exposes potential legal roots of speakers' accusations against God.

It is important, however, to distinguish between Kīnaya's case and the counteraccusatory rhetoric in the book of Job or in prayers like Ps 44. While Kīnaya, Job, and the speakers in prayers all use accusations as a means of legal defense, Kīnaya, unlike his biblical counterparts, does not "turn the tables" by accusing his accusers. The perfect analogy, in other words, would have been for Kīnaya to shift blame to the Eanna authorities instead of to a third party, just as Job and the speakers in prayers shift blame to God.

Unfortunately, this kind of perfect analogue proves elusive, because cuneiform lawsuit records are formulated from the perspective of the victors, who could use the record to prevent future claims. This convention masks original defendants as plaintiffs and original counterclaims as the initial bases of lawsuits. Magdalene does collect a handful of examples that, in one way or another, seem to refer to "table-turning."[69] Of these, the clearest two are an Aramaic text from Elephantine, dated to 451 BCE,[70] and a cuneiform text from Alalakh, over one thousand years older.[71] The Aramaic text records receipt of five shekels of silver in settlement of a lawsuit. The recipient declares satisfaction with the payment but does not neglect mentioning (twice!) that the payment originates in a lawsuit begun by the payer over disputed property "about which you complained against me" (zy qblt ʿly bgw).[72] In other words, the recipient was originally the defendant, the object of the payer's complaint. Apparently, this original defendant countersued and has ended up winning the case and receiving compensation.[73]

The earlier text from Alalakh describes a suit and countersuit between two siblings, Abbael and his sister, Bittatti, over inheritance. Initially, Abbael claims that his sister has no share in the particular property. Bittatti, however, claims against this and insists on an equal division of the property. A witness supports Bittatti's claim, and she is awarded a share. As in the case from Elephantine, the first claim has been refuted, and the counterclaim is affirmed.

These two texts, together with the broader evidence for defendants' use of accusations against others to clear themselves, illuminate the legal-procedural basis of the speakers' positions in prayers like Ps 44 or Ps 22. Just as individuals accused by other human accusers do, in fact,

---

69. Ibid., 70–71, n. 63.

70. Porten and Yardeni, *Textbook of Aramaic Documents*, 2:58–59 (B3.2).

71. D. J. Wiseman, *The Alalakh Tablets*, Occasional Publications of the British Institute of Archaeology at Ankara 2 (London: British Institute of Archaeology at Ankara, 1953), No. 7.

72. Porten and Ada Yardeni, *Textbook of Aramaic Documents*, 2:58–59 (B3.2:3–4, 5).

73. For this interpretation, see H. Z. Szubin and Bezalel Porten, "Litigation Concerning Abandoned Property at Elephantine (Kraeling 1)," *JNES* 42 (1983): 279–84.

defend themselves by accusing others, including the accusers themselves, so do the speakers in prayers turn against God.

Let us now turn to the first of the two questions pertaining to form: Would counteraccusers employ direct address in the courtroom? Studies of biblical law have suggested a distinction between accusations formulated in the second person and those made in the third person. Second-person accusations, it is claimed, characterize informal, "pre-legal" action, while third-person accusations, which suggest the presence of an adjudicating authority, are the hallmark of formal legal proceedings.[74] If this distinction is correct, then we should understand accusations to God in prayers more as expressions of informal controversy than as aspects of a lawsuit on the model of Job or Jeremiah.

In actual fact, however, the biblical evidence is itself equivocal. On the one hand, a text like the narrative of the judgment of Jeremiah (ch. 26) supports making the distinction. While the people initially accuse Jeremiah directly (and even use a question!)—"You shall die! Why have you prophesied …"—once the authorities are seated at the temple gate, the priests and prophets speak about, but not to, the accused (26:8–11).[75] Similarly, in the proceedings surrounding the slandered bride (Deut 22:13–19), the bride's father, in his own statement, quotes the accuser's "pre-legal," informal accusation, which was made in the second person (v. 17). The formal accusations, however, are lodged in the third person (vv. 14, 16).[76] On the other hand, the narrative of the proceedings leading up to the famous "Judgment of Solomon" undermines the strict correlation between form of address and degree of procedural formality. There the first woman to speak addresses her claim to the king in the third person (1 Kgs 3:17–21), but subsequent arguments are reported in the second person, including the king's own quotation of what he has heard (3:22–23).[77] So, based on the Hebrew Bible alone, accusations addressed directly to God in prayers could be no less formal than those made in the third person. It is possible that, when speakers accuse God, they adopt the tone of the women in formal judgment before King Solomon.

When we turn to Mesopotamian trial records, we find that the discourse in formal courtroom settings could, in fact, include second-person address. We begin with the Alalakh text discussed earlier, which opens as follows:[78]

---

74. Boecker, *Redeformen des Rechtslebens*, 71–74; see also Bovati, *Re-Establishing Justice*, 304–5.
75. Boecker, *Redeformen des Rechtslebens*, 71–72.
76. Compare ibid., 77–78.
77. Compare ibid., 73–74.
78. Wiseman *Alalakh* 7:1–12. For literature, see COS 3.129. My interpretation of the text has benefited from reading it together with my teacher and colleague Barry Eichler.

> Concerning the estate of Ammurabi's wife, Abbael brought suit against his sister, Bittatti. [Th]us [he (said)]: "The entire [house] is mine. Bit[ta]ti, you have no part in the house."
> [B]ittatti [(said) thus:] "... in the town of Suḫaruwa, [through] my [m]other I have a part. [W]hy do you seek an extra share? I, with you, together, we shall divide our father's estate!

The text employs the verbal construction "brought suit" (*dīnam igrēma*) to describe Abbael's action against Bittatti. It is important to note that, at least according to the text, this part of the proceedings takes place prior to the litigants' formal appearance before the king.[79] Still, because these initial actions are worthy of record, it is hard to claim that they are entirely "informal."[80] And, despite breaks in the text, it is clear that both Abbael and Bittatti address their claims to each other directly, in the second person, rather than in the third person. Abbael calls Bittatti by name and says, "You have no part [*ūl ballāti*] in the house." Similarly, Bittati's response, as we read it, includes a verb in the second person, "you seek" (*tubaʾʾu*),[81] as well as the phrase "I, with you" (*anāku ittīka*).

A close analogue to the discourse in the "Judgment of Solomon," where we see a switch from third-person to second-person address, occurs in the following Neo-Babylonian example, the record of a dispute over undivided inheritance during the reign of Nebuchadnezzar II:[82]

> PN_1, PN_2, and PN_3 and PN_4, their father's brother, came to blows against each other concerning the division of shares; they had a legal case. They arrived before the governor of Babylon, and [before?] the governor of Babylon and the elders of the citizens of Babylon they recounted their matters.
>
> PN_1 said thus, "(Regarding) the purchases which PN_4 carried out in the Gate of Bēl: the silver with which the purchases were carried out belongs

---

79. See Wiseman, *Alalakh* 7:13–14.
80. See Holtz, *Neo-Babylonian Court Procedure*, 224–32; and Magdalene, *Scales of Righteousness*, 68.
81. It is possible that the verb was preceded by the independent second-person pronoun *atta*. The reading of the verb and the reconstruction at the beginning of the line were suggested to me by Barry Eichler.
82. Cornelia Wunsch, *Urkunden zum Ehe-, Vermögens- und Erbrecht aus verschiedenen neubabylonischen Archiven*, Babylonische Archive 2 (Dresden: Islet, 2003), 138–45 (No. 42). For similar situations in Old Babylonian records, see D. O. Edzard, "'Du hast mir gegeben,' 'ich habe dir gegeben': Über das sumerische Verbum sum," *WO* 8 (1976): 159–77, here 160–61 (English edition in Andrew Fortner, "Adjudicating Entities and Levels of Legal Authority in Lawsuit Records of the Old Babylonian Era" [PhD diss., Hebrew Union College-Jewish Institute of Religion, 1996], 867–69); and Samuel I. Feigen, ed., *Legal and Administrative Texts of the Reign of Samsu-iluna*, YOS 12 (New Haven: Yale University Press, 1979), 557 (English in Fortner, *Adjudicating Entities*, 890–91).

in the common property of the patrimony! There is no more than one-sixth share (that he owns) with my father (belonging to him)!"

PN$_4$ responded to him [*īpulšu*] thus: "I used my own silver in the purchases.... (Regarding) the purchases which your father [*abūka*] carried out in the Gate of Bēl ... there was not more than 10 shekels of silver from the common property of our patrimony (involved)! ... Your father [*abūka*] sealed a tablet in his name."

The first speaker (PN$_1$), like the first woman in the biblical narrative, uses third-person address to relate his claim that his uncle (PN$_4$) has mishandled a jointly held inheritance. Then the uncle responds in the second person. Unlike in the previous example, here we cannot distinguish between the "pre-legal" speeches and what occurs during the trial's formal stages. As far as the text is concerned, all the quoted speeches take place in the presence of the adjudicatory authorities.

One last example from Old Babylonian Larsa demonstrates that litigants could, in fact, speak directly to each other throughout formal proceedings, and not just in response to claims. The case pertains to the status of Aḫassunu, a baby girl found with a slave, Kullupat. The child might be Kullupat's actual daughter, in which case she, too, is a slave, or she might be the daughter of Ṣilli-Ištar, a free man who had given her to the slave for nursing. Ṣilli-Ištar brings Aḫatum, wife of the slave owner, before Sin-iddinam, governor of Larsa. The record then reads:[83]

> Aḫatum spoke thus: "Aḫassunu is not your [Ṣilli-Ištar's] daughter [*māratka*]; she is the daughter of a female slave of my mother's household!"
>
> Ṣilli-Ištar spoke thus: "Aḫassunu, my daughter, is not a slave! I gave her to Kullupat, a female slave of your father-in-law's [*emīki*] household, for nursing."

This entire exchange follows the arrival before the governor of Larsa, the adjudicating authority. Even this formal setting allows the parties to the dispute to speak to each other, rather than to the presiding adjudicator. As recorded on the tablet, the speeches of both Aḫatum and Ṣilli-Ištar include second-person possessive pronouns indicating direct address between the litigants.

---

83. Georges Boyer, *Contribution à l'histoire juridique de la 1ʳᵉ dynastie babylonienne* (Paris: P. Geuthner, 1928), 70–74; also translated and discussed in Joannès, *Rendre la justice*, 100–101 (No. 57). For additional bibliography, see Fortner, *Adjudicating Entities*, 604. Compare also W. H. van Soldt and M. Stol, "The Old Babylonian Texts in the Allard Pierson Museum, Amsterdam," *JEOL* 25 (1977–1978): 45–55, here 45–49 (Fortner, *Adjudicating Entities*, 723–25); and *BE* 9, 69 (Holtz, *Trial Records*, 110–13 [No. 28]).

These Akkadian trial records afford us some measure of confidence when we question the posited correspondence between the degree of procedural formality and grammar. Specifically, litigants do, in fact, address each other directly, even during more formal stages of the legal process, when authorities are present. Therefore, when speakers in prayers address accusations directly to God, they might actually imagine themselves entering formal litigation with God.

Finally, we come to the particular subject of the accusation in question form. Does an accusatory question such as "My God, my God, why have You abandoned me?" (Ps 22:2) find an analogue in human courtroom parlance? Here again, the text from Alalakh proves useful. Bittatti's response to Abbael, as reconstructed by most readers, includes the question "[W]hy ([am]-mi-n[im]) do you seek an extra share?" It is with this question that Bittatti turns the tables on Abbael's suit. She, like the speakers in the prayers, specifies the wrong that her accuser has committed, thus turning the accuser into the accused.

To strengthen our case, we can look beyond this one, ultimately rare (and reconstructed, too) example of a counteraccusation by the accused to the accuser in the form of a question. Neo-Babylonian texts from the Eanna record accusatory "why" questions as part of proceedings, even though these questions are not directed by an accused to an accuser.[84] The following example is particularly relevant, because the Eanna authorities address a man in the wake of his own accusation against another man:[85]

> Ibni-Nabû, an oblate of Ištar of Uruk ... said thus to Nabû-mukīn-apli, the *šatammu* of the Eanna ... and the assembly of the *mār banî*:
> "For the past ten years, Anu-šarra-uṣur, the official in charge of the building wing, (illegally) removed many things from the storehouse in my charge."
> Nabû-mukīn-apli, *šatammu* of the Eanna, said thus to Ibni-Nabû:
> "Why [*minamma*] did you not report (this) to the *šatammu* or the royal official who was appointed before me, and, after I was appointed, (why) did you not report (it)? Now, whatever you see in his possession, bring and show us!"

Although Ibni-Nabû begins as an accuser, as the case unfolds, he becomes the accused. This change from accuser to accused occurs when Nabû-mukīn-apli, the presiding representative of the Eanna, asks Ibni-Nabû the accusatory question, "Why did you not report this?" Ibni-Nabû has

---

84. Examples include: YOS 6, 208:6–10; YOS 7, 96:1–7; YOS 7, 128:21–23; and Daniel Arnaud, "Un document juridique concernant les oblats," *RA* 67 (1973): 147–56 (lines 27–38).

85. TCL 13, 170:1–11. This text (misidentified as TCL 13, 137) is summarized in F. Rachel Magdalene, "Trying the Crime of Abuse of Royal Authority in the Divine Courtroom and the Incident of Naboth's Vineyard," in *The Divine Courtroom in Comparative Perspective*, ed. Ari Mermelstein and Shalom E. Holtz, BibInt 132 (Leiden: Brill, 2014), 167–245, here 222.

had, based on his own testimony, ten years in which he could have, and therefore should have, alerted the authorities to Anu-šarra-uṣur's malfeasances. Not having done so, Ibni-Nabû himself comes under suspicion.[86]

Nabû-mukīn-apli's question is equivalent to Bittatti's question to Abbael in the Alalakh text and to the psalmists' questions to God. It is true that, in the Neo-Babylonian example, the question comes from the adjudicating authority, rather than from one of the litigants. Nevertheless, in terms of both form and force, all of the questions are quite similar. All of them are "why" questions that convey an accusation to the addressee.

In sum, ancient Near Eastern trial records show that, when speakers in prayers accuse God, it is likely that they attempt to open a countersuit. The procedure itself and its formal manifestations—both in direct speech and in accusatory questions—find analogues in human courts. Speakers in prayers "turn the tables" on God, just as they might have done to their human legal adversaries. They address their accusation directly to God, at times in the form of a question, just as they might address their human legal adversaries.

The possibility, confirmed by biblical and extrabiblical legal texts, that some prayers can be interpreted as countersuits is, perhaps, the farthest-reaching implication of the idea of praying legally. By accusing God, speakers take fullest advantage of the prayer–courtroom connection. The idea of praying legally gives the speakers their day in court, and they use it to turn God from adjudicator into adversary. The speakers in prayers hope that, once God is confronted with their counteraccusations, matters will be settled in their favor.

The concept of prayer as a means of bringing suit against God recovers a remarkable degree of human agency in the human–divine relationship. God does not simply wield all the power over humans, who are totally dependent. Rather, when humans can sue God for justice, prayer establishes a certain balance of power.

In fact, the element of human agency unites all three of this chapter's main topics: confession, denial of wrongdoing, and accusation. It is most clearly on view when speakers accuse God, but it is present, perhaps to a lesser degree, in the two other examples we have explored here. We have seen how, in a muted but nevertheless manifestly present protest, speakers mention their suffering alongside their confession. Similarly, when they deny wrongdoing, speakers issue challenges of sorts to God. Prayer, in all these forms, allows them to "tell their side of the story" and thus to reclaim a measure of their own agency in the divine–human encounter.

---

86. See Magdalene, "Trying the Crime," 222.

4

The Audience in Prayer's Courtroom

In Ps 65:3, the speaker addresses God and says, "You who hear prayer, to you all flesh comes." This verse's two halves encapsulate the divine–human encounter that occurs during prayer. To begin with the verse's end, humans present themselves by approaching, or "coming" (*yābōʾû*), to God. God, according to the first half of the verse, takes notice by hearing. The juxtaposition of the verse's two parts suggests a causative connection: because God hears prayers, humans approach God.

These two sides of the encounter that occurs during prayer, as described in Ps 65:3, will set the agenda for this chapter. Earlier discussion exposed the legal roots of the terminology for prayer and examined how the idea of praying legally finds expression in the prayers themselves. Here the discussion turns beyond the words for prayer and the wording of prayers to study what is said to occur during prayer. It begins, so to speak, with the second half of Ps 65:3, by considering humans' approach and stance for prayer. Following that, it will return to the verse's first half and examine what God is said to do in response to prayer, including but not limited to "hearing." Throughout, I will draw connections between the descriptions of the prayer encounter and descriptions of legal encounters in human courtrooms. In this way, I will show how the idea of praying legally opens a meaningful window onto what the ancients thought was happening when they prayed.

Recent scholarship on this very question provides a valuable launching point for my argument. Several current studies of the group of ancient Near Eastern prayers known as *shuilla*s have identified the "audience concept" as a key to understanding the encounter that these ancient texts imagine. One introduction to Mesopotamian prayers explains this concept as "a fundamental situation of ancient Near Eastern culture concerning ceremonies for a meeting in which someone presents a request to someone of higher social status."[1] Scholarship has focused on the ceremonial manifestations of this concept in prayers and on the reciprocity inherent in the concept. In terms of ceremony, the very term *shuilla*, which means

---

1. Lenzi, *Reading Akkadian Prayers*, 31, with additional literature in n. 81.

"hand raising," derives from the gesture of greeting commonly depicted throughout Mesopotamian art.² This greeting recognizes the asymmetry of the relationship between the greeter, or subject, and the superior being greeted. At the same time, however, by accepting the offerings, gestures, and speech of the subject, the superior being addressed was to some degree obliged to respond favorably to the request for assistance. Through this ritual, one sought to (re-)establish such a reciprocal relationship with the deity, but the deity was regarded as free to accept or to refuse.³

In other words, the greeting opened a channel of communication to the superior. The significance of this, of course, is that it allowed ancient petitioners to bridge the perceived chasms between themselves and the divine. The goal of prayer was to gain an audience with a deity, which, in turn, could allow one to hope for, if not quite expect, a favorable response.

Interpreting prayer in the Hebrew Bible and the ancient Near East as an audience clarifies the roles played by both sides, humans and deities, during the encounter. Humans at prayer present themselves as subjects, with their prayers as their spoken parts, as it were. Deities, according to this script, play the role of the superiors.

As an understanding of the motive and rationale of prayer, the audience concept complements the idea of praying legally. The encounter between litigants and adjudicating authorities, the "social analogy" that underlies the prayer–courtroom nexus, is itself a good example of an audience. The relationship between petitioners and adjudicators parallels the subject–superior relationship. In the courtroom, the status gap stems not so much from differences in social standing (although these might play a role, too) as from the adjudicators' authority to rule on the litigants' cases. And, just as the etiquette of the audience, in general, narrows that social gap between subject and superior, here, based on the "social analogy," the law and the conventions of the courtroom create the environment in which wronged parties might turn to authorities in order to find relief.

These affinities between the audience and the courtroom encounter allow, naturally enough, for prayers to root themselves in both. Put otherwise, when prayers display their connections to the courtroom, they specify that the occasion of prayer is a particular kind of audience. Therefore, the language pertinent to the audience, in general, such as the speakers' approach to the deity or the deity's response, functions on the additional level of the particularly legal occasion.

Furthermore, the overlap between the audience and the courtroom encounter justifies the forensic interpretation of what might, at first glance,

---

2. Annette Zgoll, "Audienz—Ein Modell zum Verständnis mesopotamischer Handerhebungsrituale: Mit einer Deutung der Novelle vom *Armen Mann von Nippur*," BaghM 34 (2003): 181–203 (examples on 183, 187, and 188).

3. Lenzi, *Reading Akkadian Prayers*, 32.

appear to be neutral terms. After all, even if prayer, in general, should be considered courtroom speech, the specific mentions of hearing and seeing or approaching and standing need not be interpreted as legal terms. But, in the context of prayer, these otherwise "common" terms do more: they are the terms that create the audience setting. These terms constitute the surface evidence for the deeper, conceptual ground shared between the idea of prayer as audience and the idea of praying legally. Once we accept the charged significance of even the very basic descriptions of the interactions between humans and divinities during prayer, which is to say that these descriptions are what attune us to the audience concept in the first place, then our particularly legal interpretations follow.

Approaching and Standing before the Divine

At the most basic level, for an "audience" to take place, no matter where or between whom, the parties to this audience must encounter each other in the same space. It is for this reason that descriptions of audiences in ancient Near Eastern literature often begin with the subjects' approach or drawing near to the superior. Similarly, in all types of ancient audiences, the subjects are said to "stand before" superiors. All of this terminology emphasizes the disparities between the parties as well as how the occasion of the audience overcomes those disparities. On the one hand, it makes clear that the subjects must enter the superiors' presence, instead of the other way round, and that the subjects stand while the superiors are seated. On the other hand, though, the language of approaching and standing before superiors emphasizes that a certain distance has, in fact, been bridged, that the subjects have gained access, and that communication can begin.

The discussion here will survey and analyze examples, first from Hebrew texts and then from Akkadian ones, that refer to the subjects' approach and stance in prayer. Working separately with the materials from each language, I will draw connections between the references in prayers and similar references in contexts of the audience and the courtroom, which will show how, in both languages, overlapping terminology creates an associative network among all three spheres—the audience, prayer and the courtroom. Prayers are closely associated with terminology that denotes "approaching" and "standing." This set of terms is itself part of the broader network that connects prayer to the audience, in general, and to the specific situation of pleading one's case before adjudicators.

In the Hebrew Bible, prayers begin with an approach, or drawing near, to God. A good example occurs toward the end of Elijah's standoff with the prophets of Baal, when the prophet first "approaches" (n-g-$š$) and only afterward prays for God to be manifest and confirm Elijah's mission (1 Kgs 18:36). Likewise, the prophet Isaiah, in a condemnation of Israel's worship, singles out the nation's "approach" to God:

> Because that people has approached [*niggaš*] [Me] with its mouth
> And honored Me with its lips,
> But has kept its heart far from Me
> And its worship of Me has been a commandment of men, learned by rote.
> (Isa 29:13)

Even though this verse describes the wrong approach to God—praying dishonestly by paying lip service—it shows that "approaching" God is certainly a feature of prayer. In this text, as in the description of Elijah's prayer earlier, verbs for prayer apart from "approaching" are absent. The approach is so much a part of the encounter with God as to be practically synonymous with the act of prayer.

In addition to "approaching" God, people at prayer commonly stand. When Hannah returns to Shiloh to dedicate her son, Samuel, she reminds Eli, the priest, of their earlier encounter when she prayed to give birth to a child. She mentions not only her prayer but also her standing position: "I am the woman who stood [*hanniṣṣebet*] here with you to pray to God" (1 Sam 1:26). Similarly, as King Jehoshaphat begins his prayer for salvation from the threat of the Moabites and Ammonites, the king "stands in the congregation of Judah and Jerusalem in the House of YHWH" (2 Chr 20:5). The king prays on behalf of the entire nation, who have "assembled to beseech YHWH" (2 Chr 20:4). At the end of the king's prayer, the text indicates the people's own physical position: "all Judah stood before God, with their little ones, their womenfolk and their children" (2 Chr 20:13). In descriptions of prayer such as this one, the prepositional phrase "before God" is commonly collocated with verbs of standing.[4]

Much later, Jewish tradition would come to refer to the main prayer, recited while standing, simply as ʿămîdâ ("standing"). A one-line introductory fragment from the Ashkenazic liturgy for Yom Kippur urges the congregation as follows:

> O branch (Israel), awake! Stand, place yourself, arise, beseech and plead for life before God who dwells on high.[5]

The string of three synonyms for standing ("stand, place yourself, arise") points to the same close connection between standing and prayer. In

---

4. Compare Jer 7:10; 15:1, 19; 18:20. See Friedhelm Hartenstein, *Das Angesicht JHWHs: Studien zu seinem höfischen und kultischen Bedeutungshintergrund in den Psalmen und in Exodus 32–34*, FAT 55 (Tübingen: Mohr Siebeck, 2008), 54–58.

5. Goldschmidt, מחזור לימים הנוראים, 2:127.

particular, this line associates standing with prayers that beseech God and plead for life.

The approach and stance of petitioners to God find analogues in the human-to-human realm in two biblical narratives: the Joseph story and the book of Esther.[6] Both stories contain audience scenes in which one character (Judah or Esther) makes a plea before a superior (Joseph, viceroy of Egypt, or King Ahasuerus): Judah pleads for the release of Benjamin, and Esther pleads to save the Jews from Haman's decree. Both scenes explicitly contrast between an initial "falling" (*n-p-l*), or prostration, and a subsequent approach or standing. At first, immediately after Benjamin's arrest, the brothers return to Joseph and "throw themselves on the ground before him" (Gen 44:14). Similarly, after Esther has exposed Haman and he is hanged, she speaks again to the king "falling at his feet and weeping, and beseeching him to avert the evil plotted by Haman the Agagite against the Jews" (Esth 8:3). As both scenes continue, the pleading characters make their cases, not prone on the floor but standing: Judah "approaches" (*n-g-š*) Joseph (Gen 44:18) and Esther "stands before" (*ʿ-m-d* + *lipnê*) the king, who has extended the scepter to her (Esth 8:4). This change in position marks the difference between nearly spontaneous outbursts and pleas more formally lodged.

Both of these stories already expose connections between the audience, prayer, and the courtroom. Like Judah and Esther, people who pray make their case before an authority, God, with the hope of achieving a change. On their own, the narratives themselves and the related descriptions in the contexts of prayer do not immediately evoke courtroom scenes in the strictest legal sense. Nevertheless, litigants making their cases before human adjudicating authorities find themselves in situations similar to those of Joseph's brothers and Esther. Certainly, in the context of prayer, the idea of praying legally justifies an investigation of the legal valences of the petitioners' approach and stance.

Biblical descriptions of courtrooms do, in fact, employ the same positional terms—various terms for "approaching" and "standing before"— to describe litigants' positions in relation to adjudicating authorities.[7] The two occur in combination in the opening verse of the famous "Judgment of Solomon": "Then, two prostitutes came [*tābōʾnâ*] to the king and stood before him [*wattaʿămōdanâ ləpānāyw*]" (1 Kgs 3:16). Similarly, when the daughters of Zelophehad seek a ruling in the matter of their right, as daughters, to inherit their father, they "draw near" (*wattiqrabnâ*) and

---

6. For additional comparisons between Judah's speech and prayer, see Greenberg, *Biblical Prose Prayer*, 20–23.

7. See Bovati, *Re-Establishing Justice*, 218–23 (on approaching) and 234–36 (on standing). The discussion in the following paragraphs draws on Bovati's observations and biblical references.

"stand before" (*wattaʿămōdənâ lipnê*) Moses (Num 27:1–2).[8] It is significant that both of these texts describe two separate actions: "coming"/"drawing near" (*b-w-ʾ*/*q-r-b*) and "standing" (*ʿ-m-d*). For the purposes of conveying narrative information, either one, on its own, would have been sufficient. The occurrence of both signals that each act has its own import in the description of adjudication.[9]

Apart from these examples that combine approaching and standing, other texts describing adjudication include the litigants' approach or stance separately. Various terms, particularly verbs of motion, denote the litigants' approach for judgment. One locution describing confrontation in court consists of the verb "to come" (*b-w-ʾ*) and the prepositional phrase "in judgment" (*bə* + *mišpāṭ*).[10] Petitioners also "come for judgment" (*b-w-ʾ lammišpāṭ*) to the king (2 Sam 15:2–6); when a matter of law is unclear, they are instructed, "you shall come [*ûbāʾtā*] to the Levitical priests or to the judge" in God's chosen place to inquire (Deut 17:8–9).[11] The verbs *q-r-b* ("to draw near") and *n-g-š* ("to approach") function similarly. The two occur in parallel in a prophetic evocation of the courtroom, in which Isaiah instructs the nations, "let them approach [*yiggəšû*], then speak; together, let us draw near for trial [*lammišpāṭ niqrābâ*]" (41:1).[12] A law in the book of Deuteronomy begins with the following description of a trial: "When there is a dispute between men and they approach for judgment [*wəniggəšû ʾel hammišpāṭ*] …" (25:1). A law in the book of Exodus instructs, "the owner shall draw near [*wəniqrab*] to God," as part of the process of settling a matter of lost property (22:7). Elsewhere that same verb occurs in descriptions of characters who, like the daughters of Zelophehad, "draw near" for a ruling (Num 9:6; 36:1; Josh 17:4).[13] Along the same lines, the Israelites are described as "going up for judgment" (*ʿ-l-y lammišpāṭ*) to Deborah (Judg 4:5); petitioners "go up" to the (city) gate to resolve legal matters (Deut 25:7; Ruth 4:1).[14]

---

8. The narrative of the daughters of Zelophehad is one of four "oracular novellas," in which characters seek a ruling from Moses. A specific mention of the characters' approach for a ruling occurs in all four. See Simeon Chavel, *Oracular Law and Priestly Historiography in the Torah*, FAT 2/71 (Tübingen: Mohr Siebeck, 2014), 4 (and chart on 7).

9. Compare Isa 50:8, where the verbs *ʿ-m-d* and *n-g-š* parallel each other in the prophet's use of courtroom imagery.

10. See Isa 3:14; Ps 143:2; Job 9:32; 22:4. See Shalom E. Holtz, "The Case for Adversarial *yaḥad*," *VT* 59 (2009): 211–21, here 218. Also compare Prov 18:6, where the noun *rîb* replaces *mišpāṭ*.

11. In Lev 24:11, the community "brings," or "causes to come" (*b-w-ʾ*, C-stem), the blasphemer to Moses for a ruling.

12. See Holtz, "Adversarial *yaḥad*," 213–14.

13. On these, see Yair Hoffman, "The Root QRB as a Legal Term," *JNSL* 10 (1982): 67–73.

14. In the case of Deborah, her seat of judgment is described as in the hill country (or

Prayer and litigation have "standing" on its own in common too. People who pray "stand before God," just as the man who commits unintentional manslaughter "stands before the community for judgment" (Num 35:12; see also Josh 20:6, 9). As part of its prescribed procedure for cases of false testimony, the law in the book of Deuteronomy describes how "the two people who have the dispute stand before YHWH, the priests, and the judges" (Deut 19:17).[15] The servant of God says, "Let us stand together," as he imagines, in legal terms, a confrontation with an opponent (Isa 50:8).[16]

The positioning of the litigants and people at prayer "before" their respective audiences raises an additional point of contact between prayer and petition in court. Several biblical texts refer to prayer itself "coming before" God, in much the same way that the speakers of the prayers are, themselves, said to "come." For example, Ps 119 includes the following hopes for prayers' acceptance:[17]

[169]May my song [$rinnātî$] draw near before You [$tiqrab ləpānêkā$];
Grant me understanding in accordance with Your word.
[170]May my petition [$təḥinnātî$] come before You [$tābôʾ ləpānêkā$];
Save me in accordance with Your word.

Other texts refer to supplications "coming to" ($ʾel, lə$), rather than "before" ($lipnê$), God (Jonah 2:8; Ps 102:2).[18] The arrival of prayers, like the arrival of those who speak them, is itself a significant matter.

This, too, finds its analogue in the human-to-human legal arena. The counterpart of the arrival of the prayers is the arrival of the petitioners' legal affairs at the adjudicatory setting. Again, as with speakers and their prayers, litigants and their cases both "come" (b-w-$ʾ$). The overworked Moses tells Jethro, "When [the Israelites] have a matter [$dābār$], it comes to me [$bāʾ ʾēlay$] and I judge between a man and his fellow" (Exod 18:16; cf. 22:7). Elsewhere, we find causative conjugations indicating the "bringing" or "presentation" of the legal affairs. From the grammatical point of view, there is a subject other than the affairs themselves, but the result is

---

on a hill), so that the use of the verb for "going up" ($ʿ$-l-y) is apt and, perhaps, without any legal significance.

15. Although the litigants are said to "stand before YHWH," this should not be understood as an indication that they are to engage in prayer. Rather, the presence of YHWH in this verse indicates the procedure's occurrence in the central human court, which was to be located in the central shrine. On the secular, noncultic nature of the procedure itself, see Bruce Wells, "The Cultic versus the Forensic: Judahite and Mesopotamian Judicial Procedures in the First Millennium BCE," *JAOS* 128 (2008): 205–32, here 223–27.

16. See Holtz, "Adversarial *yaḥad*," 215–16, 218–19.

17. See also Pss 79:11; 88:3.

18. Compare Ps 18:7 and 2 Chr 30:27.

the same: the matters, rather than the people involved, "arrive." Thus, later in the narrative of Jethro and Moses, the text uses the Hebrew verbal root meaning "come" (*b-w-ʾ*), conjugated in the causative stem, to describe how the Israelites "bring" their matters (more literally, cause them to come) to Moses (Exod 18:19, 22, 26; see also Deut 1:17). Similarly, causative conjugations of the root denoting "drawing near" (*q-r-b*) describe how the subjects of the verb "bring near" or, in more idiomatic English, "bring forward" their matters. After the daughters of Zelophehad "approach" Moses themselves, Moses "brings forward their case [*wayyaqrēb ʾet mišpāṭān*] to YHWH" (Num 27:5). So too, the prophet, speaking on behalf of YHWH, invites his audience, "bring forward [*qārəbû*] your lawsuit … present [*haggîšû*] your arguments" (Isa 41:21).[19] The first verb in this sentence, "bring forward" (*qārəbû*), is an only slightly different causative counterpart (D-stem rather than C-stem) to the verb that denotes "drawing near." The second, here translated as "present," is a causative form of the verb meaning "approach" (*n-g-š*).

Attention to the language of "arrival" predicated of prayers and petitions, and not just of petitioners, leads directly to two locutions that connect prayers to God and petitions to humans, specifically human kings. The first occurs in a number of texts that describe the "cry" (*ṣəʿāqâ*) as "coming to" (*b-w-ʾ ʾel/ʿal*) God.[20] Although the locution is limited to the human–divine plane, its incorporation of the term for "cry" does return us to descriptions of prayer as "calling out" to God, analogous to "calling out" to the king for relief. The second relevant locution, used in both human-to-human and human–divine contexts, describes the "supplication falling before" (*n-p-l* + *təḥinnâ* + *lipnê*) its intended recipient.[21] It is this locution that describes Jeremiah's plea to King Zedekiah in the narratives surrounding Jeremiah's release from prison (Jer 37:20; 38:26) and, in several instances, people's supplications to God (Jer 36:7; 42:9; Dan 9:20).[22]

---

19. On the legal valence of this sentence, see Shalom E. Holtz, "The Prophet as Summoner," in *A Common Cultural Heritage: Studies on Mesopotamia and the Biblical World in Honor of Barry L. Eichler*, ed. Grant Frame et al. (Bethesda, MD: CDL, 2011), 19–34, here 25–28.

20. With *ʾel*: Gen 18:21; Exod 3:9; 1 Sam 9:16; With *ʿal*: Job 34:28. Another, similar locution describes the "groan going up" (*ʿ-l-y* + *šawʿâ*) to God (Exod 2:23; 1 Sam 5:12; compare Jer 14:2). However, as with the Israelites "going up" to Deborah (see above, with note), this locution may stem from the notion that God resides above humans, in heaven (specifically mentioned in 1 Sam 5:12).

21. In terms of grammar, the supplication occurs either as the subject of the verb (Jer 36:7; 37:20; 42:2) or as its object, with the supplicant causing the petition to fall (Jer 38:26; 42:9; Dan 9:20). Based on its distribution, the phrase is characteristic of Late Biblical Hebrew (Goldstein, *Life of Jeremiah*, 94).

22. In Jer 42:2, the locution describes the people's supplication "falling before" Jeremiah.

Before turning to the Akkadian evidence, I pause to reflect on the significance of the overlap between human subjects' "arrival" and the "arrival" of their matters. When used regarding the subjects, this terminology signals the particular importance of the petitioners' presence before authorities, be they human or divine. It marks the encounter as an "audience." That very encounter is significant, certainly as a preliminary step to a successful outcome, perhaps even as a successful outcome on its own. It is just this notion of a successful outcome that is signaled by the use of arrival terminology regarding prayers, rather than their human speakers. For the speaker in Ps 119, at least, a prayer's "arrival" before God is itself something to pray for.

We turn now to the Akkadian evidence, where we find a comparable terminological network of approaching and standing. In prayers, various verbs describe the speakers' "approach" toward the deity. One such description, in a hymn of praise to Marduk, employs the Akkadian verb *qerēbu*, cognate to the Hebrew verb for "drawing near" (q-r-b). The speaker says to Marduk, "the widow with flour, the rich man with a sheep, approach [*iqarrubū*] you."[23] In numerous examples, the verb *maḫāru*, also meaning "to approach," refers to the act of prayer, too.[24]

Some Akkadian prayers make the connection between approaching and judgment explicit. In many cases, this explicit link stems from the prayers' particular setting in divination. In that context, the entire process is seen as a form of adjudication, and the outcome is referred to as a "judgment" (*purussû*). Thus, prayers uttered as part of this process naturally make reference to the participants' "approach for judgment." For example, in an Old Babylonian diviner's prayer, the speaker says, "I approach the assembly of the gods for judgment" (*eṭeḫḫi ana dīnim*).[25] Other examples employing this verb (*ṭeḫû*) and the synonymous verb *sanāqu* are, based on references in the most comprehensive Akkadian dictionary, limited to prayers uttered in the divinatory context.[26] The verb *kašādu*, another synonym, occurs in at least one prayer, followed by a demand for judgment:

> My lord, I have approached you [*aktaldakka*]; hear my word!
> Render my judgment, decide my decision.[27]

---

23. *KAR* 25 ii, 19–20, as quoted in *CAD* Q, 233 (*qerēbu* 3a1'). Other relevant examples are listed there, too.
24. In its entry for the verb, *CAD* lists a separate submeaning "to pray to a deity" (M.1, 61 [*maḫāru* 2b]).
25. J. van Dijk, A. Goetze, and M. I. Hussey, eds., *Early Mesopotamian Incantations and Rituals*, YOS 11 (New Haven: Yale University Press, 1985), 22:11–12.
26. See note in *CAD* S, 137 (*sanāqu* A2) and relevant references in *CAD* Ṭ, 73 (*ṭeḫû* 1ab').
27. *BMS* 13:27–28.

The text here is not complete, which leaves open the question of the prayer's divinatory context. Regardless, the proximity between the "approach" and the demand for judgment underscores the verb's adjudicatory valence here.

In Akkadian, as in Hebrew, the locution "standing before" the deity describes positioning during the act of prayer. Within prayers themselves, this is most apparent from speakers' references to their own physical positions. Thus, the speaker in one *namburbi*-incantation against the evil of a snake, says to the god Shamash, "I, your servant ... stand before you" (*ana maḫarka azziz*).[28] A particularly telling example, from a prayer to Ishtar, includes both kneeling and standing, as well as a more explicit reference to the prayer–courtroom connection:

> I, sickened, I kneel, I stand before you [*maharki akmis azziz*]
> For the judgment of my case [*ana dânu dīnīya*], O torch of the gods, I seek you out.[29]

The second line quoted here explicates the purpose of the first; the speaker "stands before" Ishtar "for judgment." In other words, the speaker's stance contributes to the speaker's self-presentation as a plaintiff awaiting a ruling from the deity.[30]

The explicit positional contrast between kneeling and standing is significant too. It recalls the same transition that we have already seen in the biblical confrontations between Judah and Joseph and between Esther and Ahasuerus. Like the biblical petitioners, who first "fall" (*n-p-l*) before the authorities, the speaker in the prayer first encounters the deity while kneeling. Then, from a standing position, the speaker addresses the petition to the deity.[31]

In the context of human-to-human litigation, Akkadian lawsuit records show parallels to the terminology that occurs in the prayers, just as we find these parallels between prayers and the human courtrooms in

---

28. Duane Smith, "A Namburbi against the Evil of a Snake: Shamash 25," in *Reading Akkadian Prayers and Hymns: An Introduction*, ed. Alan Lenzi, ANEM 3 (Atlanta: Society of Biblical Literature, 2011), 421–30, here 425 (lines 10–14). See also *Maqlû* II.87, as numbered and published in Abusch, *Witchcraft Series Maqlû*, 58–59.

29. Anna-Elise Zernecke, "An Incantation Prayer: Ishtar 24," in *Reading Akkadian Prayers and Hymns: An Introduction*, ed. Alan Lenzi, ANEM 3 (Atlanta: Society of Biblical Literature, 2011), 169–78, here 172–73 (lines 9–10).

30. In other prayers, however, the kneeling itself is "for judgment" (*ana dīni*). See examples in *CAD* K, 119 (*kamāsu* B b2'). Courtroom records do not indicate that litigants would kneel.

31. Zgoll, "Audienz," 184, 194. The contrast in this prayer and elsewhere is vividly depicted in a relief of the Assyrian king Tukulti-Ninurta I, which shows the king in both positions (187, fig. 4).

Hebrew. Like the Hebrew narratives and legislative texts, Akkadian trial records frequently refer to the litigants' "approach" or "arrival." Here are three examples drawn from the corpus of Neo-Babylonian court records:

1. PN_1 raised a claim against PN_2. They **arrived** [*ikšudūma*] before [*ana maḫar*] PN_3 the governor of Babylon, the judges, and the elders of the city. They related their case.[32]

2. PN_1 **approached** [*imḫur*] PN_2 the royal official in charge of the Eanna, PN_3 the governor of Uruk, and PN_4 the *qīpi*-official of the Eanna (saying) thus: In Šabāṭu of year 6 of Nabonidus, king of Babylon, I purchased the property of PN_5 from PN_5.... PN_1 and PN_5 [argued] (their) case before them [*ina pānīšunu*].[33]

3. On 20 Kislīmu, year 4 of Cyrus, king of Babylon, king of the lands, PN_1 shall **come** [*illakamma*] to Babylon. He shall argue the case ... in the king's court of law. If he does not come, he shall pay 30-fold for these 2 sheep to the Lady of Uruk.[34]

Examples 1 and 2 come from the opening lines of two Neo-Babylonian court records. They illustrate how the litigants' arrival (*maḫāru, kašādu*) for adjudication warrants explicit mention, separate from what the people do or say during the process. They belong to the broader set of "notices of arrival in court" (*Gerichtsgang-Vermerk*) that occur throughout the long tradition of Mesopotamian trial records.[35] Eva Dombradi's study of Old Babylonian courtroom records lists seven such locutions, including the two verbs here, that can denote this stage in the process: the five Akkadian verbs *alāku, kašādu, maḫāru, sanāqu, ṭeḫû,* and two Sumerian equivalents, gaba-ri and igi-gar.[36] Texts from Nuzi regularly employ the verb *elû* in a similar manner, and the verb *qerēbu* occurs elsewhere, too.[37]

Example 3 above is a summons, written in Uruk, to the royal courthouse (*bīt dīni ša šarri*) in Babylon for a litigant, PN_1, to argue a case on

---

32. Stephanie Dalley, *A Catalogue of the Akkadian Cuneiform Tablets in the Collections of the Royal Scottish Museum, Edinburgh, with Copies of the Texts*, Art and Archaeology 2 (Edinburgh: Royal Scottish Museum, 1979), No. 69:1–5.
33. YOS 6, 92:1–23.
34. YOS 7, 31:1–12.
35. For the German term, see Dombradi, *Die Darstellung des Rechtsaustrags*, 1:60–69.
36. Ibid. For additional references, see *CAD* M.1, 59–61 (*maḫāru* 2a); S, 137 (*sanāqu* A2). On the different legal usages of the Sumerian locution igi-gar, see Adam Falkenstein, *Die neusumerischen Gerichtsurkunden*, 3 vols., ABAW NF 39, 40, 44 (Munich: Bayerischen Akademie der Wissenschaften, 1956), 1:60–61.
37. On *elû*, see *CAD* E, 119 (*elû* 1c2'). Also compare *CAD* E, 123–24 (*elû* 2d2'), where this verb refers to claimants who might "turn up" to contest legal transactions. On *qerēbu*, see *CAD* Q, 233 (*qerēbu* 3a2').

appeal.[38] In the present context, its particular significance is its emphasis on the appellant's "coming" (*alāku*).[39] The verb occurs twice, once in the notice of what PN_1 must do and again in the statement of the penalty he will incur for failure to comply. In the second occurrence, this verb, rather than anything pertaining to actually "arguing the case," is the only indication of what is to be done.

Equivalent to expressions of the litigants' own independent motion toward the adjudicatory forum are locutions that indicate that the litigants were "brought" there. One Neo-Babylonian trial record begins with the notice that a plaintiff "brought" (*ubilamma*) a defendant "before the judges of Cyrus."[40] Another petitioner, after describing his case against a fraudulent boatman, concludes his speech to the judges by saying, "Now, I have brought him before you [*ina mahrīkunu ublaš*]. Render our decision!"[41] In yet another case, the judges address the defendants with an order that they present their supposed creditor: "Bring [him] before us!" (*ana mahrīni bilā*).[42]

According to Akkadian trial records, litigants in Mesopotamia, like their counterparts in biblical sources, "stand before" the judges. This is most clearly seen in notices that adjudicating authorities "made a litigant stand before them" (*maḥaršunu ušzizzū*).[43] These notices employ the causative (C-stem) form of the common verb meaning "to stand" (*izuzzu*), which implies that the object of the verb, namely, the person appearing in court, is in fact standing. The basic (G-stem) form of the verb, with the litigants themselves as the subject, rather than the object, occurs, for example, in a letter preserved at Ugarit. There, the author writes to the king of Ugarit, "let these men come [*lillikūni*] stand before me with their adversaries [*itti bēlē dīnīšunu ana pānīya lizzizū*] and I will settle their case immediately."[44] Similarly, one Middle Babylonian courtroom record begins with

---

38. For brief discussion, with references to earlier literature, see Holtz, *Trial Records*, 163–65 (No. 39).

39. This verb is the standard verb meaning "to go." Here the translation "come" is based on the inclusion of the ventive *–am*.

40. Cyr. 312:1–5.

41. YOS 19, 101:24.

42. BM 32165+:20, as edited by Cornelia Wunsch, *Das Egibi-Archiv: I. Die Felder und Gärten*, 2 vols., CM 20A, 20B (Groningen: Styx, 2000), 1:230–31 (No. 90A).

43. E.g., Nbn. 13:5–6. Other Neo-Babylonian examples are collected in *CAD* U/W, 390 (*uzuzzu* 23a). Note that this form of the verb is used more broadly in reference to other objects (animate and otherwise) presented before the court.

44. RS 17.83:11–18 (J. Nougayrol, *Textes accadiens des archives sud*, vol. 4.1 of *Le palais royal d'Ugarit*, ed. Claude F.-A. Schaeffer, MRS 9 [Paris: Klincksieck, 1955], 216). Additional relevant examples are included in the references collected in *CAD* U/W, 379 (*uzuzzu* 4a2'). Note that the subject of this verb, in legal contexts, can also be other parties, including witnesses and the judges themselves.

the notice that it pertains to "the case in which [the named parties] stood [*izzizūma*] and (in which) they judged them."[45]

Many of these Akkadian verbal expressions, those of motion toward the adjudicatory venue as well those referring to litigants' position once there, expose an additional, more basic aspect of the terminology that describes the "staging" of the courtroom scene: the action occurs "before" (*maḫar* or *ina maḫar*) or "in the presence of" (*ina pāni*) the adjudicators. In the examples already cited, these prepositional phrases often denote the direction or location to which the litigants "go" or are "brought," as well as where they "stand" during the adjudication. Another Neo-Babylonian example indicates, without any verb of motion or positioning, that "before [*ina maḫar*] the *sukkallu*, the 'great ones' and the judges of Nabonidus king of Babylon they [the litigants] argued (their) case."[46] In fact, we find that not only litigants come to this location, but also evidence, in the form of livestock, is "brought and made to stand before" adjudicating authorities.[47]

As a connection between litigation and prayer, the significance of placement "before" the authority is a motif in the following selection from a hymn to Shamash, sun god and god of justice:

> Those whose mouth says "No"—(their case) is before you [*šakin ina maḫrīka*]
> Speedily you discern what they say;
> You hear and examine them; you determine the case [*tumassi dīnšu*] of the wronged.
> Every single person is entrusted to your hands;
> You manage their omens; that which is perplexing you make plain.
> You hear, Shamash, prayer, supplication, and benediction,
> Obeisance, kneeling, ritual murmurs, and prostration.
> The feeble man calls you from the hollow of his mouth,
> The humble, the weak, the wronged, the poor,
> He daily, constantly and unceasingly approaches you [*imaḫḫarka*].
> He whose family is remote, whose city is distant,
> The shepherd [amid] terror of the steppe approaches you [*imaḫḫarka*],
> The herdsman in warfare, the keeper of sheep among enemies.
> O Shamash, the caravan approaches you [*imaḫḫarka*], those journeying in fear,
> The traveling merchant, the agent carrying capital.
> O Shamash, the fisherman with his net approaches you [*imaḫḫarka*],

---

45. Herbert Petschow, *Mittelbabylonische Rechts- und Wirtschaftsurkunden der Hilprecht-Sammlung Jena*, ASAW Philologisch-Historische Klasse 64.4 (Berlin: Akademie-Verlag, 1974), 13:1–4.

46. Nbn. 1113:6–8. For discussion, with references to earlier literature, see Holtz, *Trial Records*, 70–73 (No. 20).

47. YOS 7, 7:37–40.

> The hunter, the bowman who drives the game,
> With his bird net, the fowler approaches you [*imaḫḫarka*].
> The prowling thief, the enemy of Shamash,
> Along the tracks of the steppe the marauder approaches you [*imaḫḫarka*].
> The roving dead, the vagrant soul,
> O Shamash, they approach you [*imḫurūka*], you hear all.
> You do not obstruct those that approach you [*imḫurūka*] ...
> For my sake, O Shamash, do not curse them![48]

Language describing placement "before" Shamash runs as a common thread throughout this part of the hymn. The excerpt begins by describing Shamash as the great, all-seeing judge, who "determines the case" against the dishonest ("those whose mouth says No"). It is their case, as Wilfred Lambert's translation correctly elucidates, that is "set before" (*šakin ina maḫar*) the god. In the latter part of the selection, the verb *maḫāru*, meaning "to approach," repeatedly refers to the action of the wide array of people from all walks of life (and even the dead!) praying to the god. The related terminology underscores the connection between prayer and adjudication: cases are said to be "before" (*ina maḫar*) the divine judge and petitioners "approach" (*maḫāru*) the great judge to put their cases before him.

The Akkadian evidence presented here closely parallels what we find in the Hebrew Bible. Prayer and litigation, in both bodies of literature, resemble each other as occasions of an "audience." We have made this point by observing the general similarities between the positional terminologies of the courtroom and of prayer in Hebrew and Akkadian. In both bodies of literature, approach or arrival marks the occasion of both prayer and litigation, as does the positioning, or stance, of the subject.

To conclude these general observations, let us consider one additional specific case of this terminological overlap in Akkadian, which may shed comparative light on a similar Hebrew locution. In some Akkadian prayers, the speakers use a phrase consisting of the verb *nadû* ("to place") with the noun *rigmu* ("complaint") as its object. For example, one speaker says to a deity, "In anguish, I complain [*rigme addīki*; lit., 'place my complaint'] bitterly to you."[49] This same verb–noun combination, and a nearly identical one with the related noun *rugummāʾu*, occurs in Old Assyrian legal texts. There one litigant is said to "place" (*nadû*) the complaint (*rigmu* or *rugummāʾu*) "to" (*ana*) the other litigant: PN$_1$ *rugummāʾu ana* PN$_2$ *iddi u*

---

48. *BWL* 134:124–148. Translation follows *BWL*, 135.

49. Stephen Langdon, ed., *Babylonian Penitential Psalms to Which Are Added Fragments of the Epic of Creation from Kish in the Weld Collection of the Ashmolean Museum*, OECT 6 (Paris: Geuthner, 1927), pl. 4, K. 4926, as cited in *CAD* R, 344 (*rigmu* 5). For additional references, see *CAD* N.1, 94 (*nadû* 6) and R, 333–34 (*rigmu* 5).

PN₂ *ana* PN₁ *rugummêšu iddi*.⁵⁰ As in the other Akkadian examples already presented, this specific case nicely illustrates how the same terminology describes the presentation of a complaint to deities and humans alike.

Moreover, based on its constituent parts, the Akkadian locution *rigma nadû* may illuminate the Hebrew idiom *n-p-l* + *təḥinna*. Specifically, the unusual use of the verb *n-p-l*, which usually means "to fall" and, in the causative stem, "to drop" demands explanation. Akkadian *nadû* often means "to drop." In combination with a noun like *rigmu*, meaning "complaint," the Akkadian presents a tempting parallel to the Hebrew. Both appear to consist of equivalent parts: a verb (*nadû/n-p-l*) meaning "to drop" and a noun (*rigmu/təḥinnâ*) meaning "complaint." Could the Akkadian verb lie behind the idiomatic usage of *n-p-l* in Hebrew?

While this is an intriguing possibility, we should be aware of some drawbacks. First, the Akkadian locution probably employs the verb *nadû* in its meaning "to place,"⁵¹ along the lines of the verb *šakānu*, another verb meaning "to place" that also commonly takes *rigmu* as an object.⁵² More crucially, the two idioms do not quite describe the same actions. In the Old Assyrian legal texts, the subject of the verb complains to the legal opponent, rather than to an adjudicator. In Hebrew, on the other hand, the subject complains to the authority. This is entirely in keeping with the noun *təḥinnâ*, which suggests an imbalance of power between the persons performing the action and their intended audience. In short, for the two locutions to be linked historically, we would have to imagine that the Hebrew has undergone a considerable transformation from any purported Akkadian origin. Even so, each expression, in its own way and within its own linguistic matrix, underscores broader connections between the audience concept and the idea of praying legally.

Legal Aspects of Prophetic Intercession

Until this point, we have observed that the terminology of approaching and standing, in general, marks a nexus between the audience, prayer, and the courtroom. In order to demonstrate the value of these observations, in this section I will apply them to the specific case of prophetic intercessory prayer. This particular kind of prayer occurs when prophets

---

50. Kültepe g/k 100:5–10, as edited in Kemal Balkan, "Contribution to the Understanding of the Idiom of the Old Assyrian Merchants of Kanish," *Or* 36 (1967): 393–415, here 409–10. See *CAD* N.1, 94 (*nadû* 6), R, 344 (*rigmu* 6b) and R, 405 (*rugummû*).

51. See *CAD* N.1, 80 (*nadû* 2).

52. *CAD* R, 334 (*rigmu* 6b).

pray to prevent impending punishment. Through prayer, prophets "stand in the breach" between God and Israel (Ezek 22:30).[53]

Our particular interest in prophetic intercession stems, in part, from scholarship that has posited a legal interpretation of the phenomenon. For example, Yochanan Muffs, in his foundational study of the role of prophets as intercessors, invokes the metaphor of "the defense attorney" to characterize Moses, who intercedes on behalf of Israel in the wake of the golden calf incident (Exod 32:7–14). Here are some selections from Muffs's interpretation of Moses's intercessory speech:

> Pay attention to the strategy of the defense attorney who avails himself of all the rhetorical devices of argumentation, legitimate as well as spurious, to save the defendant.... The defense attorney reminds the Lord that Israel is not Moses's people, but God's …

> Moses argues further, "Remember Abraham, Isaac, and Jacob, your servants, to whom You personally promised to redeem their children" (Exod 32:13). Here we have a compelling legal and emotional argument. Could it be that God is not as trustworthy as an ordinary human being? … Moses is saying to God, "You cannot behave in such an arbitrary fashion. After all, You are a King bound by the fetters of Your own justice. You are obligated to realize what You have promised, like it or not!"[54]

It is Muffs's last point, about the covenant with the patriarchs, that marks the direction toward a legal understanding of Moses's role. In fact, I have already drawn on this observation near the beginning of the previous chapter, in my reading of the communal prayer in Jer 14. There, as here, evocation of the covenant serves as a legal argument in the community's defense.

Muffs, however, expands this particular legal connection into a broader understanding of the entire scene as one of legal defense. Casting Moses as the "defense attorney" implies that we have a courtroom scene in Exod 32, where Israel is "the defendant" and God the King is also God the Judge.

In their breadth, Muffs's ideas closely resemble Pietro Bovati's interpretation of intercession within the framework of the courtroom. Like Muffs, Bovati regards intercession as a "kind of speech for the defense" in a lawsuit.[55] Further, he writes:

---

53. The fundamental study on prophetic intercession remains Muffs, *Love and Joy*, 9–48; on this particular verse, see 31–32. For up-to-date bibliography on the general subject, see references in Marian W. Broida, *Forestalling Doom: "Apotropaic Intercession" in the Hebrew Bible and the Ancient Near East*, AOAT 417 (Münster: Ugarit-Verlag, 2014).

54. Muffs, *Love and Joy*, 12–13.

55. Bovati, *Re-Establishing Justice*, 237 n. 34.

The peculiarity of this form of supplication lies in its being made on behalf of the guilty by someone who is not guilty.... The intercessor is well aware that crime has been committed, and is in no way conniving at it; it is worth remembering in this context that the great intercessors of biblical tradition were indeed representatives for the prosecution: from Moses ... to Samuel ... and the prophets, who were sent to denounce sin and threaten appropriate retribution. But if the guilty manages ... to bring about a change of function by the accuser ... so that the accuser no longer speaks *against* but *on behalf of* the guilty, putting across the defense, then it is a reasonable assumption that nobody will speak up to accuse the guilty, who will thus be able to experience the joy of pardon.[56]

The courtroom is extensively present in Bovati's interpretation of intercessory prayer. As in Muffs's reading, when prophets and others intercede on behalf of a sinner, they "put across the defense." For Bovati, though, the prophets' role as legal defenders hinges on their role as "representatives for the prosecution." Prophetic intercessions carry weight precisely because the prophets switch sides, as it were, from prosecution to defense. By invoking these categories, Bovati, like Muffs, insists that we view intercession scenes through the lens of the courtroom.

What justifies this legally tinged view of prophetic intercession? Is it grounded in what the biblical texts actually mean, or is it simply a convenient heuristic-rhetorical trope that elucidates the text by drawing analogies to a situation with which modern readers might be more familiar? As I have already observed, following Muffs, Moses's invocation of the sworn covenant with the patriarchs in Exod 32:13 constitutes a kind of legal argument that evinces his more-general role as a "defense attorney." Similar evidence is encountered in the story of Abraham's (ultimately failed) intercessory negotiations with God to save Sodom (Gen 18:23–33).[57] There Abraham concludes his opening speech with the rhetorical question, "Shall the Judge of all the earth not do justice?" (Gen 18:25). Abraham's reference to God as "judge of all the earth" (*šōpēṭ kol-hāʾāreṣ*) situates the entire scene in the courtroom. Once God is explicitly cast in the role of the judge, then Abraham can be viewed as a defense attorney of sorts, and Abraham's entire speech can be understood as a legally conceived argument on behalf of Sodom.

---

56. Ibid., 132–33.
57. See Muffs, *Love and Joy*, 10–11. Sustained legal treatments of this passage can be found in James K. Bruckner, *Implied Law in the Abraham Narrative: A Literary and Theological Analysis*, JSOTSup 335 (Sheffield: Sheffield Academic Press, 2001), 124–70; and Timothy D. Lytton, "'Shall Not the Judge of the Earth Deal Justly?': Accountability, Compassion, and Judicial Authority in the Biblical Story of Sodom and Gomorrah," *Journal of Law and Religion* 18 (2002–2003): 31–55.

Our legal understanding of the language of approaching and standing in prayer adds evidence in favor of the legal interpretation of prophetic intercession. Bovati himself adduces the locution ʿ-m-d lipnê, which he takes to have the sense of "to intercede," as the basis for understanding intercession as a "kind of speech for the defense."[58] Given the general uses of this locution, especially in prayer contexts, Bovati's lexicographical claim may go beyond what the words themselves convey. One can certainly imagine that the term refers to prayer in general, even "service," rather than specifically "intercession."[59] We might even imagine a more literal, physical meaning instead of a legal one. According to Ezek 22:30, a crucial verse for understanding prophetic intercession, the prophets' role should have been to "mend the fence and stand in the breach" before God.[60] A "mended fence" would have provided the barrier necessary to prevent a wrathful God from reaching the nation. By "standing in the breach before God," the prophet could have achieved the same goal: maintaining the physical barrier between God and the people. By this reading, the job of the prophet is more defensive lineman than defense attorney, to "stand before," that is, to block, God and thus protect the people.

Nevertheless, the locution ʿ-m-d lipnê does, indeed, occur in descriptions of prophetic intercession and certainly connects these scenes to those of prayer in general. In addition to the presence of this locution in God's own statement on intercession (Ezek 22:30), Jeremiah, for his part, adopts it to describe himself as "standing before You [God] to speak in their [Israel's] favor, to calm Your anger against them" (Jer 18:20; see also 15:1, 19). As argued above, outside of the specific context of prophetic intercession, this locution illustrates the intersection between the audience taking place during prayer and the audience taking place in the courtroom. If so, then there is a good basis to the argument that Jeremiah's "standing before" God to intercede on behalf of Israel should, in some way, be related to the litigants' "standing before" the judge, like the inadvertent homicide (Num 35:12) or the two women in the judgment of Solomon (1 Kgs 3:16).

As with the phrase ʿ-m-d lipnê, locutions denoting approach and standing (without the "before" element) occur also in contexts of intercession. According to Ps 106:30, Phinehas "stands" (wayyaʿămôd) in prayer to stop a plague. Before Abraham begins his oral arguments on behalf of Sodom, Gen 18:23 specifically notes that he "approaches" (wayyiggaš).[61] Again,

---

58. Bovati, *Re-Establishing Justice*, 237 n. 34; see also Bruckner, *Implied Law*, 95–96.

59. On the prophet as a servant, see Muffs, *Love and Joy*, 10.

60. On the significance of Ezek 22:30 for understanding prophetic intercession, see Muffs, *Love and Joy*, 31, 35. See also Ps 106:23.

61. See Bruckner, *Implied Law*, 96. Note that the immediately preceding clause "Abraham was still standing before YHWH" (Gen 18:22) includes the locution ʿ-m-d lipnê,

the legal significance of these terms in descriptions of prayer in general certainly pertains to the particular example of intercession. People who approach and stand in prayer resemble petitioners in general, like Judah or Esther, who stand before an authority to make their case. As we have seen, litigants, who also plead their cases, present themselves similarly. The comparable positional terminology in contexts of intercession allows us to say the same for prophets who "approach" and "stand before" God to intercede on behalf of the nation: their role is to plead the nation's case.

Before turning to the Akkadian materials, I note briefly that a later Hebrew prayer retains this association between a near equivalent to intercessory prayer and the language of approaching and standing. It is the petition "Behold I am bereft of deeds" (*hinənî heʿānî mimmaʿaś*), which, in the Ashkenazi and Eastern European traditions, the prayer leader recites before the additional prayer on the high holidays.[62] The leader announces:

> I have come to stand [*bāʾtî laʿămōd*] and plead before You [*ləpānêkā*] on behalf of Your people Israel, who have commissioned me ... grant success to my mission: to stand [*laʿămōd*] and seek mercy on behalf of myself and those who have commissioned me.

This prayer gives expression to the broader idea of the prayer leader's role as "messenger of the congregation" [*šəliaḥ ṣibbûr*]. As a spokesperson for the congregation, the leader, to some extent, continues and replaces the prophet in the role of intercessor. The use of language that emphasizes arrival and standing before God highlights this conceptual continuity.

The comparable legal valences of the Akkadian terminology for approaching and standing during prayer, in general, remain relevant to our present discussion of prophetic intercession. The Akkadian evidence surveyed in the previous section provides an additional layer of support for establishing the legal significance of the prophets' prayers on behalf of the nation.

Apart from the general support that the Akkadian materials provide, we can also point to a possible, more specific situational parallel to prophetic intercession from the realm of the courtroom. One recent study of the Old Babylonian system of justice, as it is attested in the letters from Mari, shows that disadvantaged individuals sought legal advocatory assistance from the more privileged. This study concludes that "although there were no professional 'lawyers' in the Old Babylonian period, certain people in society functioned as agents and helpers

---

discussed earlier (Bovati, *Re-Establishing Justice*, 237 n. 34). In this verse, however, it is more likely that the phrase's narrative purpose is to set up the contrast between the visiting men, who move on to Sodom, and Abraham, who remains. Contrast Bruckner, *Implied Law*, 95.

62. Goldschmidt, מחזור לימים הנוראים, 1:147.

for people who had been wronged. In this capacity, they provided a service similar to that provided by present-day lawyers."[63] These "agents," in addition to possessing technical legal language and knowledge, may also have had personal connections with adjudicatory authorities.[64] Individuals of lesser status and education would have relied on these agents to make their cases.

The legal-social system expected the more privileged to provide legal assistance to those less fortunate. This expectation finds expression not only in its practical manifestations in the Mari letters but also in a Neo-Babylonian literary text known by the modern English title, "Nebuchadnezzar King of Justice." This text describes how the king corrects the lawlessness and the breakdown of legal institutions that existed during the reigns of earlier rulers.[65] In the part of the text that reports examples of the wide-ranging corruption under previous kings, we read the following: "Regent and prince would not take the part of the cripple and widow before the judge [*itti akû u almat la izzazzū maḫar dayyāni*], and if they approached the judge [*imaḫḫarā*] he would not judge their case."[66] Under normal, proper circumstances, those in power are expected to support the legal causes—"take the part"—of those in need by playing an advocatory role of some kind.

Even at the conceptual level, the regent and the prince in the "King of Justice" text and the "agents" attested in the Mari letters seem to play a role analogous to that of the prophet who "takes Israel's part" by interceding with God on behalf of Israel. Like the prophets who intercede, the "agents" assist the disadvantaged to make a strong argument.[67]

The language of the Neo-Babylonian text allows us to press the analogy even further. The idiom that describes what the "regent and prince" are expected to do, translated by the editor as "take the part of," actually

---

63. Shirley Graetz, "To Whom Can a Wronged Person Turn for Help in the Old Babylonian Period?," in *Marbeh Ḥokmah: Studies in the Bible and the Ancient Near East in Loving Memory of Victor Avigdor Hurowitz*, ed. S. Yona et al. (Winona Lake, IN: Eisenbrauns, 2015), 237–60, here 254.

64. Ibid., 251–53.

65. BM 45690. First published in CT 46, 45 with a full edition in W. G. Lambert, "Nebuchadnezzar King of Justice," *Iraq* 27 (1965): 1–11. For updated bibliography on the text, including reference to current scholarly opinion on its relevance to the reign of Nabonidus, rather than Nebuchadnezzar, see Janice Barrabee, "The King of Justice: A Reconsideration of the River Ordeal in BM 456901" [sic], in Frame, *Common Cultural Heritage*, 1–18, here 1–2.

66. CT 46, 45 ii.5–6.

67. For a biblical analogue outside the realm of prophecy, in the human-to-human courtroom, we might compare the speech by the elders on behalf of Jeremiah (Jer 26:17–19). Later rabbinic tradition allows judges themselves to offer defense in capital cases (b. Sanh. 43b).

consists of the verb *izuzzu* ("to stand") and the preposition *itti* ("with").[68] So, a more literal translation would render the text as "regent and prince would not stand with the cripple and widow before the judge." Thus, the situational similarity between the prophets and the Babylonian leaders as advocates is underscored by similar terminology. Both the prophets and the leaders "stand before" the judge—a human one, in the case of the leaders, and God, in the case of the prophets.

There are, however, limits to the terminological similarity between the actions expected of the Babylonian leaders and those of the biblical prophets. Although both "stand before" the authorities, the Babylonian texts describe the leaders as standing "with" (*itti*) the underprivileged. Hebrew texts, in contrast, do not describe the prophets as standing "with" the people as advocates. Still, the situational and the limited terminological parallels remain in place. The interceding prophets stand with Israel, or take Israel's side, in concept, if not exactly in language. The situational parallels, and, to some extent the linguistic ones too, all ground the legal interpretation of prophetic prayer in the law as practiced.

Furthermore, our attention specifically to the positional terminology returns us to the general connections between prayer, the "audience concept," and the courtroom. As I have suggested, in all three of these contexts, the language of approaching and standing connotes the subjects' gaining of access to the superiors, the bridging of the gap that enables communication. Just this aspect of the audience, without any mention of a successful outcome, places demands on the subjects that might end the encounter before it even gets under way. It is not just any subject that can approach a superior to present a plea; certain subjects have better connections and know-how that allow them to approach and stand before the superiors. For these reasons, subjects come to rely on prophetic intercessors and their counterparts as they make their cases.

These observations underscore a contrast between our understanding of prayer, in general, and the specific case of prophetic intercessory prayer. Our discussion in the previous section suggested that the audience concept in prayer, through its invocation of known etiquette, allows humans to access the divine. Within this conceptual framework, the use of positional terminology marks the point of access, that humans and divinities share the requisite space for a petition to be submitted. All of this implies that prayer-as-audience, and even prayer-as-courtroom-audience, makes prayer available to all humans. Intercessory prayer, in contrast, is the realm of only the few. Only those most familiar with the conventions of the audience, in the courtroom or elsewhere, can gain access. Here,

---

68. See *CAD* U, 380–81 (*uzuzzu* 5b).

the language of approach and stance leaves the gap between subject and superior in full view, even as that terminology connotes that it has been successfully spanned.

God's Forensic Senses: Hearing and Seeing

Near the outset of this chapter, I quoted the observation that, by invoking the audience concept, prayer seeks "to (re)-establish such a reciprocal relationship with the deity."[69] We have, until now, explored the human, or subject, side of this relationship that manifests itself during prayer. Humans present themselves as subjects, more specifically as subjects making legal pleas by means of their legally formulated prayers. They underscore their spoken message by means of their approach and stance toward the superior. Crucially, however, there is another side to the audience, that of the superior. Subjects, by following their assigned parts in the audience drama, expect (or at least hope) that the superiors, too, will play theirs. What humans say and how they say it serve the ultimate goals of the audience: acceptance by the superior and a favorable response.

This section turns to this other side of the reciprocity between subject and superior and analyzes what occurs during prayer, from the deities' end. Specifically, I will examine the sensory terminology of hearing and seeing that describes how deities are said to take notice of the subjects' pleas. These terms mark the initial, most-basic divine response to prayer. Even before any action is taken in favor of the subject, the deities' hearing or seeing indicates that a certain transfer of agency has occurred from the subject to the superior. Indeed, as so many prayers indicate, just being "seen" or "heard" by the divine is itself something worth praying for.

The sensory terminology predicated of the deities, like the terminology describing the speakers' approach and stance, also participates in the broader motif that connects the audience, the courtroom, and prayer. At the most basic level, the fact that deities are said to "hear" justifies the application of the modern term "audience" to the occasion of prayer, even though ancient Near Eastern sources lack a specific equivalent term. Interpreting prayer as an "audience" makes sense, in part, because the English word "audience" derives from a word meaning "to hear." I observed above that the positional terms are fundamental to creating the shared space between subject and superior that allows the audience to take place. Here I point to something equally fundamental: the presumption that the superior will hear the subject turns that encounter into an "audience."

In contrast to hearing, the English term *audience* on its own shares no etymological connection with the sense of sight. Nevertheless, when it

---

69. Lenzi, *Reading Akkadian Prayers*, 32.

comes to the ancient Near Eastern sources, especially the Hebrew Bible, the two senses are closely related.⁷⁰ In the context of prayer, we see this quite clearly in the common and nearly formulaic notices that God has seen the Israelites' plight and has heard their cries, too.⁷¹ More generally, speakers in prayers ask God both to "hear their voices" (e.g., Pss 5:2–3; 27:7) and to "see their plight" (e.g., Pss 9:14; 35:22). Both senses, then, refer to an expected outcome for prayer. In an "audience," a superior might see as well as hear.

Our claim here is that these sensory descriptions connect prayer not only to the audience concept but also, more specifically, to the idea of praying legally. Deities, when they see and hear the petitioners, act in a manner resembling that of human adjudicators. The deities' side of the audience, like the human subjects' speeches and actions, should be understood as a nexus between the prayer and courtroom.

In making this claim I will build on the work of earlier scholars, especially Bovati, who have interpreted both hearing and seeing as forensic actions.⁷² In keeping with my own focus on prayer, I will highlight the contextual factors that underscore the particularly forensic use of these terms in prayers. As I have done throughout, I will draw on Hebrew and Akkadian evidence to describe the ways in which these terms function in human-to-human adjudicatory contexts. Doing so will allow us to illustrate how the deities' responses to prayers are more than indications of awareness of the speakers and their situations. In hearing and seeing, the deities act as adjudicating authorities, who give, or are asked to give, legal consideration to the prayer. I will address each sense separately, first hearing and then seeing.

Biblical prayers themselves associate God's hearing with the judicial process. The earlier discussion of the demand for judgment observed in passing that in Ps 17 and 54, where the demand occurs in the prayers' opening lines, it is coupled with a demand to be heard. Here are the relevant texts:

¹⁷:¹⁻²Hear, O YHWH, what is just;
Heed my cry, give ear to my prayer,
Uttered without lips of guile.
From before You, let my judgment emerge!
Your eyes behold what is right.

---

70. Avrahami, *Senses of Scripture*, 69–74. For meaningful speculation about a possible distinction between Hebrew and Akkadian in this regard, see 277–78.
71. Exod 2:24–25; 3:7; 4:31; Deut 26:7; 2 Kgs 13:4; 14:26; Neh 9:9.
72. On hearing, see Bovati, *Re-Establishing Justice*, 311–28; compare the brief observations in Magdalene, *Scales of Righteousness*, 121, 243; and Avrahami, *Senses of Scripture*, 134. On seeing, see Bovati, *Re-Establishing Justice*, 71, 244.

⁵⁴:³⁻⁴O God, by Your name, deliver me,
And with Your might, judge me [*tədînēnî*]!
O God, hear my petition [*təpîllātî*],
give ear to the words of my mouth.

Psalm 17:1–2, when read in sequence, suggest a progression from hearing to judgment. The emphatically threefold cry to be heard (v. 1)[73] leads directly to the jussive call for God to judge the petitioner's case—"From before You, let my judgment go out" (v. 2). In Ps 54, the sequence is reversed, with judgment following hearing, rather than preceding. Here, too, though, the close association between judgment and hearing remains.

A similar forensic concept of God's hearing prayer (and seeing, too) emerges from the following passage in Elihu's address to Job (Job 35:12–14):

¹²Then they cry out, but He does not respond
Because of the arrogance of evil men.
¹³Surely it is false that God does not listen,
That Shaddai does not see it [*lōʾ yəšûrennâ*].
¹⁴Though you say, "You do not see it,"
The case is before Him [*dîn ləpānāyw*]; so wait for Him.[74]

These verses appear in a section that describes those who complain of oppression but forget God (35:9–16). Consequently, according to Elihu, God ignores these people's prayers (v. 12). Under normal circumstances, however, God does, in fact, hear prayers; it is false to say that God does not hear or see them (vv. 13–14a). God's hearing and seeing are part of the judicial process (*dîn*). The machinery of justice may take time to operate, and humans misinterpret delays in the process as unresponsiveness, even rejection, on the part of God the judge. For the righteous who have filed their petitions and await a hearing and a decision, Elihu counsels patience.

Similar contextual connections between demands to be heard and forensic language occur in Akkadian religious literature. In the first incantation of the anti-witchcraft series *Maqlû*, the speaker makes the following demand: "Stand by me, O great gods, hear my suit [*šimâ dabābī*]! Judge my case [*dīnī dīnā*], grant me a decision [*alaktī limdā*]!"[75] Along the same lines,

---

73. Compare 17:6, another emphatically repetitive cry to be heard
74. This translation follows the NJPS. For literature supporting this rendering, see David J. A. Clines, *Job 21–37*, WBC 18A (Nashville: Thomas Nelson, 2006), 791. Clines mentions this understanding as an alternative with which he disagrees in part (see discussion on 801–2). The basic connection between God's hearing and the legal process remains, even in other interpretations.
75. *Maqlû* I.13–14. For the specifically legal meaning of the word *dabābu*, rendered here as "my suit," see *CAD* D, 8–10 (*dabābu* 4).

the speaker in a prayer to the goddess Gula motivates a demand to be heard with a particularly legal reason:

> I call out to you, my lady, stand nearby and listen to me [*izizzimma šimî yâti*]!
> I seek you out ...
> Because judging a case, handing down the decision [*aššum dīni dâni purussâ parāsi*],
> Because restoring and maintaining are within your power,
> Because you know how to save, to spare, and to rescue ...[76]

In both texts, the gods' judgment comes right after the gods' hearing. The speaker in the opening of *Maqlû* couples the demand for hearing with an explicit demand for judgment. In the Gula prayer, the goddess's judicial capability is the speaker's first reason for asking to be heard. All of this suggests that in this prayer, hearing, like judgment itself, is a particularly legal activity.

In all of these prayers, hearing and judgment are two steps in the legal process. Speakers who link demands to be heard with demands for judgment express their confidence in the process. A different picture emerges from the opening verses of Ps 143, where the speaker wishes to disconnect hearing from judgment:

> ¹O YHWH, hear my prayer, give ear to my plea.
> In Your faithfulness (and) justice, answer me.
> ²But do not enter into judgment with Your servant,
> Since before You, no living being can ever be in the right.

As in the previous examples, God's hearing precedes judgment here. The speaker asks to be heard but adopts a legal tactic of asking God not to enter into litigation.[77] Under normal circumstances, judicial hearing is a first step to achieving justice; in Ps 17, for example, the speaker asks to be heard and then anticipates a favorable judgment. In contrast, the speaker in Ps 143 fears that, upon hearing the plea, God might switch roles from judge to litigant.[78] Since the outcome can never be favorable, it is best to avoid any lawsuit that might evolve out of the judicial hearing.

---

76. Lenzi, *Reading Akkadian Prayers*, 254 (Gula 1a:2–6).

77. For the suggestion that these two verses reflect a contrast, see the translation in Allen, *Psalms 101–150*, 280.

78. Thus, Allen renders 143:2a thus: "do not enter into legal proceedings with your servant" (*Psalms 101–150*, 280). Compare John Goldingay, *Psalms*, 3 vols., BCOTWP (Grand Rapids: Baker Academic, 2008), 3:673. Some have suggested that the speaker wishes to avoid rejection of the plea or an unfavorable ruling by God, in the part of judge rather than litigant. See, e.g., Amos Ḥakham, *Psalms with the Jerusalem Commentary* [Hebrew], 3 vols. (Jerusalem: Mosad Harav Kook, 2003), 3:432; and Hossfeld and Zenger, *Psalms 3*, 573, as well as the notes

The speaker's legal maneuver in Ps 143 brings to mind one section of the long model prayer of the Hittite king Muwatalli. In this particular section, Muwatalli instructs the gods on how to relate to his pleas:

> Thereafter, I shall make the matters of my own soul into a plea. Divine lords, lend me your ear, and listen to these my pleas! And the words which I will make into a plea to the divine lords, these words, divine lords, accept and listen to them! And whatever words you do not wish to hear from me, and I nevertheless persist in making them into a plea to the gods, they merely emerge from my human mouth; refrain from listening to them, divine lords.[79]

Like the speakers in the psalms and the Akkadian texts, Muwatalli begins by asking the gods to hear. Since the idea of arguing, or pleading one's case, lies at the heart of the Hittite conception of prayer, this request to be heard should be understood forensically, which is to say that it is equivalent to a petition for a hearing. In this particular example, however, Muwatalli understands that he may say more than is necessary to make his case before the gods. Speaking too much can have undesirable results; he might say something that the gods "do not wish to hear" and they might use this against him when they reach their decision. Therefore, he asks the gods to ignore anything irrelevant or undesirable that may "emerge from his human mouth."

For Muwatalli and the speaker in Ps 143, hearing, the sensory term that designates the divine reaction to or perception of prayer, is part of the forensic conception of prayer. Both speakers imagine themselves as petitioners making their cases before a judge, who, they hope, will hear their arguments and rule in their favor. Their shared legal conception of prayer gives rise to concerns about where the process might lead. Both attempt to head off these potentially adverse legal outcomes by asking the judges to focus on the arguments. The speaker in Ps 143 does this by asking that the hearing not devolve into a case against him. Muwatalli hopes to curtail the process even earlier, by asking the gods to conduct their hearing selectively.

At their root, the demands to be heard in prayers evoke the act, in the human-to-human sphere, of "crying out" to the king for relief. The act itself, as we have already argued, offers a situational and terminological parallel to the act of prayer. In terms of our specific subject here, God's hearing the "cry" of the person at prayer suggests a parallel between the role of God and the role of the king to whom petitioners bring their cries.[80]

---

by Allen (*Psalms 101–150,* 281) and Goldingay (*Psalms,* 3:673). However, the collocation b-w-ʾ (G-stem) bamišpāṭ refers to the action of fellow litigants, rather than the action of the judge.

79. CTH 381, i 25–32. Translation follows Singer, *Hittite Prayers,* 87 (No. 20).
80. See Bovati, *Re-Establishing Justice,* 324–327.

In fact, Hebrew texts that describe human-to-human petitions allow us to identify examples of demands to be heard analogous to those that occur in prayers. One such example occurs in the narrative of Jeremiah's plea before Zedekiah (Jer 37:13–21), a scene discussed in the opening chapter. In the waning days of the kingdom of Judah, the officers of Judah imprison the prophet in the house of the scribe Jonathan. King Zedekiah seeks out Jeremiah in secret, in order to hear God's message. Jeremiah reports that the king of Babylon will take Zedekiah prisoner. Then Jeremiah seizes the opportunity to seek clemency from the king. He pleads, "Now, please hear me, O Lord King, and let my plea come before you: Do not send me back to the house of the scribe Jonathan, and let me not die there" (Jer 37:20). While the emotional aspects of Jeremiah's speech are hard to ignore, the prophet is, in the end, seeking a legal ruling: he wants the king to overturn the punishment that the officers have given him. Thus, his opening words, "please hear me," are more than a way of directing the king's attention. Rather, the call to be heard also signals that Jeremiah is demanding the king's legal consideration.[81]

A demand to be heard with a similar legal function occurs in the Yavneh Yam inscription, also known as the Meṣad Ḥashavyahu ostracon.[82] This extrabiblical Hebrew text is a letter that has been interpreted as "an extrajudicial petition," which means that its language carries some legal force.[83] The author of the letter is a petitioner who narrates his grievance to an officer and, quite like Jeremiah, hopes that the officer (here playing a role analogous to that of King Zedekiah) will address it. The situational parallel between the petitioner and Jeremiah is underscored by the petitioner's opening words: "May my lord the officer hear his servant's word" [yšmʿ ʾdny hśr ʾt dbr ʿbdh]. Like Jeremiah, the petitioner begins his appeal with a demand to be heard and expects a favorable decision once the authority has "heard."

These two specific examples demonstrate how speakers' demands to be heard in prayers mark the overlap between prayer, the audience concept, and the courtroom. In making their demands to be heard, speakers, as subjects, take on a role like that of Jeremiah or the petitioner in the Yavneh Yam inscription. With their cries, speakers signal more than asking their superiors to pay attention; there is an implicit demand for action on their behalf. In hearing, the deities, as superiors, play the role of King Zedekiah or the officer. They give the cries legal consideration.

These legal overtones of the "hearing" by the superiors, be they humans or deities, manifest themselves not only in descriptions of hopes for audiences' successful outcomes but also in descriptions of audiences

---

81. Magdalene, *Scales of Righteousness*, 121, 243.
82. For the basic comparison, see F. W. Dobbs-Allsopp, "The Genre of the Meṣad Ḥashavyahu Ostracon," *BASOR* 295 (1994): 49–55, here 51.
83. Ibid.

that fail. The possibility that God might not hear a prayer occurs in explicit statements by God, as well as by petitioners.[84] It is also implied in statements that acknowledge God's having heard:[85] for, if God *always* hears cries, why acknowledge that God has heard?

God's not hearing suggests a further analogy to the human legal sphere. In the human realm, the king or another adjudicator has the right to ignore the petitioner: the Israelite king, Ahab, dismisses just this kind of "crying" petitioner (1 Kgs 20:39–40).[86] A corrupt authority might abuse this prerogative by not judging the cases of the poor, who, presumably, could not pay the requisite fees.[87] Thus, Prov 21:13 warns, "Who stops his ears [ʾōṭēm ʾoznô] at the cry of the wretched, he too will call out and not be answered." This verse stands out for its specific reference to the authority's sense of hearing and to its implicit reference to the analogy between prayer and the human action of "crying out." Hearing is the normal, righteous response to "the cry of the wretched" (*zaʿăqat-dal*); a wicked authority "stops his ear." The just desert occurs when the unhearing person tries to get a hearing from God, who will not consider his prayer.[88]

Finally, beyond the biblical evidence, we find an analogous legal use of "hearing" in Neo-Babylonian trial records.[89] The Akkadian verb *šemû*, etymologically cognate to Hebrew *š-m-ʿ* and semantically parallel to other verbs of hearing, occurs as a regular feature of these documents' reports.[90] Usually the sentence "the judges heard their arguments" (*dayyānū dibbīšunu išmû*) follows the quotation of the litigants' statements. In this position, the verb of hearing serves as the second part of a frame for the quoted statement; the first part of the frame is the verb of speech (*qabû*), which introduces the quotation.[91] This framing of the speech seems natural

---

84. See, e.g., Isa 1:15; Jer 7:16; 11:11, 14; 14:12; Ezek 8:18. Prayers themselves also mention that God does not "answer" (*ʿ-n-y*), which is analogous to God's not hearing: e.g., Pss 18:42; 22:3. See Avrahami, *Senses of Scripture*, 130–41.

85. See Pss 4:4; 6:9–10; 10:17; 18:7; 22:25; 28:6; 31:23; 34:7, 18; 40:2; 61:6; 66:19; 116:1; 145:19.

86. The petitioner is really a disguised prophet, but this has little bearing on the king's right to dismiss the cry. Also compare 2 Sam 15:3.

87. E.g., Exod 23:6; Isa 1:23; 10:2; 32:7; Jer 5:28; Amos 5:12; Prov 22:22. Also compare Jer 22:16; Ps 82:3; Prov 29:7, 14; 31:9.

88. The interpretation of Prov 21:13b as a reference to prayer occurs already in the Targum to this verse. Modern commentators who uphold this interpretation include Richard J. Clifford, *Proverbs: A Commentary*, OTL (Louisville: Westminster John Knox, 1999), 191; and Michael V. Fox, *Proverbs 10–31: A New Translation with Introduction and Commentary*, AYB 27A (New Haven: Yale University Press, 2009), 685.

89. Compare the use of the Hebrew verb "to hear" (*š-m-ʿ*) in Deut 17:4.

90. For similar references in legal records from other periods see *CAD* Š.2, 282–83 (*šemû* 2b3').

91. See Holtz, *Neo-Babylonian Court Procedure*, 28–37, 243–45.

enough: people speak to the judges and the judges hear what is said. At the same time, however, the notice of the judges' "hearing" is superfluous, since the records begin by stating that the litigants speak to the judges (*ana dayyānī*); noting that the judges hear what is spoken to them adds very little to the legal record. Thus, by their very existence, the notices that "the judges heard their arguments" must provide procedural, rather than merely perceptual, information. In other words, "hearing" is an action of legal record. The verb refers to the end of the initial arguments before the judges, when they "hear" or consider the arguments before proceeding to gather evidence and reach their judgment.[92]

When petitioners in prayers ask to be heard, they hope their addressees will perform an action analogous to the "hearing" performed by the Neo-Babylonian judges. As an aspect of both the human–divine encounter in prayer and the human-to-human encounter in the courtroom, "hearing" marks a point of transition in the audience. In the human litigation records, this is the first action predicated of the adjudicating authorities; the action moves, as it were, into the adjudicators' arena. In prayers, when speakers ask to be heard, they act in a manner that recalls our earlier interpretation of the demand for judgment.[93] There we noted how, at times, the demand for judgment marks a pivotal point between human despair and a "remedy sought." Being "heard," based on what we have seen here, is the most basic first step toward achieving legal relief.

As with hearing, the forensic interpretation of God's seeing emerges from context. Here are four examples of prayers that associate God's seeing with God's judgment:

Jeremiah 12:1–3

> ¹You will be in the right, O YHWH, if I bring suit against you,
> Yet I shall present charges against You:
> Why does the way of the wicked prosper?
> Why are the treacherous at ease?
> ²You have planted them, and they have taken root,
> They spread, they even bear fruit.
> You are near in their mouths,
> But far from their inner thoughts.
> ³Yet You, YHWH, have known me. You see Me!
> Test my heart—it is with You!
> Drive them out like sheep to the slaughter,
> Prepare them for the day of killing!

---

92. Neo-Babylonian letters from the king and other authorities show these authorities referring to this very procedure. Examples are collected in *CAD* D, 133–34 (*dibbu* A, 5).

93. See the discussion in chapter 2 above.

Psalm 35:22–24

> [22]See,[94] O YHWH, do not be silent; my Lord, do not be distant from me!
> [23]Arise and awake for my case, my God, my Lord, for my suit.
> [24]Judge me in accordance with Your righteousness, O YHWH, my God,
>   let them not rejoice over me.

Psalm 119:153–54

> [153]See my affliction and rescue me,
> for I have not neglected Your teaching.
> [154]Champion my cause [*rîbâ rîbî*] and redeem me;
> according to Your promise, let me live.

Lamentations 3:55–66

> [55]I have called Your name, O YHWH,
> From the depths of the Pit.
> [56]Hear my plea;
> Do not let Your ear ignore my groan, my cry!
> [57]You have drawn near whenever I call You;
> You have said, "Do not fear!"
> [58]Champion my cause, O YHWH,
> redeem my life.
> [59]See, O YHWH, the wrong done to me;
> Judge my case!
> [60]See all their malice,
> all their thoughts against me;
> [61]Hear their taunts, O YHWH,
> all their thoughts against me.
> [62]The lips and thoughts of my adversaries,
> against me all day long.
> [63]Observe how, at their ease or at work,
> I am the butt of their gibes.
> [64]Repay them as they deserve, O YHWH,
> according to their deeds.
> [65]Give them anguish of heart,
> Your curse upon them!
> [66]In wrath, chase and destroy them,
> from under the heavens of YHWH!

Alongside the more explicitly forensic language (like "suit" or "case"), all four speakers refer to God's seeing. Just after Jeremiah's "charges" (*mišpāṭîm*) against God, the prophet proclaims his own innocence and challenges God on the basis that God "sees" (Jer 12:3). In the three other

---

94. This translation interprets the suffix form here (*rā᾿îtā*) as a precative perfect. The NJPS renders the verb as "You have seen," which is certainly possible. The same exegetical ambiguity pertains to the suffix forms in Lam 3:55–61. The translation decisions do not affect the connection between God's vision and God's judgment.

prayers, the speakers refer to God's seeing (and, in Lam 3:56, hearing) in the immediate vicinity of their demands for judgment. All of these collocations of judgment and vision suggest that vision is, in fact, more than an act of sensory perception. Rather, God sees as part of the adjudicatory process.

Two letters, one Neo-Assyrian and the other Neo-Babylonian, offer a valuable situational parallel to the occurrences of vision terminology in the Hebrew letters. Both letters are addressed to the king, and, in both, the common Akkadian verb for seeing, *amāru*, describes the action that the authors ask the king to perform:

> (1) May the king, my lord, pay heed to the case of his servant, may the king investigate [*lēmur*, lit., "see"] the entire case [*dibbi gabbu*]![95]
> (2) May the king immediately investigate my claims [*dibbī ... līmuršunūtu*]![96]

The writers of both these letters demand an investigation into a case (*dibbu*), in language that brings to mind the biblical prayers. Thus, we might even interpret the prayers as a close equivalent to the letters, a prayed petition before God the king and judge.

At the same time, there is an important difference between the Akkadian examples and those in Hebrew. In the Akkadian letters, the verb *amāru* ("to see") occurs with the complement *dibbu*, a term denoting "legal case" that belongs squarely in the forensic realm and refers specifically to the petitioner's claim or lawsuit. In contrast, in the Hebrew prayers, the same obviously legal object for the verb of seeing (*r-ʾ-y*) does not occur. Instead, in the Hebrew examples above and elsewhere, the verb stands alone or with an object that refers to the speakers' plight or the wrong they are experiencing.[97] This difference suggests that when the speakers refer to God's vision, they are referring to another, perhaps more specific, aspect of the process.

What, then, is the legal function of God's vision? All of these prayers share a common occasion or cause for turning to God: perceived persecution by enemies. The speakers all mention God's seeing alongside more explicit demands that God remedy the situation by judging their cases and punishing their enemies. If, according to these prayers, punishment is the result of God's judgment, then God's vision is the basis upon which God is asked to reach that judgment. In these contexts, Bovati correctly

---

95. *ABL* 1285:13. For discussion of this phrase and the parallel occurrence of the verb *qâlu* ("to give heed") earlier in this line in light of the Yavneh Yam inscription, see Victor Avidgor Hurowitz, "ABL 1285 and the Hebrew Bible: Literary Topoi in Urad-Gula's Letter of Petition to Assurbanipal," *SAAB* 7 (1993): 10–11.

96. BIN 1, 93:20.

97. See Gen 29:32; 31:42; Exod 2:25; 3:7, 9; 4:31; Deut 26:7; 1 Sam 1:11; 9:16; 24:15; 2 Sam 16:12; 2 Kgs 20:5 // Isa 38:5; 2 Kgs 13:4; 14:26; Jer 12:3; Pss 10:14; 31:8; 35:22; 106:44; 119:153–54; Lam 3:36, 59; Neh 9:9; 1 Chr 12:18 (compare Exod 5:21; 2 Chr 24:22).

characterizes the verbs of visual perception as "suggest[ing] the investigative phase necessary for right judgment."[98] The speakers, as plaintiffs, ask God to investigate their situation, to obtain or examine the evidence that will support their claim and lead to a just conclusion.

A parallel to this technical legal nuance of the verb "to see" occurs in Neo-Babylonian legal records from the Eanna temple of Uruk. In these texts, "seeing" (*amāru*) is one of the actions that the assembly of the Eanna performs as it gathers the evidence to reach a decision. The assembly "sees," that is to say, it inspects or examines, items such as an iron tool used in an attempted prison escape, a dagger drawn against gatekeepers of the Eanna, or the marks on the hands of individuals considered to be property of the Eanna.[99] One record states that, after the assembly heard the confession of a man who has misappropriated a jar of dates, "they brought the jar of dates that he had carried off ... and the assembly saw [*īmurū*] (it)."[100] The notice that the assembly "saw" what is "brought" to the Eanna must refer to more than an act of visual perception on the part of the assembly. This statement, like the notices about the judges' "hearing" arguments, indicates that seeing was a matter of some legal consequence.

When the speakers in the Hebrew prayers refer to God's seeing, they imagine a legally significant act akin to the investigative actions of the Eanna assembly. The speakers' plights in the Psalms should be understood as near equivalents of the objects that the authorities "see." As the speakers make their case, they present their plights as the evidence for God to examine and consider.

This legal interpretation of God's vision in the Hebrew prayers finds support in the prelude to the negotiations between Abraham and God over the destruction of Sodom. The narrative begins with God's own declaration, "I will go down to see [*waʾerʾê*] whether they have acted altogether according to the outcry that has reached Me; if not, I will take note" (Gen 18:21). Here, as Avrahami correctly observes, "God himself sets out (through motion and sight) personally to examine and investigate what he heard."[101] For our purposes, it is also significant that, in this verse as well

---

98. Bovati, *Re-Establishing Justice*, 244; for extended discussion, see 70–71, 244–47.

99. *CAD* A.2, 17 (*amāru* A2i5'). According to this entry in *CAD*, the use of the verb "of the assembly with regard to objects, etc., presented as evidence" is limited to the Neo-Babylonian period. The corpus of Old Babylonian litigation records, however, shows a related, if not exactly the same, use of the verb *amāru*. There, the verb refers to the examination of written tablets by judges prior to rendering judgment. See Dombradi, *Die Darstellung des Rechtsaustrags*, 1:89. As Dombradi's presentation indicates, this visual inspection is apparently different from the "hearing" (*šemû*) of the tablets' contents.

100. YOS 7, 42:15–18.

101. Avrahami, *Senses of Scripture*, 264. See also Bruckner, *Implied Law*, 93–94, 144; and the brief note in Bovati, *Re-Establishing Justice*, 241 n. 38. Note also Avrahami's general observation on "the centrality of sight within the juridical system of the Hebrew Bible,"

as in the immediately preceding one, God specifically refers to the outcry (*zaʿăqâ/ṣaʿăqâ*) coming from the city. It is this outcry that leads to God's investigation and dictates its goals.

These verses from the Sodom story give us God's perspective, as it were, on the conception of prayer as outcry. The cries of people at prayer impel God to take legal action; the outcry leads to investigation. In light of this, we understand why the outcries themselves, which is to say the prayers addressed to God, ask God to see. The speakers are aware that, following the outcry, God will "see," or investigate, their claim. Armed with this knowledge, they pray with the hope of directing God to take the next step toward favorably resolving their case.

---

which she interprets as "the dominant metaphor used to describe the public's involvement in the [legal] process (*Sense of Scripture*, 225). My interpretation here is somewhat different because it reflects my focus on the act of seeing predicated upon God.

Conclusion

Why Pray Legally?

The introduction to this book invoked the category of metaphor as a means of understanding the connections between prayers and the courtroom. Prayers themselves, together with the discourse surrounding them, are built on the "social analogy" of argument in court. Following Berend Gemser and Moshe Greenberg, I have interpreted the presence of legal language in prayer as evidence for how ancient peoples conceived of human–divine communication. Reading prayers together with legal texts, as we have done throughout this book, makes sense because litigation is a central metaphor of ancient prayer.

These concluding reflections return to the subject of metaphor. Joseph Lam, in his recent study of metaphors for sin in the Hebrew Bible, offers thoughts on the advantages of metaphoric language in general. Throughout his work, Lam considers not only the contours of particular metaphoric networks for sin but also what is gained from the use of these metaphors: "*why* these metaphors were employed at all."[1] Here I ask this question of our particular subject. What does invoking the courtroom contribute to prayer? In short, why pray legally?

In asking this question from the perspective of religious metaphors, I wish to avoid speculation regarding possible historical sources for the idea of praying legally. It is certainly possible that an overlap between the realms of law and prayer stems from some historical reality. Copying legal formulations would have been part of ancient scribes' training, so that the same scribes who would have composed prayers were likely to have been familiar with the technicalities of legal writing as well. Similarly, it is certainly possible that temples were themselves physical venues of adjudication. If so, then the courtroom and prayer would have found a natural meeting point there.

Nevertheless, even if the historical circumstances favored the nexus between the courtroom and prayer, consideration of the metaphor's function allows us to investigate why someone would have taken advantage of these favorable circumstances. We can formulate this, perhaps somewhat

---

1. Lam, *Patterns of Sin*, 86 (emphasis in original); see also 154–55, 205–6.

bluntly, as a question of origins: did those earliest scribes (whoever and wherever they may have been), when they wrote prayers, just happen to use legal language they knew from their legal training, or perhaps was law seen as an effective religious metaphor even at the point of origin? Moreover, even if the origins remain out of view, we must still account for the pervasiveness, across time and space, of the courtroom imagery in prayer. Again, the known links between the cultures we have studied here give only a partial explanation for this metaphor's remarkable staying power. For the idea of praying legally to survive, it must have proven itself to be effective enough for humans to continue employing it.

The question of historical origin raises another theoretical point that should be addressed here before I return to my specific question. Throughout, this book has considered the idea of praying legally as a metaphor in its own right. There are good reasons, however, for arguing that the prayer–courtroom connection may, in fact, be a subset of the broader conception of deities as kings.[2] We have seen this, in the biblical context, in Pss 9–10, where God's kingship manifests itself in God's attention to and judgment of the oppressed. If gods are conceived of as kings and kings are conceived of as judges, then the idea of petitioning royally conceived deities as one might petition human judges follows quite naturally. Still, even as a submetaphor of the broader complex of royal metaphors, the particularly legal imagery warrants its own investigation. Even if the idea of praying legally ultimately originates in the royal court in general, prayers definitely exhibit a robust connection to the court of law in particular. Why?

At the end of his study, Lam attributes the use of metaphors to two features: "their capacity for expressing the inchoate and the perspectives they apply to a concept."[3] In both of these ways, metaphoric language is empowering, especially in the domain of relationships between humans and the divine sphere. This entire area of human existence would remain "inchoate" or, more accurately, ineffable, but for metaphors' expressive capacity. It is this capacity of metaphors that enabled ancient humans to describe their encounters with all kinds of forces—natural as well as emotional—that otherwise would overwhelm. At the same time, per the second feature that Lam identifies, metaphors give humans perspectives on their relationship with these forces.[4] We might say, then, that metaphors tamed these forces. Through metaphor, the powerfully unfamiliar became something to which humans can relate.

---

2. Brettler, *God Is King*, 109–16.
3. Lam, *Patterns of Sin*, 208.
4. This is similar to Job Jindo's observation, quoted extensively in the introduction, that metaphors "reorient" discourse (*Biblical Metaphor Reconsidered*, 44–45).

We can, therefore, explain the courtroom metaphor's presence in prayer as a particular example of metaphor's empowering capacity. When prayer is conceived of as a legal plea or petition, it becomes far more than abject begging before an all-powerful being. It is, instead, an opportunity for humans to be heard. To aptly characterize this opportunity, we might apply modern English expressions and say that prayer gives humans a chance to "make their case" or "have their day in court." The occasion of prayer is more than a silent audience that negotiates the perceived gap between humans and deities merely by creating an encounter between them. Rather, the courtroom metaphors in prayer give humans, who might otherwise be dumbfounded even by the thought of such an encounter, the power to speak up, indeed to argue.[5]

Following the legal imagery, we can press further and conclude that, by means of the courtroom metaphor in prayer, speakers acquire standing, in the legal sense of this term, before divine adjudicators. This sense of standing has implications for our understanding of prayer, in general. To adumbrate these, let us consider two examples of how praying legally serves speakers in prayer by affording them rather specific legal status. The first example comes from the sixth incantation in the anti-witchcraft ritual *Maqlû* (I.73–121):[6]

> O Nusku, these are the figurines of my sorcerer,
> These are the figurines of my sorceress,
> The figurines of my warlock and witch,
> The figurines of my sorcerer and the instigating-sorceress,
> The figurines of my enchanter and enchantress,
> The figurines of my male and female poisoner,
> The figurines of my male and female irritators,
> The figurines of my male and female enemies,
> The figurines of my male and female persecutors,
> The figurines of my male and female litgants [*bēl dīni*],
> The figurines of my male and female accusers [*bēl amāti*],
> The figurines of my male and female adversaries [*bēl dabābi*],
> The figurines of my male and female slanderers,
> The figurines of my male and female evildoers,
> Whom you, Nusku, the judge, know, but whom I do not know—
> Who witchcraft, spittle, enchainment, evil machinations,

---

5. Compare a similar observation by Daniel Schwemer about figurative language in anti-witchcraft incantations: "The verbalization of the threat in similes, analogies, metaphors, allegories as well as by means of personification and prosopopoeia transforms the abstract fear and the incomprehensible suffering into a concrete enemy that can be fought, controlled and, ultimately, removed" ("'Form Follows Function'? Rhetoric and Poetic Language in First Millennium Akkadian Incantations," *WO* 44 [2014]: 263–88, here 267–68).

6. Abusch, *Witchcraft Series Maqlû*, 48–51.

Sorcery, rebellion, evil-speech, love-magic and hate-magic,
Distortion of justice, cutting of life, speech-paralysis, calming-anger,
Confusion, vertigo, madness,
Have conjured against me, and caused to be conjured against me, have sought against me and have caused to be sought against me.
These are they. These are their figurines.
Since they are not present, I bear their figurines.
You, Nusku, the judge, who captures evildoer and enemy, capture them, so I will not be harmed!
Those who have made figurines of me, who imitated my face,
Who have bound my mouth, shaken my neck,
Pressed against my chest, bent my spine,
Weakened my heart, seized my libido,
Made me angry with myself, weakened my strength,
Poured out my arms, bound my knees,
Filled me with fever, stiffness and debility,
Fed me bewitched bread,
Given me bewitched water to drink,
Washed me with contaminated water,
Anointed me with salves of evil herbs,
Betrothed me to a dead person,
Brought the waters of my life to the grave,
Caused god, king, lord and prince to be angry with me.
You, O Girra, burner of warlock and witch,
Destroyer of the wicked, seed of warlock and witch,
Demolisher of evildoers, are you!
I call upon you, like Šamaš, the judge,
Judge my case, decide my decision [*dīnī dīn purussâya purus*]!
Burn my warlock and my witch!
Consume my enemies, devour those who do evil against me!
May your angry storm capture them!
Like water from a waterskin, trickling, may they come to an end!
As if by a blow from a stone, let their fingers be cut back!
By your exalted command, which cannot be altered,
And by your true assent, which cannot be changed.

At its essence, this text follows a pattern identified earlier in the discussion of the demands for judgment. As in *Maqlû*'s opening incantation, in this one too the demand for judgment signals a climactic transition. It follows the speaker's presentation of the opponents in effigy and description of the harms they have done, and it precedes the speaker's statement of "remedy sought" from the gods. Through the demand for judgment, the speaker, here the patient, moves from despair to hope.

As argued above, this structure imitates the form of plaintiffs' speeches in human courtrooms. In taking on the role of plaintiff, the patient "follows the script," as it were. In the same vein, the presentation of the figurines of the suspected antagonists should itself be interpreted as a legally significant act in the ritual. It represents the patient-plaintiff's fulfillment of the obligation to bring the opponents to the adjudicatory venue, a known requirement of trial procedure in human courtrooms in the ancient Near East.[7] Thus, both rhetorically and procedurally, this incantation evokes the courtroom with remarkable similitude.

At the same time that the incantation's overall structure points to the courtroom, its details underscore a certain paradox in the ritual: the patient's actions are remarkably similar to those of the accused opponents.[8] The opening lines call the deity's attention to the figurines, representing no fewer than thirteen categories of opponents (male and female), which the patient presents as effigies. The text continues by describing the means by which the opponents have worked their evil against the patient. They, too, have fashioned figurines, which have allowed them to torment the patient and to cause the graphically detailed suffering. The incantation, formulated as the patient's own words, creates a clear distinction between the good speaker and the evil opponent, and even invites us (and, more importantly, the deities), to side with the patient. But a closer look at the described actions undercuts this dichotomy; the speaker and the witch are, in effect, doing the same thing.

This paradox explains why the incantation evokes the courtroom to such an impressive degree. If, indeed, both speaker and opponents engage in remarkably similar actions, then the incantation's legal imagery suggests that the only distinction between them is that the patient's activities are licit, while those of the opponents are illicit. The patient must convince the deities to accept this distinction and interpret the ritual actions as ones done within the scope of the law, rather than as actions performed without legal sanction. Meticulous adherence to trial procedure becomes, then, part of the patient's strategy in achieving this goal. Following the courtroom's rhetorical and procedural rules stakes the clear claim that the patient, unlike the opponents, acts legally.

Thus, at the level of the ritual, the patient's sense of standing, acquired by means of this incantation's overt connections to the courtroom, brings law to the patient's side. We can interpret this as a technical matter, as a way of ensuring that the court of the gods grants the patient's claim a hearing and a favorable judgment. From this perspective, failure to comply with courtroom procedure risks rejection of the claim on technical grounds.

---

7. These observations on this section of *Maqlû* are fully developed in Holtz, "Maqlû I.73–121 and Trial Procedure," 140–48.

8. Daniel Schwemer, *Abwehrzauber und Behexung: Studien zum Schadenzauberglauben im alten Mesopotamien; Unter Benutzung von Tzvi Abuschs Kritischem Katalog und Sammlungen im Rahmen des Kooperationsprojektes Corpus of Mesopotamian Anti-witchcraft Rituals* (Wiesbaden: Harrassowitz, 2007), 128, 162–63, 185, 210–12. Compare similar observations on Greek prayers by Versnel, "Beyond Cursing," 62–67.

Worse still, the gods might find the patient, rather than the opponents, guilty of illicit activity.

At the same time, we can interpret these technicalities as part of the broader empowerment achieved by praying legally. The sense that the speaker has legal standing, that law is on the speaker's side, gives rise to the expectation that justice will be served. The opponents and their witchcraft may have harmed the speaker, but the adjudicatory process in the divine courtroom will provide redress and resolution. The patient has made every effort to comply with required trial procedure. Having done so, the patient can confidently demand judgment and seek a remedy from the gods.

The second example of how speakers in prayers invoke the law to acquire standing comes from prayers that mention oaths sworn in the past. We have seen this posture in Kuzullum's prayer, with which we opened chapter 2. There, the speaker turns to the deities because an opponent has violated an oath. The deities invoked were witnesses to that original oath and thus have jurisdiction over the matter at hand. A similar use of this point of law occurs in the Middle Assyrian Epic of Tukulti-Ninurta I, which narrates the victory of the Assyrian king, Tukulti-Ninurta I, over the Kassite king of Babylonia, Kaštiliaš IV.[9] In one scene, intruding Kassite merchants are captured on Assyrian soil and made to stand before the god Šamaš. Tukulti-Ninurta I then prays, and includes a demand for judgment in his prayer:[10]

> O Šamaš, [...] lord I respected (?) your oath, I feared your greatness,
> He who does not [...] transgressed before your [...] I observed your ordinance.
> When, before your divinity, our fathers made a pact,
> (And) they established an oath between them, they invoked your greatness.
> Since times past, the unaltering judge of our fathers, the hero, were you!
> And now, the god who sees our loyalty, the one who sets (things) straight, are you!
> Why, then, since times past, has the king of the Kassites contravened your plan (and) your judgment?
> He has not feared your oath, he has transgressed your command, he has schemed falsehood.
> He has committed crimes before you. O Šamaš, judge me [*di-na-an-ni*]!

---

9. An edition of the epic, with translation and extensive commentary, can be found in Peter Bruce Machinist, "The Epic of Tukulti-Ninurta I, A Study in Middle Assyrian Literature" (PhD diss., Yale University, 1978). For a newer translation, still based on Machinist's text, see Foster, *Before the Muses*, 298–317.

10. II.A obv. 13'–24', as published in Machinist, "Epic of Tukulti-Ninurta I," 76–79 (text and translation), 214–237 (commentary), 403–9 (notes).

> But he who committed no crime [against] the king of the Kassites [...].
> By your great [...] grant [...] to the one who keeps the oath.
> [He who does not obey] your command, in the defeat of battle, destroy his people!

This prayer follows the pattern familiar from other prayers we have seen. Tukulti-Ninurta I's accusation, that the Kassite king has violated a treaty oath, culminates with the demand, "judge me," followed by Tukulti-Ninurta I's statement of "remedy sought"—"in the defeat of battle, destroy his people!"

Tukulti-Ninurta I presents the same legal argument as Kuzullum. The king reminds Šamaš of the legal instrument governing Assyrian–Babylonian relations: an oath sworn between earlier rulers. The Kassites' bad actions violate this oath's terms, but this is not simply a matter between two human kings and their nations. Because this oath was solemnized before Šamaš, violations of its terms are transgressions against the deity. It is on these legal grounds that Tukulti-Ninurta I prays to Šamaš, in much the same way that Kuzullum turns to Nanna and Šamaš in his own prayer. Both pray legally because law gives them standing before the deities and empowers them to demand just judgment.

A very similar legal point constitutes the basis of some of the biblical "protest prayers." There the prayers' legal angle stems not from God having witnessed the oath, as in the prayers of Tukulti-Ninurta I and Kuzullum, but from God having sworn to the nation. Thus, Moses follows his accusatory question—"Why, YHWH, should Your anger burn against Your people"—by demanding that YHWH remain faithful to the covenant with the patriarchs (Exod 32:11–13). The community in Jer 14 adopts a similar strategy: their accusatory "why" question—"Why have You smitten us, so that we have no cure?" (19)—comes shortly before their own invocation of the covenant—"Remember, do not annul Your covenant with us" (21). In these cases, the people make their accusation directly to God, who has breached the oath sworn to them.

In sum, there are two ways in which speakers assert their own legal standing by drawing on specific points of law. In the *Maqlû* incantation, the patient adheres to courtroom style to distinguish the ritual from what might have been done by the opponent. Other prayers, such as Tukulti-Ninurta I's and our biblical examples, base their claims on the legalities of sworn oaths. Our reading of these prayers in light of the idea of legal standing brings us to what we may call the psychology of these prayers. These prayers are effective because they offer an assurance that law is on the speakers' side.

We can extend these psychological effects to explain courtroom imagery in other prayers, too. Whenever speakers demand judgment, they assert their standing as well as their belief that adjudication will remedy their distress. Whenever speakers cry out to be seen or heard, they insist on obtaining a fair hearing in the court of last resort. They are confident that, while human justice has failed them, divine justice just might provide relief. In short, the law gives speakers at prayer a measure of control in otherwise desperate circumstances.

The imagined courtroom setting of prayer even allows speakers to move beyond just asking for relief. As we have seen, some speakers use the occasion of prayer to express protest and even to "turn the tables" with a countersuit. In doing so, they call attention to the divine adjudicators' own shortcomings and the concomitant injustices that have been caused. Courtroom procedure in prayer levels the playing field, as it were, between humans and divine adjudicators. An encounter that might have been heavily tilted in favor of one side becomes something of a bilateral process, with clear expectations not only from humans but also from deities. Indeed, at times humans might even gain an upper hand in this encounter.

We arrive, then, at one answer to the question with which we have framed this conclusion: Why pray legally? Arguably, the empowering value of law as a source of standing constitutes the bedrock of this idea. By conceiving of prayer as an argument in court, humans gained much more than a way to talk about (and to) powers perceived to be greater. They also gained a sense that, through prayer, justice would be served.

Bibliography

Abusch, I. Tzvi. "*Alaktu* and *Halakhah*: Oracular Decision, Divine Revelation." *HTR* 80 (1987): 15–42.
———. *The Magical Ceremony Maqlû: A Critical Edition*. AMD 10. Leiden: Brill, 2016.
———. *Mesopotamian Witchcraft: Toward a History and Understanding of Babylonian Witchcraft Beliefs and Literature*. AMD 5. Leiden: Brill, 2002.
———. *The Witchcraft Series Maqlû*. WAW 37. Atlanta: SBL Press, 2015.
Allen, Leslie C. *Psalms 101–150*. WBC 21. Waco, TX: Word Books, 1983.
Andersen, Francis I. *Habakkuk: A New Translation with Introduction and Commentary*. AB 25. New York: Doubleday, 2001.
Ap-Thomas, D. R. "Notes on Some Terms Relating to Prayer." *VT* 6 (1956): 225–41.
———. "Some Aspects of the Root HNN in the Old Testament." *JSS* 2 (1957): 128–48.
Arnaud, Daniel. "Un document juridique concernant les oblats." *RA* 67 (1973): 147–56.
Assmann, Jan, Bernd Janowski, and Michael Welker. "Richten und Retten: Zur Aktualität der altorientalischen und biblischen Gerechtigkeitskonzeption." Pages 220–46 in *Die rettende Gerechtigkeit*. Edited by Bernd Janowski. Beiträge zur Theologie des Alten Testaments 2. Neukirchen-Vluyn: Neukirchener Verlag, 1999.
Avrahami, Yael. *The Senses of Scripture: Sensory Perception in the Hebrew Bible*. LHBOTS 545. New York: T&T Clark International, 2012.
Balkan, Kemal. "Contribution to the Understanding of the Idiom of the Old Assyrian Merchants of Kanish." *Or* 36 (1967): 393–415.
Barmash, Pamela. *Homicide in the Biblical World*. Cambridge: Cambridge University Press, 2005.
Barr, James. "Why? In Biblical Hebrew." *JTS* 36 (1985): 1–33.
Barrabee, Janice. "The King of Justice: A Reconsideration of the River Ordeal in BM 456901" [sic]. Pages 1–18 in *A Common Cultural Heritage: Studies on Mesopotamia and the Biblical World in Honor of Barry L. Eichler*. Edited by Grant Frame et al. Bethesda, MD: CDL, 2011.

Basson, Alec. *Divine Metaphors in Selected Hebrew Psalms of Lamentation.* FAT 2/15. Tübingen: Mohr Siebeck, 2006.

Bautch, Richard J. "Lament Regained in Trito-Isaiah's Penitential Prayer." Pages 83–99 in *The Origins of Penitential Prayer in Second Temple Judaism,* vol. 1 of *Seeking the Favor of God.* Edited by Mark J. Boda, Daniel K. Falk, and Rodney A. Werline. EJL 21. Atlanta: Society of Biblical Literature, 2006.

Beaulieu, Paul-Alain. *Legal and Administrative Texts from the Reign of Nabonidus.* YOS 19. New Haven: Yale University Press, 2000.

Beentjes, Pancratius Cornelis. "King Jehoshaphat's Prayer: Some Remarks on 2 Chronicles 20, 6–13." *BZ* 38 (1994): 264–70.

Berger, Yitzhak. "The David–Benjaminite Conflict and the Intertextual Field of Psalm 7." *JSOT* 38 (2014): 279–96.

Berlin, Adele. "On the Meaning of *pll* in the Bible." *RB* 96 (1989): 345–51.

Blank, Sheldon H. "The Confessions of Jeremiah and the Meaning of Prayer." *HUCA* 21 (1948): 331–54.

———. "The Curse, Blasphemy, the Spell, and the Oath." *HUCA* 23 (1950–1951): 73–95.

———. "An Effective Literary Device in Job 31." *JJS* 2 (1950–1951): 105–7.

Boecker, Hans Jochen. *Redeformen des Rechtslebens im Alten Testament.* WMANT 14. Neukirchen-Vluyn: Neukirchener Verlag, 1970.

Botha, Phil J. "Psalm 108 and the Quest for Closure to the Exile." *OTE* 23 (2010): 574–96.

Bottéro, Jean. "Symptômes, signes, écritures." Pages 70–197 in *Divination et rationalité.* Edited by J. P. Vernant et al. Recherches anthropologiques. Paris: Seuil, 1974.

Bovati, Pietro. *Re-Establishing Justice: Legal Terms, Concepts and Procedures in the Hebrew Bible.* Translated by Michael J. Smith. JSOTSup 105. Sheffield: Sheffield Academic Press, 1994.

Boyce, Richard Nelson. *The Cry to God in the Old Testament.* SBLDS 103. Atlanta: Scholars Press, 1988.

Boyer, Georges. *Contribution à l'histoire juridique de la 1re dynastie babylonienne.* Paris: P. Geuthner, 1928.

Brettler, Marc Zvi. *God Is King: Understanding an Israelite Metaphor.* JSOTSup 76. Sheffield: Sheffield Academic Press, 1989.

Broida, Marian W. *Forestalling Doom: "Apotropaic Intercession" in the Hebrew Bible and the Ancient Near East.* AOAT 417. Münster: Ugarit-Verlag, 2014.

Bruckner, James K. *Implied Law in the Abraham Narrative: A Literary and Theological Analysis.* JSOTSup 335. Sheffield: Sheffield Academic Press, 2001.

Buss, Martin. "The Idea of Sitz im Leben—History and Critique." *ZAW* 90 (1978): 157–70.

Charney, Davida H. *Persuading God: Rhetorical Studies of First-Person Psalms*. Hebrew Bible Monographs 73. Sheffield: Sheffield Phoenix Press, 2015.

Chavel, Simeon. *Oracular Law and Priestly Historiography in the Torah*. FAT 2/71. Tübingen: Mohr Siebeck, 2014.

Clifford, Richard J. *Proverbs: A Commentary*. OTL. Louisville: Westminster John Knox, 1999.

Clines, David J. A. *Job 21–37*. WBC 18A. Nashville: Thomas Nelson, 2006.

Cohen, Chaim. "The Ancient Critical Misunderstanding of Exodus 21:22–25 and Its Implications for the Current Debate on Abortion." Pages 437–58 in *Mishneh Todah: Studies in Deuteronomy and Its Cultural Environment in Honor of Jeffrey H. Tigay*. Edited by Nili Sacher Fox, David A. Glatt-Gilad, and Michael J. Williams. Winona Lake, IN: Eisenbrauns, 2009.

Cottrill, Amy C. *Language, Power, and Identity in the Lament Psalms of the Individual*. LHBOTS 493. New York: T&T Clark, 2008.

Craigie, Peter C., and Marvin Tate. *Psalms 1–50*. WBC 19. Nashville: Thomas Nelson, 2004.

Crowe, Loren D. "The Rhetoric of Psalm 44." *ZAW* 104 (1992): 394–401.

Czander, Giovanna Raengo. "'You Are My Witnesses': A Theological Approach to the Laws of Testimony." PhD diss., Fordham University, 2008.

Dahood, Mitchell. *Psalms: Introduction, Translation, and Notes*. 3 vols. AB 16, 17, 17A. Garden City, NY: Doubleday, 1966–1970.

Dalley, Stephanie. *A Catalogue of the Akkadian Cuneiform Tablets in the Collections of the Royal Scottish Museum, Edinburgh, with Copies of the Texts*. Art and Archaeology 2. Edinburgh: Royal Scottish Museum, 1979.

Dijk, J. J. A. van, A. Goetze, and M. I. Hussey. *Early Mesopotamian Incantations and Rituals*. YOS 11. New Haven: Yale University Press, 1985.

Dijkstra, Meindert. "Lawsuit, Debate and Wisdom Discourse in Second Isaiah." Pages 251–71 in *Studies in the Book of Isaiah: Festschrift Willem A. M. Beuken*. Edited by Jacques Van Ruiten and Marc Vervenne. BETL 132. Leuven: Leuven University Press, 1997.

Dobbs-Allsopp, F. W. "The Genre of the Meṣad Ḥashavyahu Ostracon." *BASOR* 295 (1994): 49–55.

Dombradi, Eva. *Die Darstellung des Rechtsaustrags in den altbabylonischen Prozessurkunden*. 2 vols. FAOS 20. Stuttgart: Franz Steiner, 1996.

Dougherty, Raymond Philip. *Records from Erech, Time of Nabonidus (555–538 B.C.)*. YOS 6. New Haven: Yale University Press, 1920.

Edzard, D. O. "'Du hast mir gegeben,' 'ich habe dir gegeben': Über das sumerische Verbum sum." *WO* 8 (1976): 159–77.

Egwim, Stephen C. *A Contextual and Cross-Cultural Study of Psalm 109*. BTS 12. Leuven: Peeters, 2011.

Elgavish, David. "'Concerning the Droughts': Jeremiah 14:1–15:9—Structure and Significance." Pages 51–64 in *"My Spirit at Rest in the North Country" (Zechariah 6.8): Collected Communications to the XXth Congress of the International Organization for the Study of the Old Testament, Helsinki 2010*. Edited by Hermann Michael Niemann and Matthias Augustin. BEATAJ 57. Frankfurt am Main: P. Lang, 2011.

Falkenstein, Adam. *Die neusumerischen Gerichtsurkunden*. 3 vols. ABAW, NF 39, 40, 44. Munich: Bayerischen Akademie der Wissenschaften, 1956.

Feder, Yitzhaq. "Pleading One's Case before God: A Hittite Analogy for תפלה." *ZAW* 125 (2013): 650–53.

Feigin, Samuel I. *Legal and Administrative Texts of the Reign of Samsu-iluna*. YOS 12. New Haven: Yale University Press, 1979.

Figulla, H. H. "Lawsuit concerning a Sacrilegious Theft at Erech." *Iraq* 13 (1951): 95–101.

Fortner, Andrew. "Adjudicating Entities and Levels of Legal Authority in Lawsuit Records of the Old Babylonian Era." PhD diss., Hebrew Union College-Jewish Institute of Religion, 1996.

Foster, Benjamin R. *Before the Muses: An Anthology of Akkadian Literature*. 3rd ed. Bethesda, MD: CDL, 2005.

Fox, Michael V. *Proverbs 10–31: A New Translation with Introduction and Commentary*. AYB 18/2. New Haven: Yale University Press, 2009.

Füglister, Notker. "'Die Hoffnung der Armen ist nicht für immer verloren': Psalm 9/10 und die sozio-religiöse Situation der nachexilischen Gemeinde." Pages 101–24 in *Biblische Theologie und gesellschaftlicher Wandel: Für Norbert Lohfink, SJ*. Edited by Georg Braulik et al. Freiburg: Herder, 1993.

Gadd, C. J., and Samuel Noah Kramer. *Ur Excavations Texts VI: Literary and Religious Texts*. UET 6. London: British Museum, 1966.

Garner, Bryan A., ed. *Black's Law Dictionary*. 9th ed. St. Paul, MN: Thomson Reuters, 2009.

Gemser, B. "The *rîb*- or Controversy-Pattern in Hebrew Mentality." Pages 120–37 in *Wisdom in Israel and in the Ancient Near East*. Edited by M. Noth and D. Winton Thomas. VTSup 3. Leiden: Brill, 1960.

Gesenius' Hebrew Grammar. Edited by E. Kautzsch. Translated by A. E. Cowley. Oxford: Clarendon, 1910.

Goldingay, John. *Psalms*. 3 vols. BCOTWP. Grand Rapids: Baker Academic, 2008.

Goldschmidt, Daniel, ed. מחזור לימים הנוראים: לפי מנהגי בני אשכנז לכל ענפיהם כולל מנהג אשכנז (המערבי) מנהג פולין ומנהג צרפת לשעבר. 2 vols. Jerusalem: Koren, 1970.

Goldstein, Ronnie. *The Life of Jeremiah: Tradition* [sic] *about the Prophet and Their Evolution in Biblical Times*. [Hebrew.] Biblical Encyclopaedia Library 30. Jerusalem: Bialik Institute, 2013.

Graetz, Shirley. "To Whom Can a Wronged Person Turn for Help in the Old Babylonian Period?" Pages 237–60 in *Marbeh Ḥokmah: Studies in the Bible and the Ancient Near East in Loving Memory of Victor Avigdor Hurowitz*. Edited by S. Yona et al. Winona Lake, IN: Eisenbrauns, 2015.

Greenberg, Moshe. *Biblical Prose Prayer as a Window to the Popular Religion of Ancient Israel*. Taubman Lectures in Jewish Studies. Berkeley: University of California Press, 1983.

Greenfield, Jonas C. "The Zakir Inscription and the Danklied." Pages 174–91 in *Proceedings of the Fifth World Congress of Jewish Studies, The Hebrew University, Mount Scopus-Givat Ram, Jerusalem, 3–11 August 1969*. Ed. Pinchas Peli. Vol. 1, *Ancient Near East, Bible, Archaeology, First Temple Period*. Jerusalem: World Union of Jewish Studies, 1972.

Gunkel, Hermann, and Joachim Begrich. *Introduction to Psalms: The Genres of the Religious Lyric of Israel*. Translated by James D. Nogalski. Mercer Library of Biblical Studies. Macon, GA: Mercer University Press, 1998.

Ḥakham, Amos. *The Bible: Job with the Jerusalem Commentary*. Jerusalem: Mosad Harav Kook, 2009.

———. *Psalms with the Jerusalem Commentary*. 3 vols. Jerusalem: Mosad Harav Kook, 2003.

Halberstam, Chaya. "Justice without Judgment: Pure Procedural Justice and the Divine Courtroom in *Sifre Deuteronomy*. Pages 49–68 in *The Divine Courtroom in Comparative Perspective*. Edited by Ari Mermelstein and Shalom E. Holtz. BibInt 132. Leiden: Brill, 2014.

Halton, Charles. "An Eršaḫunga to Any God." Pages 447–64 in *Reading Akkadian Prayers and Hymns: An Introduction*. Edited by Alan Lenzi. ANEM 3. Atlanta: Society of Biblical Literature, 2011.

Harper, Robert Francis. *Assyrian and Babylonian Letters Belonging to the K. Collection of the British Museum*. 14 vols. Chicago: University of Chicago Press, 1892–1914.

Harrelson, Walter. "'Why, O Lord, Do You Harden Our Heart?' A Plea for Help from a Hiding God." Pages 163–74 in *Shall Not the Judge of All the Earth Do What Is Right?: Studies on the Nature of God in Tribute to James L. Crenshaw*. Edited by David Penchansky and Paul L. Redditt. Winona Lake, IN: Eisenbrauns, 2000.

Hartenstein, Friedhelm. *Das Angesicht JHWHs: Studien zu seinem höfischen und kultischen Bedeutungshintergrund in den Psalmen und in Exodus 32–34*. FAT 55. Tübingen: Mohr Siebeck, 2008.

Heinemann, Joseph. *Prayer in the Period of the Tanna'im and the Amora'im: Its Nature and Patterns*. [Hebrew.] Jerusalem: Magnes, 1964.

Hilprecht, H. V., ed. *The Babylonian Expedition of the University of Pennsylvania, Series A: Cuneiform Texts*. 31 vols. Philadelphia: University of Pennsylvania Press, 1893–1914.

Hoffman, Joel M. "*Avinu Malkeinu*: A New and Annotated Translation." Pages 41–58 in *Naming God: Avinu Malkeinu—Our Father, Our King*.

Edited by Lawrence A. Hoffman. Woodstock, VT: Jewish Lights, 2015.

———. "*Un'taneh Tokef*: Behind the Translation." Pages 33–48 in *Who by Fire, Who by Water:* Un'taneh Tokef. Edited by Lawrence A. Hoffman. Woodstock, VT: Jewish Lights, 2010.

Hoffman, Lawrence A. "The History, Meaning, and Varieties of *Avinu Malkeinu*." Pages 3–15 in *Naming God:* Avinu Malkeinu—*Our Father, Our King*. Edited by Lawrence A. Hoffman. Woodstock, VT: Jewish Lights, 2015.

———, ed. *Naming God:* Avinu Malkeinu—*Our Father, Our King*. Woodstock, VT: Jewish Lights, 2015.

———. "*Un'taneh Tokef* as Poetry and Legend." Pages 13–25 in *Who by Fire, Who by Water:* Un'taneh Tokef. Edited by Lawrence A. Hoffman. Woodstock, VT: Jewish Lights, 2010.

———, ed. *Who by Fire, Who by Water:* Un'taneh Tokef. Woodstock, VT: Jewish Lights, 2010.

Hoffman, Yair. "The Root *QRB* as a Legal Term." *JNSL* 10 (1982): 67–73.

———. "The Song of Vineyard." [Hebrew.] Pages 69–82 in הצבי ישראל: *Studies in Bible Dedicated to the Memory of Israel and Zvi Broide*. Edited by Jacob Licht and Gershon Brin. Tel Aviv: Tel Aviv University, 1976.

Holtz, Shalom E. "The Case for Adversarial *yaḥad*." *VT* 59 (2009): 211–21.

———. "Maqlû I.73–121 and Trial Procedure." *JANER* 17 (2017): 140–48.

———. *Neo-Babylonian Court Procedure*. CM 38. Leiden: Brill, 2009.

———. *Neo-Babylonian Trial Records*. WAW 35. Atlanta: Society of Biblical Literature, 2014.

———. "Praying as a Plaintiff." *VT* 61 (2011): 258–79.

———. "The Prophet as Summoner." Pages 19–34 in *A Common Cultural Heritage: Studies on Mesopotamia and the Biblical World in Honor of Barry L. Eichler*. Edited by Grant Frame et al. Bethesda, MD: CDL, 2011.

Hossfeld, Frank-Lothar, and Erich Zenger. *Psalms 3: A Commentary on Psalms 101–150*. Translated by Linda M. Maloney. Hermeneia. Minneapolis: Fortress, 2011.

Hubbard, Robert L. "Dynamistic and Legal Processes in Psalm 7." *ZAW* 94 (1982): 267–79.

Hurowitz, Victor Avigdor. "ABL 1285 and the Hebrew Bible: Literary Topoi in Urad-Gula's Letter of Petition to Assurbanipal." *SAAB* 7 (1993): 9–17.

Irsigler, Hubert. "Speech Acts and Intention in the 'Song of the Vineyard' Isaiah 5:1-7." *OTE* 10 (1997): 39–68.

Janowski, Bernd. *Arguing with God: A Theological Anthropology of the Psalms*. Translated by Armin Siedlecki. Louisville: Westminster John Knox, 2013.

Japhet, Sara. *I and II Chronicles*. OTL. Louisville, KY: Westminster John Knox, 1993.

Jindo, Job Y. *Biblical Metaphor Reconsidered: A Cognitive Approach to Poetic Prophecy in Jeremiah 1–24*. HSM 64. Winona Lake, IN: Eisenbrauns, 2010.

Joannès, Francis. *Rendre la justice en Mésopotamie: Archives judiciaires du Proche-Orient ancien (IIIe-Ier millénaires avant J.-C.)*. Temps et Espaces. Saint Denis: Presses Universitaires de Vincennes, 2000.

Kasher, Rimon. "The Saving of Jehoshaphat." [Hebrew.] *Beth Miqra* 31 (1985–1986): 242–251.

Kensky, Meira Z. *Trying Man, Trying God: The Divine Courtroom in Early Jewish and Christian Literature*. WUNT 2/289. Tübingen: Mohr Siebeck, 2010.

King, Leonard W. *Babylonian Magic and Sorcery*. London: Luzac, 1896.

Knoppers, Gary N. "Jerusalem at War in Chronicles." Pages 57–76 in *Zion, City of Our God*. Edited by Richard S. Hess and Gordon J. Wenham. Grand Rapids: Eerdmans, 1999.

Köcher, Franz. *Die babylonisch-assyrische Medizin in Texten und Untersuchungen*. Berlin: De Gruyter, 1963–.

Kozuh, Michael. *The Sacrificial Economy: Assessors, Contractors, and Thieves in the Management of Sacrificial Sheep at the Eanna Temple of Uruk (ca. 625–520 B.C.)*. EANEC 2. Winona Lake, IN: Eisenbrauns, 2014.

Kugel, James L. "Topics in the History of the Spirituality of the Psalms." Pages 113–44 in *Jewish Spirituality from the Bible through the Middle Ages*. Edited by Arthur Green. World Spirituality 13. New York: Crossroad, 1986.

Lai, Barbara M. Leung. "Psalm 44 and the Function of Lament and Protest." *OTE* 20 (2007): 418–31.

Lam, Joseph. *Patterns of Sin in the Hebrew Bible: Metaphor, Culture, and the Making of a Religious Concept*. Oxford: Oxford University Press, 2016.

Lambert, David A. *How Repentance Became Biblical: Judaism, Christianity, and the Interpretation of Scripture*. Oxford: Oxford University Press, 2016.

Lambert, W. G. *Babylonian Wisdom Literature*. Oxford: Clarendon, 1960.

———. "Nebuchadnezzar King of Justice." *Iraq* 27 (1965): 1–11.

Lambert, W. G., and A. R. Millard. *Babylonian Literary Texts*. CT 46. London: The Trustees of the British Museum, 1965.

Lebrun, René. "Observations sur la prière Hittite." Pages 31–57 in *L'expérience de la prière dans les grandes religions*. Edited by Henri Limet and Julien Ries. Homo Religiosus 5. Louvain-la-Neuve: Centre d'Histoire des Religions, 1980.

Lenzi, Alan, ed. *Reading Akkadian Prayers and Hymns: An Introduction*. ANEM 3. Atlanta: Society of Biblical Literature, 2011.

Lohfink, Norbert. *In the Shadow of Your Wings: New Readings of Great Texts from the Bible*. Translated by Linda M. Maloney. Collegeville, MN: Liturgical Press, 2003.

Lytton, Timothy D. "'Shall Not the Judge of the Earth Deal Justly?': Accountability, Compassion, and Judicial Authority in the Biblical Story of Sodom and Gomorrah." *Journal of Law and Religion* 18 (2002–2003): 31–55.

Machinist, Peter Bruce. "The Epic of Tukulti-Ninurta I, A Study in Middle Assyrian Literature." PhD diss., Yale University, 1978.

Magdalene, F. Rachel. *On the Scales of Righteousness: Neo-Babylonian Trial Law and the Book of Job*. BJS 348. Providence, RI: Brown Judaic Studies, 2007.

———. "Trying the Crime of Abuse of Royal Authority in the Divine Courtroom and the Incident of Naboth's Vineyard." Pages 167–245 in *The Divine Courtroom in Comparative Perspective*. Edited by Ari Mermelstein and Shalom E. Holtz. BibInt 132. Leiden: Brill, 2014.

Makela, Finn. "Metaphors and Models in Legal Theory." *Les Cahiers du Droit* 52 (2011): 397–415.

Maré, Leonard P. "Psalm 44: When God Is Responsible for Suffering." *Journal for Semitics* 21 (2012): 52–65.

Maul, Stefan M. "How the Babylonians Protected Themselves against Calamities Announced by Omens." Pages 123–29 in *Mesopotamian Magic: Textual, Historical, and Interpretive Perspectives*. Edited by Tzvi Abusch and Karel van der Toorn. AMD 1. Groningen: Styx, 1999.

———. *Zukunftsbewältigung: Eine Untersuchung altorientalischen Denkens anhand der babylonisch-assyrischen Löserituale (Namburbi)*. BaF 18. Mainz: Philipp von Zabern, 1994.

Mayer, Werner. *Untersuchungen zur Formensprache der Babylonische 'Gebetsbeschwörungen.'* StPohl: Series Maior 5. Rome: Pontifical Biblical Institute, 1976.

Michel, Cécile. "Hommes et femmes prêtent serment à l'époque paléo-assyrienne." Pages 105–23 in *Jurer et maudire: Pratiques politiques et usages juridiques du serment dans le Proche-Orient ancien; Actes de la table ronde organisée le samedi 5 Octobre 1986 à l'université de Paris, X-Nanterre*. Edited by Francis Joannès and Sophie Lafont. Méditerranées 10–11. Paris: L'Harmattan, 1996.

———. "Règlement des comptes du défunt Huraṣānum." *RA* 88 (1994): 121–28.

Miller, Patrick D. "The Ruler in Zion and the Hope of the Poor: Psalms 9–10 in the Context of the Psalter." Pages 187–97 in *David and Zion: Biblical Studies in Honor of J.J. M. Roberts*. Edited by Bernard F. Batto and Kathryn L. Roberts. Winona Lake, IN: Eisenbrauns, 2004.

Moran, William L. "UET 6, 402: Persuasion in the Plain Style." *JANESCU* 22 (1993): 113–20.

Morrow, William S. *Protest against God: The Eclipse of a Biblical Tradition.* Hebrew Bible Monographs 4. Sheffield: Sheffield Phoenix Press, 2006.

Mowinckel, Sigmund. *The Psalms in Israel's Worship.* Translated by D. R. Ap-Thomas. 2 vols. Grand Rapids: Eerdmans, 1962. Reprint, 2004.

———. *Psalm Studies.* Translated by Marc E. Biddle. 2 vols. HBS 2. Atlanta: SBL Press, 2014.

Muffs, Yochanan. *Love and Joy: Law, Language, and Religion in Ancient Israel.* New York: Jewish Theological Seminary of America, 1992.

Neubauer, Karl Wilhelm. "Der Stamm Ch N N im Sprachgebrauch des Alten Testaments." Th.D. diss., Kirchlichen Hochschule Berlin, 1964.

Nies, James B., and Clarence E. Keiser. *Historical, Religious and Economic Texts and Antiquities.* BIN 2. New Haven: Yale University Press, 1920.

Nissinen, Martti. *Prophets and Prophecy in the Ancient Near East.* WAW 12. Atlanta: Society of Biblical Literature, 2003.

Nougayrol, Jean. *Le palais royal d'Ugarit IV: Textes Accadiens des Archives Sud.* MRS 9. Paris: Imprimerie Nationale, 1956.

Oshima, Takayoshi. *Babylonian Prayers to Marduk.* ORA 7. Tübingen: Mohr-Siebeck, 2011.

Paul, Shalom M. "Heavenly Tablets and the Book of Life." *JANESCU* 5 (1973): 345–53.

Petschow, Herbert. *Mittelbabylonische Rechts- und Wirtschaftsurkunden der Hilprecht-Sammlung Jena.* ASAW 64/4. Berlin: Akademie-Verlag, 1974.

Pohl, Alfred. *Neubabylonische Rechtsurkunden aus den Berliner Staatlichen Museen.* AnOr 8. Rome: Pontifical Biblical Institute, 1933.

Porten, Bezalel. *Archives from Elephantine: The Life of an Ancient Jewish Military Colony.* Berkeley: University of California Press, 1968.

———. "Cowley 7 Reconsidered." *Or* 56 (1987): 89–92.

Porten, Bezalel, and Ada Yardeni. *Textbook of Aramaic Documents from Ancient Egypt.* 4 vols. Winona Lake, IN: Eisenbrauns, 1986.

Provan, Iain W. "Past, Present and Future in Lamentations III 52–66: The Case for a Precative Perfect Re-Examined." *VT* 41 (1991): 164–75.

Reiner, Erica. *Šurpu: Collection of Sumerian and Akkadian Incantations.* AFO Beiheft 11. Graz: E. Weidner, 1958.

Renger, Johannes. "Notes on the Goldsmiths, Jewelers and Carpenters of Neo-Babylonian Eanna." *JAOS* 91 (1971): 494–503.

Rom-Shiloni, Dalit. "Between Protest and Theodicy: The Dialogue between Communal Laments and Penitential Prayers in Biblical Prayers." [Hebrew.] *Shnaton* 16 (2005–2006): 71–96.

———. "Psalm 44: The Power of Protest." *CBQ* 70 (2008): 683–98.

———. "Socio-Ideological *Setting* or *Settings* for Penitential Prayers?" Pages 51–68 in *The Origins of Penitential Prayer in Second Temple Judaism*, vol. 1 of *Seeking the Favor of God.* Edited by Mark J. Boda, Daniel K. Falk, and Rodney A. Werline. EJL 21. Atlanta: Society of Biblical Literature, 2006.

Roth, Martha T. "Hammurabi's Wronged Man." *JAOS* 122 (2002): 38–45.
Sachs, Abraham J., and Hermann Hunger. *Diaries from 261 B.C. to 165 B.C.,* vol. 2 of *Astronomical Diaries and Related Texts from Babylonia*. DÖAW. PH 210. Vienna: Österreichische Akademie de Wissenschaften, 1989.
San Nicolò, Mariano. "Parerga Babylonica XI: Die *maš'altu*-Urkunden im neubabylonische Strafverfahren." *ArOr* 5 (1933): 287–302.
Sawyer, J. F. A. "Types of Prayer in the Old Testament: Some Semantic Observations on Hitpallel, Hithannen, etc." *Semitics* 7 (1980): 131–43.
Scheil, V. "La libération judiciaire d'un fils donné en gage sous Neriglissor en 558 av. J.-C." *RA* 12 (1915): 1–13.
Schmelzer, Menahem. "Penitence, Prayer and (Charity?)." Pages 291–99 in *Minḥah le-Naḥum: Biblical and Other Studies Presented to Nahum M. Sarna in Honour of His 70th Birthday*. Edited by Marc Brettler and Michael Fishbane. JSOTSup 134. Sheffield: Sheffield Academic Press, 1993.
Schmidt, Hans. "Das Gebet der Angeklagten im Alten Testament." Pages 143–55 in *Old Testament Essays: Papers Read before the Society for Old Testament Study at Its Eighteenth Meeting, Held at Keble College, Oxford, September 27th to 30th, 1927*. London: Charles Griffin, 1927.
———.*Das Gebet der Angeklagten im Alten Testament*. BZAW 49. Giessen: Töpelmann, 1928.
———. *Die Psalmen*. HAT 15. Tübingen: J. C. B. Mohr, 1934.
Schwemer, Daniel. *Abwehrzauber und Behexung: Studien zum Schadenzauberglabuen im alten Mesopotamien; Unter Benutzung von Tzvi Abuschs Kritischem Katalog und Sammlungen im Rahmen des Kooperationsprojektes Corpus of Mesopotamian Anti-Witchcraft Rituals*. Wiesbaden: Harrassowitz, 2007.
———. "Empowering the Patient: The Opening Section of the Ritual *Maqlû*. Pages 311–39 in *Pax Hethitica: Studies on the Hittites and their Neighbours in Honour of Itamar Singer*. Edited by Yoram Cohen, Amir Gilan, and Jared L. Miller. StBoT 51. Wiesbaden: Harrassowitz, 2010.
———. "'Form Follows Function'? Rhetoric and Poetic Language in First Millennium Akkadian Incantations." *WO* 44 (2014): 263–88.
Scurlock, Jo Ann. *Magico-Medical Means of Treating Ghost-Induced Illnesses in Ancient Mesopotamia*. AMD 3. Leiden: Brill, 2006.
Seeligmann, I. L. "Zur Terminologie für das Gerichtsverfahren im Wortschatz des biblischen Hebräisch." Pages 251–78 in *Hebräische Wortforschung: Festschrift zum 80. Geburtstag von Walter Baumgartner*. Edited by Benedikt Hartmann et al. VTSup 16. Leiden: Brill, 1967.
Singer, Itamar. *Hittite Prayers*. WAW 11. Atlanta: Society of Biblical Literature, 2002.
Smith, Duane."A Namburbi against the Evil of a Snake: Shamash 25." Pages 421–30 in *Reading Akkadian Prayers and Hymns: An Introduction*.

Edited by Alan Lenzi. ANEM 3. Atlanta: Society of Biblical Literature, 2011.

———. "A Ritual Incantation-Prayer against Ghost-Induced Illness: Shamash 73." Pages 197–215 in *Reading Akkadian Prayers and Hymns: An Introduction*. Edited by Alan Lenzi. ANEM 3. Atlanta: Society of Biblical Literature, 2011.

Sokoloff, Michael. *A Dictionary of Jewish Palestinian Aramaic of the Byzantine Period*. Ramat-Gan: Bar-Ilan University Press, 2002.

Soldt, W. H. van, and M. Stol. "The Old Babylonian Texts in the Allard Pierson Museum, Amsterdam." *JEOL* 25 (1977–1978): 45–55.

Speiser, E. A. "The Stem PLL in Hebrew." *JBL* 82 (1963): 301–6.

Starr, Ivan. *The Rituals of the Diviner*. BMes 12. Malibu, CA: Undena, 1983.

Strassmaier, J. N. *Inschriften von Cyrus, König von Babylon (538–529 v. Chr.)*. Leipzig: Eduard Pfeiffer, 1890.

———. *Inschriften von Nabonidus, König von Babylon (555–538 v. Chr.)*. Leipzig: Eduard Pfeiffer, 1889.

Szubin, H. Z., and Bezalel Porten. "Litigation Concerning Abandoned Property at Elephantine (Kraeling 1)." *JNES* 42 (1983): 279–84.

Throntveit, Mark A. *When Kings Speak: Royal Speech and Royal Prayer in Chronicles*. SBLDS 93. Atlanta: Scholars Press, 1987.

Tigay, Jeffrey H. "Psalm 7:5 and Ancient Near Eastern Treaties." *JBL* 89 (1970): 178–86.

Toorn, Karel van der. "Ḥerem-Bethel and Elephantine Oath Procedure." *ZAW* 98 (1986): 282–85.

Tremayne, Arch. *Records from Erech: Time of Cyrus and Cambyses (538–521 B.C.)*. YOS 7. New Haven: Yale University Press, 1925.

Veldhuis, Niek. "On Interpreting Mesopotamian Namburbis." *AfO* 42/43 (1995/1996): 145–54.

Versnel, H. S. "Beyond Cursing: The Appeal to Justice in Judicial Prayers." Pages 60–106 in *Magika Hiera: Ancient Greek Magic and Religion*. Edited by Christopher A. Faraone and Dirk Obbink. Oxford: Oxford University Press, 1997.

Weinfeld, Moshe. *Social Justice in Ancient Israel and in the Ancient Near East*. Jerusalem: Magnes, 1995.

Wells, Bruce. "The Cultic versus the Forensic: Judahite and Mesopotamian Judicial Procedures in the First Millennium BCE." *JAOS* 128 (2008): 205–32.

———. "Introduction: The Idea of a Shared Tradition." Pages xi–xx in vol. 1 of *Law from the Tigris to the Tiber: The Writings of Raymond Westbrook*. Edited by Bruce Wells and F. Rachel Magdalene. Winona Lake, IN: Eisenbrauns, 2009.

———. *The Law of Testimony in the Pentateuchal Codes*. BZABR 4. Wiesbaden: Harrassowitz, 2004.

Wells, Bruce, F. Rachel Magdalene, and Cornelia Wunsch. "The Assertory Oath in Neo-Babylonian and Persian Administrative Texts." *RIDA* 57 (2010): 13–29.

Westbrook, Raymond. "International Law in the Amarna Age." Pages 265–84 in vol. 2 of *Law from the Tigris to the Tiber: The Writings of Raymond Westbrook*. Edited by Bruce Wells and F. Rachel Magdalene. Winona Lake, IN: Eisenbrauns, 2009.

———. "A Matter of Life and Death." Pages 251–64 in vol. 2 of *Law from the Tigris to the Tiber: The Writings of Raymond Westbrook*. Edited by Bruce Wells and F. Rachel Magdalene. Winona Lake, IN: Eisenbrauns, 2009.

———. "Witchcraft and the Law in the Ancient Near East." Pages 289–300 in vol. 1 of *Law from the Tigris to the Tiber: The Writings of Raymond Westbrook*. Edited by Bruce Wells and F. Rachel Magdalene. Winona Lake, IN: Eisenbrauns, 2009.

Westermann, Claus. *Praise and Lament in the Psalms*. Translated by Keith R. Crim and Richard N. Soulen. Atlanta: John Knox, 1965.

Williamson, Robert, Jr. "Lament and the Arts of Resistance: Public and Hidden Transcripts in Lamentations 5." Pages 67–80 in *Lamentations in Ancient and Contemporary Cultural Contexts*. Edited by Nancy C. Lee and Carleen Mandolfo. SBLSymS 43. Atlanta: Society of Biblical Literature, 2008.

Wiseman, D. J. *The Alalakh Tablets*. Occasional Publications of the British Institute of Archaeology at Ankara 2. London: British Institute of Archaeology at Ankara, 1953.

Wright, David P. *Inventing God's Law: How the Covenant Code of the Bible Used and Revised the Laws of Hammurabi*. Oxford: Oxford University Press, 2009.

Wunsch, Cornelia. *Das Egibi-Archiv: I. Die Felder und Gärten*. CM 20. Groningen: Styx, 2000.

———. *Urkunden zum Ehe- Vermögens- und Erbrecht aus verschiedenen neubabylonischen Archiven*. Babylonische Archive 2. Dresden: Islet Verlag, 2003.

Zernecke, Anna-Elise. "An Incantation Prayer: Ishtar 24." Pages 169–78 in *Reading Akkadian Prayers and Hymns: An Introduction*. Edited by Alan Lenzi. ANEM 3. Atlanta: Society of Biblical Literature, 2011.

Zgoll, Annette. "Audienz—Ein Modell zum Verständnis mesopotamischer Handerhebungsrituale. Mit einer Deutung der Novelle vom *Armen Mann von Nippur*." *BaghM* 34 (2003): 181–203.

Index of Subjects

Akkadian literature
  analogues to biblical prayers in, 2, 40
    prayer–courtroom connection, 27–28, 42, 48–49, 123–24 (see also under prayer)
    prophetic intercession, 111–14
    audience approaching and standing for prayers, 95, 101–7, 111–14
  law collections of, 35
  Mari letters, 34–35
  and meta-tradition of law and religious thought, 15
  prayer in, 10, 42–43, 46, 49, 94, 101, 105–6, 116–17
    confession in, 66 (see also confession)
    and court records, 11–12, 14–15
    demand for judgment in, 47–50
    eršaḫunga prayers, 68
    incantations, 41–42
    namburbi prayers, 47–51, 60, 102
    oaths in, 77–78
  trial records, 2, 12, 63, 91–92
  words connected with law and praying
    alāku ("to come"), 103–4, 116
    amāru ("to see"), 123–24, 124n99
    dabābī ("my suit"), 116, 116n75
    dânu/dīn ("to judge"/"judge"), 2, 11, 22, 24, 25, 35, 40, 41–42, 45, 48–49, 116, 130
    ḫabālu ("to wrong"), 40, 42, 46
    maḫāru ("to approach"), 101, 103, 104
    mašʻaltu ("interrogation"), 70–71
    purussû ("decision"), 42, 48–49, 101
    qerēbu ("to approach"), 101, 103

  rigma nadû ("to drop a complaint"), 107
  šemû ("hearing"), 120–21
  shuilla ("hand–raising" prayer), 93–94
  sullû ("to petition"), 27–28
  See also Hittite prayers; Maqlû; Neo-Babylonian literature; Old Babylonian literature
ancient Near Eastern literature. See Akkadian literature; Hittite prayers; Maqlû; Neo-Babylonian literature; Old Babylonian literature
audience
  ancient: standing before superiors, 95, 107, 113
  courtroom and, 94–125
  of prayer, 94–125

"calling/crying out," 34–37, 45–46, 57–59, 124–25 (see also under prayer)
communication. See human–divine communication; human–human axis
confession, 63–75
  addressed to God, 66
  and interrogation, 70–72
  and judgment, 66, 73
  legal aspects of, 64–75
  made under duress, 72
  and ordeal, 66–67
  as prayer, 72–73
  and punishment, 69
  sincerity of, 72–73
  as submission, 67, 70, 72–73
  and suffering, 68–70, 73–74
  vs. contrition or penitence, 66
counteraccusation, 63
  against God, 85–92

counteraccusation (*cont.*)
  as legal defense, 87
  in second person or third person, 88–90
courtroom
  accusations against God and, 84–85
  affliction and, 44, 46
  audience in, 93–125
  biblical trial procedure and, 7–8
  book of Job and, 13–14
  connected to language of prayer, 17–37
  divine, 23–26, 36–37, 40, 42, 49, 60, 69, 72, 132
  human, 2, 11, 15, 20, 22, 49, 65, 69, 77, 91, 93, 99n15, 102, 130, 131
  imagery of, 7–8
  oaths in, 77–78
  oppression and poverty in context of, 46
  as setting for prayers, 4, 65–66
  as social analogy, 8, 10–11, 15
  təpillâ and, 22–27
  as vehicle or source of metaphor, 11
  witnesses or accusers in, 65
  See also under prayer
covenant
  as binding agreement between God and nation, 65
  as legal defense, 108

God/deities
  accusation against, 82–92
  acting as human adjudicators, 115
  adjucatory authority of, 58–59
  as adversary, 92
  "coming" to, in prayer, 93
  confession addressed to, 66
  as enemy, 83–84
  as father, 2
  forensic senses of, 114–25
  hearing and seeing, 93, 114–25
  as judge, 2, 21, 22, 24, 43, 44–45, 47, 49, 84, 108
  as king, 2, 128
  as patron, 43
  response of
    to poor, 43–45
    to prayer, 3, 22, 32 (*see also under* prayer)
  subversion of justice by, 25n27
Greek literature: judicial prayers in, 2n7

hearing. *See under* God/deities; prayer
Hebrew terminology related to law and prayer
  ʿ-m-d ("stand"), 97, 110
  ʿ-n-y + bə ("testify against"), 65
  b-w-ʾ ("come"), 98–100
  gəzar dîn ("legal decision"), 22–23, 25
  d-y-n ("judge"), 3n12, 46–47, 48–49, 116
  hitpallēl ("pray"), 3, 17–37
  z-ʿ-q ("call out"), 31–32, 34–35
  ḥ-n-n (pertaining to requests for favor, mercy), 31–33
  mišpāṭ ("judgment," "justice"), 21, 32, 37, 43, 45, 98, 100, 122
  n-g-š ("approach"), 95–96, 97, 98, 100, 110–11
  n-p-l ("fall"), 97, 100, 102, 107
  p-l-l ("pray"), 17–18
  ṣədāqâ ("almsgiving"), 23
  ṣ-ʿ-q ("call out"), 3, 31–32, 34–35, 100, 125
  q-r-ʾ ("call"), 31–32, 34–35
  q-r-b ("drawing near"), 98–100
  r-ʾ-y ("see"), 123–24, 125
  rîb ("legal dispute"), 6–7
  ś-ṭ-n ("accuse"), 30
  š-m-ʿ ("hear"), 120–21, 120n89
  š-p-ṭ ("to judge"), 20, 44–45, 48–49, 53, 56, 58
  təḥinnâ ("prayer"), 32–37, 100, 107
  təpillâ ("prayer"), 3, 17–37, 116 (*see also* prayer; təpillâ)
    Akkadian and Hittite analogues to, 27–29
    as antidote to divine decree, 22–23
    connected to courtroom, 17, 20–21, 22–27 (*see also under* prayer)
    directed to God, 21

Index of Subjects   149

directed to a human, 20–21
meaning "plea" or "petition," 17
preceding *mišpāṭ*, 27
təšûbâ ("repentance"), 23
Hittite prayers
of King Muwatalli, 118
terminology of, 28–29
human–divine communication/relationship
calling out, 36
as "coming" to God, 93
courtroom metaphor and, 10, 127
"hearing" and, 121
metaphor and, 128–29
prayers as sources of insight into, 10
human–human communication, 19–20, 32, 49
approaching and standing and, 97–99, 102
calling/crying out and, 36, 118–19
"hearing" and, 121
petitions and, 119
təpillâ and, 29–30

imprecation, 19–20
innocence, oath of, 75–82, 83
interrogation, 70–72
investigation
divine, 74–77
Israel
as plaintiff, 6

Job
counteraccusation and, 86–92
judgment
"calling out" and, 35–36, 134
confession and, 66
demand for, 46–60, 82, 121, 133–34
in biblical narrative contexts, 52–55
in biblical poetic prayers, 55–59
and courtroom parlance, 63
position of, in legal texts, 49–51
position of, in prayers, 54–56, 58–59, 63
and remedy sought, 52, 55, 56, 58, 63, 81, 121
structure of, 53–54

and downtrodden, 45
justice and, 32
prayer and, 21, 32
protection and, 45
relief and, 58
"seeing" connected with, 123–24
terminology of, 76
justice
divine: dissatisfaction with, 64
perversion of, 37
prayer and, 134
poverty and need for, 43

law
biblical, 7
salvation and, 45–46
as source of standing, 134
legal terminology, 6–7n21, 7, 11

Maqlû (Babylonian anti–witchcraft ritual), 2–3, 11–13, 129–32, 133
demand for judgment in, 51–52
forensic language in, 116–17
metaphor
cognitive significance of, 9
as conceptual constructs, 9
of courtroom, 10, 127
as frame of mind 9
and human communication, 128–129
metaphoric language, 127
of lawsuit, 8–9
as mode of orientation, 9
poems and, 9
and prayer, 10, 127
praying legally as, 128
problem of, 10–15
value of, 8–10
vehicle or source of, 11

Neo–Babylonian literature
"Nebuchadnezzar King of Justice," 112–14
petitioners in, asking to be heard, 121
trial records, 49–51, 59–60, 91–92, 103–5
counteraccusation in, 86–87

Neo-Babylonian literature (*cont.*)
  trial records (*cont.*)
    demand for judgment in, 55,
      58–59
    "hearing" in, 120–21
    tribunals at Eanna temple, 69–72,
      78–79, 91–92, 124
    structure of decision records,
      52–54
    trial procedure, 129–32

oath of innocence, 61
Old Babylonian literature
  court records, 103
  forensic language in, 40
  gods as ultimate arbiters in, 40
  prayer, 39–41
oppression
  salvation and, 44–45, 46

penitential prayers, 1, 2, 14–15, 23–25,
  59, 73
poor
  judgment for, 45, 46
  response of God to, 43–45
prayer
  accusation against God, 82–92
  affliction and, 44
  ancient theory of, 17
  approach and stance in, 95–107, 114
  audience concept and, 94–125
    allowing humans to access the
      divine, 113
  as "coming before" God, 99, 100
  confessions in, 72–75
  as crying out to God, 3, 31–32,
    34–37, 43, 45–46, 57–59, 100,
    124–25
  deities as superiors in, 94
  demand for judgment in, 121
  and divine decree, 26–27
  divine–human encounter in, 93
    hearing, seeing, approaching,
      standing, 95–107
  effectiveness of, 26, 59
  forensic conception of, 1, 20, 118
  God hearing, 93
  as human response to adverse
    rulings by God, 24
  intercessory, 113
  and judgment, 21, 25 (*see also* judgment)
  laments as, 3–4
  as legal appeal, 26, 31, 37, 59–60, 61
  legal language and, 2, 5–6, 11, 13,
    127–28
  as legal petition, 3, 129
  legal standing and, 131–34
  and litigation, 106, 127
  as making one's case before God,
    17, 31, 37, 129
  metaphoric language and, 9–10 (*see
    also* metaphor)
  oaths in, 75–82
  as overturning decree, 25–27
  and petition, 47
  petitionary: connection of, to lawsuits, 4
  prayer–courtroom connection, 1, 6,
    7, 15, 17, 24, 27, 47–48, 54–55,
    59, 61, 63, 92, 94, 102, 107, 115,
    127–28
    and adjudicatory process, 63
    concretization of, 26
    and conception of deities as
      kings, 128
    courtroom imagery, 128
    courtroom as metaphor, 129
    courtroom procedure, 134
    courtroom as setting for prayers,
      4, 65–66, 134
    human subjects and deities'
      response, 115
    inherent in language of prayer,
      17–18
    in modern biblical scholarship,
      3–8
    in postbiblical Jewish texts, 1
    prayer as courtroom audience,
      113
    prayer as courtroom speech, 1,
      95
    social analogy of, 94, 127
  proper timing of, 26–27

as protest, 64, 133–34
response of God to, 3, 21
   as favorable legal verdict, 3
social analogy and, 10–11, 15
speaker in prayers
   as appellant, 59
   asking to be heard, 121
   as community on trial, 2
   as defendant, 61, 63
   and patron–client relationship, 43
   as oppressed or wronged, 59–60
   as plaintiff, 47, 49, 58, 59–61, 84
   as poor or destitute, 42–43
   positioning of, 95–100, 113
   as subject, 94, 114
terminology of
   derived from forensic sphere, 10
   positional, 113
   See also Hebrew terminology related to law and prayer
wording of, 10
prophetic intercession
   and Akkadian writings, 111–14
   courtroom context of, 108–9
   and Israelite courtrooms, 7, 108
   legal aspects of, 107–14
   as speech of defense, 108–9
Psalms
   and Akkadian *namburbi* prayers, 47–50
   descriptions of human litigation in, 4
   individual and communal complaints or laments, 2, 4, 46
   rîb pattern in, 6
   trial context of Ps 69, 4–5

seeing
   as legally significant act, 124
   See also under God/deities; prayer

self–abasement
   adjudication and, 44
   language of, 42–43
self–curse, 77–79, 80
sin(s) (*ḥăṭāʾâ*), 20
   as accusatory witnesses, 65
   articulation of, 66
   metaphor and, 127
   prayer and, 20
   recorded as "debt notes," 2
   as testifying against, 65
speech
   between God and humans, 3
   social analogy and, 3, 5
   legal language and, 5
suffering
   confession and, 68–69, 73–74
   of Job, 70–72
   prayer as appeal for relief from, 31
   as punishment, 69
   as torturous investigation, 74–75

təpillâ (Hebrew word for prayer), 3
   Akkadian and Hittite analogues to, 27–29
   as antidote to divine decree, 22–23
   connected to courtroom, 17, 20–21, 22–27
   denoting human communication, 3
   denoting an argument in court, 3
   directed to God, 21
   directed to a human, 20–21
   meaning "plea" or "petition," 17
   preceding *mišpāṭ*, 27
   and root *p–l–l*, 17–18

wrongdoing: denial of, 75–82

Index of Ancient Sources

Hebrew Bible

Genesis
16:5	49
18:21	100n20, 124
18:22	110n61
18:23–33	109
18:23–25	84
18:23	110–11
18:25	109
29:32	123n97
30:6	3n12
31:42	123n97
44:14	97
44:18	97

Exodus
2:23	100n20
2:24–25	115n71
2:25	123n97
3:7	115n71, 123n97
3:9	100n20, 123n97
4:31	115n71, 123n97
5:21	49, 123n97
9:27	66–67
18:16	99
18:19	100
18:22	100
18:26	100
20:13	65
21:22	18n3
22:7	98, 99
23:6	43n13, 120n87
32	108
32:7–14	108
32:11–13	84, 133
32:13	65, 109

Leviticus
24:11	98n11

Numbers
9:6	98
27:1–2	98
27:5	100
35:12	99, 110
36:1	98

Deuteronomy
1:17	100
10:18	43n11
13:15	4n14
17:4	4n14, 120n89
17:8–9	98
19:15–18	4n14
19:17	99
22:13–19	88
24:14–15	36, 43
24:17	43n13
25:1	98
25:7	99
26:7	115n71, 123n97

Joshua
17:4	98
20:6	99
20:9	99

Judges
4:5	99
20:60	20n15
21:22	33

1 Samuel
1:11	123n97
1:26	96
2:8	42–43n7
5:12	100n20
9:16	100n20, 123n97
24:15	123n97

2 Samuel
14:12	34n47
15:2–6	98
15:3	120n86
16:12	123n97
19:29	34n47
22:28	43n7

1 Kings
3:16	97–98, 110
3:17–21	88
3:22–23	88
3:28	21n19
8	22, 24, 27
8:44	21
8:45	21, 32
8:46–48	21
8:49	21, 32
8:50	22
8:59	21n18, 32
18:36	96
20:39–40	120
20:39	34n47

2 Kings
4:1	34n47
6:26	34n47
8:3	34
8:5	34
13:4	115n71, 123n97
14:26	115n71, 123n97
20:5	123n97

Isaiah
1:15	120n84
1:17	43n13
1:23	43n13, 120n87
3:14	98n10
5:1–7	49
5:3b	51

Index of Ancient Sources

6:3	23	26:17–19	112n67	17	49, 115–16, 117
10:1–2	43n13	29:23	24	17:1–2	115–16
10:2	120n87	36:7	100, 100n21	17:1	47
29:13	96	37:12–21	33, 119	17:2	47
32:7	120n87	37:20	33, 100, 100n21, 119	17:2–3	76n33
38:5	123n97	38	33n44	17:6	116n73
38:14	44n15	38:14–28	33	18:7	99n18, 120n85
41:1	98	38:26	33, 100, 100n21	18:28	43n7
41:21	100	42:2	100nn21, 22	18:42	120n84
45:14	19n10	42:9	100, 100n26	22	83–84, 85, 87–88
50:8	98n9, 99			22:2	91
60:18	45n16	Ezekiel		22:3	120n84
63:17–64:4	83n55	3:12b	23	22:25	120n85
64:11	42n7, 83n55	8:18	120n84	25:9	43n11, 45
		18:8	21n19	25:18	42n7
Jeremiah	9	22:29	43n13	26	49, 75–79, 80
5:28	43n13, 120n87	22:30	108, 110, 110n60	26:1	47
6:6–7	45n16			27:7	115
7:5	21n19	Amos		27:12	4n14
7:10	96n4	5:12	120n87	28:6	120n85
7:16	120n84			31:8	42n7, 123n97
11:11	120n84	Jonah		31:10–13	6
11:14	120n84	2:8	99	31:23	120n85
11:20	76n33, 85n62			33:5	4n13
12:1–3	76n33, 121	Habakkuk		34:7	43n7, 120n85
12:1	84–85	1:2–4	36–37	34:18	120n85
12:3	80n46, 122, 123n97	1:2–3	85	35:11	4n14
14	108, 133	1:2	45	35:13–15	6
14:2–9	65			35:17	83n56
14:2–6	67	Psalms		35:22–24	122
14:2	100n20	4:4	121n85	35:22	115, 123n97
14:7	67	5:2–3	115	39:11–12	83n56
14:8–9	83n55	6:9–10	120n85	40:2	120n85
14:12	120n84	7	79–82	41:5–11	67–68
14:19–22	65	7:4–6	80n45	42–43	55–59
14:19	83n55, 133	7:9–10	76n33	42:10–11	56
14:21	65, 133	9–10	44–45, 128	43:1–4	56
15:1	96n4, 110	9:2–5	44	43:1	58
15:18	83n56	9:8–10	45	43:2	83n56
15:19	96n4, 110	9:14–15	44	44	79–83, 84n59, 85, 87–88
18:20	96n4, 110	9:14	42n7, 115	44:10–15	82–83
20:7	83n56	10:1	83n56	44:21–22	4n14, 80
20:8	45n16, 85n62	10:13–15	4n14	44:25	42n7
20:13	43n7	10:14	123n97	48:12	4n13
22:1–17	43n12	10:16–18	44–45	51:5–6	73
22:16	120n87	10:17	120n85	54	46–47, 49, 115–16
26	88	14:6	43n7	54:3–4	115–16

154 *Praying Legally*

Psalms (*cont.*)		113:7	43n7	34:28	100n20
60:3–6	83n55	116:1	120n85	35:9–16	116
60:12	83n55	116:6	42n7	35:12–14	116
61:6	120n85	119	101	36:6	43n11
65:3	93	119:50	42n7		
66:19	120n85	119:71	42n7	Ruth	
67:5	4n13	119:75	42n7	4:1	99
68:11	43n7	119:92	42n7		
69	4–5, 6	119:107	42n7	Lamentations	
72:2–4	43n12	119:122	44n15	1:9	42n7
72:12–14	43n12	119:153–54	122, 123n97	3	55, 57–59
74:1	83n55	119:153	42n7	3:1	42n7
74:10–11	83n55	119:169–70	99	3:19	42n7
79:8	42n7	131	76–79	3:36	57n43, 123n97
79:11	99n17	137:5–6	80n45	3:50	57n43
80:5–6	83n55	139:1	4n14	3:55–66	122–23
80:13	83n55	139:23–24	4n14	3:55–61	122n94
82:3	120n87	140:2	45	3:55–59	36–37, 57
88:3	99n17	140:5	45	3:59	58, 123n97
88:8–9	483n56	140:13	43n7, 43n11, 45	3:56–61	57n43
88:8	42n7	142:7	42n7	3:56	123
88:16–19	83n56	143	117–18	5:1–16	67
89:39–50	83n55	143:1–2	117	5:20	83n55
90:15	42n7	143:2	82n52, 98n10, 117n78	5:22	83n55
96:13	4n13				
97:2	4n13	145:19	120n85	Esther	
97:8	4n13	146:7	4n13, 43n11	8:3	97
98:9	4n13	147:19	4n13	8:4	97
99:4	4n13				
102:2	99	Proverbs		Daniel	
102:11	83n56	18:6	98n10	9:16	73n31
102:24	42n7	20:14	43n12	9:20	100, 100n21
103:6	4n13, 43n11	21:13	120, 120n88		
106:23	110n60	22:22	120n87	Ezra	
106:30	110–11	29:7	120n87	9:7	73n31
106:44	123n97	20:14	120n87		
106:47	73n31	31:9	120n87	Nehemiah	
107:41	43n7			9	74n32, 76n34
108:12	83n55	Job	13–14, 84	9:9	115n71, 123n97
109	30–31	9:15	33	9:32–37	73–74
109:1–5	30	9:32	98n10		
109:4	30–31	19:7	45n16	1 Chronicles	
109:6–20	19	19:23–24	4n14	12:18	123n97
109:6	30	22:4	98n10		
109:7	19–21, 27, 29–30	23:4–11	76n33	2 Chronicles	
109:20	30	31:11	18n3	6:35	21n18
109:29	30	31:35	4n14	6:39	21n18

Index of Ancient Sources 155

20	52–54	VIII.6.1:10–2′	48n21	Elephantine papyri	
20:4	96	VIII.6.2:15–33	47–48,	(Porten and	
20:5	96		47n21	Yardeni)	
20:13	96			B3.2	87n70
30:27	99n18	AnOr		B3.2:3–4, 5	87n72
24:22	123n97	8, 27:4–5	71n21	B7.2	35n52, 87

Dead Sea Scrolls
1QapGen
XX   52–53, 59
XX, 12–16   54–55

Rabbinic Writings
Genesis Rabbah
44:12   22–23, 25

Deuteronomy Rabbah
11   25–26

Sipre Deuteronomy
                      25n26

Sipre Numbers
42   26n28

Babylonian Talmud
b. Roš Haš. 17b–18a   26
b. Sanh. 43b   112n67

Other Jewish Writings
Ashkenazic liturgy for
  Yom Kippur   96
Hinənî heʿānî mimmaʿaś
                      111
Untannê Tōqep Qəduššat
  Hayyôm   23–24

Ancient Near Eastern
  Writings (see Abbre-
  viations for identifi-
  cation of sources)
ABL
1285:13   123, 123n95

Akkadian *namburbi*
  prayers (Maul)
VIII.2.2:2″–15″   48n21

BE
9, 60:10   28n32
9, 69   90n83
10, 44:8   28n32
10, 55:10–11   28n32

BIN
1, 93:20   123, 123n96
2, 134:1–11
                49–50, 50n27

BM
32165+:20   104, 104n42
45690   112n65

BMS
13:27–28   101n27

Boyer, *Contribution,*
                     70–74

BWL
134:124–148   105–6,
                     106n48
135   106n48

CT
45, 46 ii.5–6   112n66
46, 45   112n65

CTH
71   29n36
378.III   29n36
381, i 25–32   118, 118n79

Cyr.
312:1–5   104, 104n40

DÖAW.PH 210
168.A15′–A18′   71n23

Epic of Tukulti-Ninurta I
  (Machinist)
II.A obv. 13′–24′   132–33

Gula 1a:2–6   117, 117n76

Ishtar
24:9–10   102n29

KAR
25 ii, 19–20   101n23
267:27–30   41

Köcher BAM 323:19–35
                         41

Kültepe
g/k 100:5–10   106–7,
                     107n50

Maqlû
I.1–36   51–52
I.13–14   116n75
I.73–121   129–32
I.114   2n6
II.24   2n6
II.87   102n28
II.108   2n6
II.131   2n6

Mari letters   34–35,
                     111–12
A. 1121 + A. 2731:53–55
                      34n48
A. 1968.6′–11′   34n49

Meṣad Ḥashavyahu
  Ostracon   12n39, 119

Nbn.
13:5–6   104, 104n43
1113:6–8   105, 105n46

Nebuchadnezzar King of Justice, 112–14

RS
17.83:11–18   104, 104n44

TCL
13, 137   91n85

13, 181   78–79, 78n39
13, 170:1–11   91n85

UET 6, 402   39–40

Wiseman, Alalakh, No. 7
               87–92

YOS
6, 92:1–23   103, 103n33
6, 92:20   51n32
6, 123:8–17   86–87, 86n67
6, 208:6–10   91n84
6, 223:1–7   70–71, 70n19
7, 7:37–40   105n47
7, 31:1–12   103, 103n34
7, 42:15–18   124, 124n100
7, 43–50   70n16
7, 77–87   70n16
7, 96–146   70n16
7, 96:1–7   91n84
7, 10:1–5   71n21
7, 128:21–23   91n84
11, 22:11–12   101n25
12, 557   89–90, 89n82
19, 101:24   104, 104n41